Profiting from Technical Analysis and Candlestick Indicators

Profiting from Technical Analysis and Candlestick Indicators

Powerful Methods for Accurately Timing Trades

Michael C. Thomsett

Editor-in-Chief: Amy Neidlinger
Executive Editor: Jeanne Levine
Operations Specialist: Jodi Kemper
Cover Designer: Chuti Prasertsith
Managing Editor: Kristy Hart
Senior Project Editor: Betsy Gratner
Copy Editor: Karen Annett
Proofreader: Katie Matejka
Compositor: Nonie Ratcliff
Manufacturing Buyer: Dan Uhrig

Publishing as FT Press
Upper Saddle River, New Jersey 07458

Printed in the United States of America
First Printing December 2014

ISBN-10: 0-13399337-X
ISBN-13: 978-0-13-399337-0

Pearson Education LTD.
Pearson Education Australia PTY, Limited.
Pearson Education Singapore, Pte. Ltd.
Pearson Education Asia, Ltd.
Pearson Education Canada, Ltd.
Pearson Educación de Mexico, S.A. de C.V.
Pearson Education—Japan
Pearson Education Malaysia, Pte. Ltd.

Library of Congress Control Number: 2014950977

Contents

Acknowledgments

I extend my gratitude to Executive Editor at Pearson/FT Press, Jeanne Glasser Levine, for her guidance, enthusiasm, and long-time association and friendship. Also, thanks to Betsy Gratner, Senior Project Editor, to Kristy Hart, Amy Neidlinger, Karen Annett, and to the entire production staff at FT Press. A special thanks to Michael Stoppa, my Web master and partner at ThomsettOptions.com, for his dedicated help in designing the Web site and the virtual portfolio where the theories explained in this book were first tested. Finally, thanks to all the readers of past books whose correspondence, suggestions, and compliments are always welcome.

About the Author

Michael C. Thomsett is the author of more than 80 books, including many FT Press projects (*Stock Profits: Getting to the Core, Put Option Strategies, The Options Trading Body of Knowledge, Options Trading for the Conservative Investor, Options Trading for the Institutional Investor*, and *Trading with Candlesticks*). He also has written several other books on the topics of technical analysis, candlesticks, and options trading. Thomsett is the cofounder of the education site ThomsettOptions.com, where he manages a virtual portfolio emphasizing technical analysis and candlestick charting as required trading skills; there, he has executed trades using the system explained in *Profiting from Technical Analysis and Candlestick Indicators*. He is a frequent speaker at investment and trading conventions and trade shows, and he teaches several classes for Moody's and the New York Institute of Finance. Thomsett lives in Nashville, Tennessee.

Introduction

The Self-Fulfilling Prophecy

Traders relying on candlestick charts have a problem. Whether experienced retail investors or managers of institutional portfolios, one of their greatest challenges in chart analysis is creating and maintaining objectivity.

The tendency is to seek reversal and confirmation that agree with the initial belief. So once you spot an initial signal (such as momentum moving into the overbought range), the next step is to seek bearish confirmation. Upon finding a signal, or two or three signals that confirm the bearish reversal, traders take action—closing long positions or opening short positions based on the discovered bearish signals.

This is where the problem lies.

In seeking *only* bearish signals, do you ignore contradictory bullish signals at the same time? A bullish pattern may be ignored, for example, with the latter session used as the first of a new bearish signal. But which signal is correct?

Are traders at risk for seeking only those signals confirming what they initially see on the price pattern? If so, chances for a poorly timed trade increase. With the purpose of signal identification and confirmation to accurately identify reversal and time trades, it is essential that an objective and open process is created for two contradictory purposes. First, traders seek confirmation for the initial reversal signal spotted because the entire exercise of chart analysis is designed to spot reversal before it occurs. By doing so, you are able to enter your trade before the greater market sees the same thing. Second, however, you will vastly improve your timing of trades if you also seek contradictory signals and then attempt to interpret them accurately. What initially seems like a clear reversal signal could become a false signal to be followed by a different set of indicators forecasting continuation of the current trend.

Traders as a group tend to seek what they expect to find on the chart; this creates a large blind spot and vulnerability. Even those who consider themselves entirely objective are at risk for this type of error, seeking a set of signals that become a *self-fulfilling prophecy*.

This book proposes that a candlestick indicator by itself is not reliable for timing of trades. You need confirmation through distinct and separate signals forecasting the same reversal (or continuation), but you also need more. In the process of seeking confirmation, the candlestick only becomes a valuable forecaster of future price direction under one premise: The chances of confirmation or contradiction are given equal weight. In other words, a series of very specific methods need to be brought to bear to ensure that all possible signals are recognized and analyzed. In the desire to spot reversal and confirmation, the tendency to ignore any signals contradicting that idea reduces the reliability of chart analysis.

Several supporting principles are brought into this revised analysis. It is based on statistical principles as well as the scientific method, under which an indicator is subjected to objective analysis, which may have either a positive or a negative outcome. In this application of the principle, a positive outcome is confirmation of likely reversal or trend continuation. A negative outcome is a contradictory indicator, which draws into question whether the initial signal is correct or a false lead. Either of these outcomes is valuable, leading either to trade execution or caution and a delay in action.

Augmenting the concept that candlesticks are useful only when applied within an objective search for confirmation or contradiction are a few additional principles. Every chartist will benefit from being aware of these.

First, reversal signals vary in their strength based on *proximity* to resistance or support. When a reversal occurs close to these borders of the current trading range, it is much stronger than the identical signal found at midrange.

Second, when reversal occurs at the point that price trends above resistance or below support, it is the strongest possible proximity, meaning reversal is more likely than anywhere else—assuming the first signal can be strongly confirmed by other price, volume, or momentum signals. The move above resistance or below support lends to even greater likely reversal when price gaps accompany that breakout. At this point, a candlestick reversal signal is quite strong, as long as it is confirmed.

By the same series of arguments, breakouts may be accompanied by candlestick continuation signals. These are particularly strong following a resistance/support or support/resistance flip (in which the prior border becomes a new, opposite one). This tends to add great strength. For example, if price moves above resistance and is accompanied by a candlestick continuation signal, and the new assumed level of support is at the same price location as prior resistance, this is one form of strong confirmation, making it likely that the new range will not reverse.

These concepts contain many variables, but can be demonstrated with a detailed analysis of chart patterns; with the study of candlesticks in the context of their interaction with traditional Western technical analysis of prices; and with a range of moving average, volume, and momentum signals acting as confirmation.

One aspect of this analysis used throughout this book is recognition that among the dozens of candlestick indicators, many are reliable only about half of the time. Even those candlesticks leading to expected price movement between 50% and 70% of the time serve little use in predicting price movement. These weaker signals may be useful if and when confirmed independently, or when they confirm other signals. However, it makes sense to limit an analysis of candlestick patterns in a logical manner. For this reason, the arguments for strong and objective analysis of trends and prediction of reversal are limited to only ten of the strongest candlestick indicators. These are explained in detail in Chapter 3, "Candlestick Patterns—Recognizing Evolving Strength or Weakness."

Why use only the strongest candlestick signals? The belief that objective analysis has to begin with solid and reliable information leads to a conclusion that exceptionally strong candlestick indicators form a solid basis and a starting point in the analysis. This is based on a statistical rule for sampling. In a population sample, the statistician needs to ensure that the sample is representative of the larger group. Thus, a survey of "likely voters" should include only those who have voted in recent elections, and not those who *might* vote or might not. A survey of shoppers in a product survey should include the family member likely to do the majority of shopping, and not the occasional shopper seeking a fast in-and-out of the store, regardless of price, product nutrition, or brand loyalty.

The same idea should apply to candlestick analysis. Some studies of candlesticks focus on the attributes of the indicator itself and its location within the price chart. However, even those examples that include explanations of false signals often do not focus on the narrowing down of likely outcomes. By limiting the discussion to ten of the strongest candlestick signals, this book presents the best case for utilizing candlesticks in a context of accuracy and reliability.

1

Charting Techniques—Predicting the Future

For many, charting itself—and technical analysis in general—is an uncertain science, more guesswork than fact and far from reliable.

Most theories of prices and trends agree on one point: Short-term pricing is chaotic and short-term trends are difficult to predict. However, charting provides short-term forecasts about price movement in one respect: Due to the chaotic nature of short-term price movement, many price moves are overreactions to immediate news, and these are likely to correct within one to three subsequent days. For example, earnings surprises often lead to big moves in price, even when the surprise is minor. A repetitive tendency can be observed, in which the immediate reaction to the surprise is extreme, and the next step is a reversal to correct the exaggerated price movement.

This occurs because the "crowd mentality" of the market tends to create predictable movement that itself is an overreaction to any news. Because of this, the correcting countermove is inevitable. It is quite rare for an overreaction to news to go uncorrected. It can happen without any doubt, but the astute chartist understands how this move and countermove is most likely to occur in each case when the unexpected (earnings surprises, merger rumors, or changed guidance) occurs. First is an overreaction, and second—often immediately—is a correction of the first move, fixing most if not all of the movement.

So the market may be broadly unpredictable, especially in the degree to which it reacts to news. However, the type of reaction consisting of move and countermove is predictable.

When this observation about the price swings is enhanced with the addition of several price pattern indicators (as well as changes in volume and momentum), it becomes easier to predict how price is likely to behave in the short term.

These concepts are by no means "settled science." In fact, candlestick charting and all forms of technical analysis have different levels of value to different traders and investors, and between retail traders and institutional managers. Many are ultraconservative and rely on fundamental analysis, the study of financial statements in an attempt to identify value investments for long-term, buy-and-hold strategies. This is a completely acceptable approach to investing as long as the conservative investor accepts the problem that published financial statements tend to be out of date by the time they are publicly available.

Technical analysis is also flawed if it is used to the exclusion of fundamental input. For this reason, it makes sense to consider both fundamental (historical) and technical (price) data in the development of a strategy to manage a portfolio. For many on the institutional side, the analysis of a company and the timing of buying or selling shares often are based on the process of asset allocation. However, allocation may be divided into many different categories, and knowing where to emphasize the next market move is just as difficult as technical analysis based on price patterns, reversal and confirmation, and candlesticks. Asset allocation is a reactive form of selection among products, rather than a proactive means for anticipating and forecasting price trends and reversals.

Because the controversy between technical and fundamental analysis cannot be settled or agreed upon by either side, the supposition in this book is that a solution may be found in applying empirical research, or research based on the attempt at objective observations.

Can this scientific method of empirical research be applied to a price chart? Or are there too many variables to be able to predict price direction with any reliability? The answer rests with the application of empirical data to actual stock charts, drawing analysis and conclusions, and attempting to demonstrate that a consistent degree of accuracy is, indeed, possible. The point of view that price movement is not predictable and even random (random walk hypothesis) cynically presumes that no forms of analysis can be effective. Hopefully, this theory can be dispelled with demonstrated successful forecasting above the random walk's 50% assumptions. This concept was first introduced in the year 1900, with the conclusion that stock price movement is entirely random and unpredictable.[1]

If this were true, no systems or methods would make any difference because all selections of stocks to trade would represent 50% probability of profit or loss. Given the wealth of methods for identifying likely reversal or continuation of current trends, the random walk hypothesis is an unlikely theory.

Another theory, the efficient market hypothesis (EMH), states that all current pricing of stocks have discounted all publicly known information, and therefore all pricing is fair. In that case, once again, beating the averages would be impossible. In fact, strict application of EMH would mean that a trader may buy any stock and will get a fair price at all times. The theory states that higher-than-average returns cannot be achieved based on historical prices or volume.[2]

Most traders know that this is not the case; the amount of effort that is expended in trying to anticipate changes in price, volume, and momentum demonstrates that a majority of traders instinctively understand that there is nothing random and nothing efficient about the markets.

The larger question must be: How can traders analyze and predict price movements? This is a challenging idea because some studies have concluded that traders react to news in the market in only two ways: by underreacting or overreacting. If this is true, then the efficient market hypothesis is suspect.[3]

This book methodically studies a number of stock price charts and applies a short list of ten candlestick indicators in conjunction with other signals, to determine whether the elusive "beat the market" goal can be met.

The Desire for 100%

Most traders accept the reality that no signals, even in combination, provide 100% accuracy concerning the next price move. However, all traders desire that "sure thing" that a 100% indicator provides.

Although 100% is impossible in terms of timing trades even with the best technical information, it is possible to beat the averages. If the beginning assumption is that any trade has a 50% chance of succeeding or failing, then the goal has to be to improve those odds in your favor. Given the uncertainty of trading and trade timing, for many a 60% or 65% success rate is an improvement. This is especially applicable to portfolio management if:

1. Every trade opened involves a similar dollar exposure, so that the application of a success rate is not weighted by a small number of trades involving larger-than-average risks.
2. Traders set goals for closing positions based on percentages or dollar values of profits as well as levels of loss.
3. Traders adhere to their self-imposed goals. This is probably the most difficult "rule" to follow because so many traders act like gamblers rather than scientists, hoping to recover a paper loss by holding too long even as the level of loss increases. This ensures a losing position in the long run because losses are not mitigated. The same issue is found in profitable situations. Once a profit goal

is reached, it is difficult for traders to close a position and take profits because the possibility of even-greater profits presents itself. In some percentage of cases (perhaps more than half), the profits will evaporate rather than grow.

Realizing that 100% is not only unlikely but also impossible, how can a trader develop a system to create consistent net profits? How can a particular set of signals be applied with consistency to increase those odds?

If you are content with a 60% or 65% success rate, then basic technical signals can be used effectively to accomplish the goal, even though the outcome is minimal. However, if you would prefer a 75% or better success rate, there is a solution. It is found in the judicious application of a small number of candlestick signals, confirmed by other signals (candlesticks, traditional Western technical signals, volume indicators, or momentum oscillators). Candlestick price indicators are not universally effective, but if limited to applications in specific proximity and strength moments, they are effective.

Articulating Risks in Trading Policy

This book and the examples developed throughout are based on a hypothesis: Focusing on a small number of highly reliable candlestick indicators, confirmed by other indicators, when price proximity is most likely to act as expected, will lead to better-than-average timing of trades.

The degree of profits derived from these trades relies on two key factors. First, trade dollar amounts should be identical in each case to ensure that the target outcome is applicable given both profits and losses. Second, setting a specific goal for closing trades based on levels of either profits or losses is a key to accomplishing the desired outcome.

The majority of traders, including professional and experienced retail traders as well as institutional portfolio managers, do not consistently follow these basic and logical rules. They tend to fall into a speculative mode, especially when losses occur, in the interest of recapturing the amount lost. This is ill-advised. So the hypothesis is based on some commonsense goals that must be set and then followed, even though it is difficult to remain consistent.

For example, assume for the sake of discussion that the average trade is $1,000. The goal is set that the position will be closed when it becomes profitable at 50% or when it loses 50% of the invested value. So a $1,000 trade is closed either at $1,500 or $500.

If the goal is further defined that a 75% success rate is expected (based on application of the principles described in the hypothesis), then four trades would result as:

- Trade # 1 (profitable) $1,000 invested, closed at $1,500, profit of $500
- Trade # 2 (profitable) $1,000 invested, closed at $1,500, profit of $500
- Trade # 3 (profitable) $1,000 invested, closed at $1,500, profit of $500
- Trade # 4 (not profitable) $1,000 invested, closed at $500, loss of $500

Overall net profit $1,000, 25% based on profits occurring 75% of the time

This is but one example of how the assumptions are based. The selection of a 75% profitable experience may be modified upward or downward based on how conservative or aggressive a portfolio manager is, and on the levels of risk involved in trades. Likewise, the selection of 50% profit or loss is also random. An aggressive trader may prefer a 100% profit versus a 75% loss, for example. Given the same outcomes as mentioned previously, profitable trades would be closed at $2,000 and loss position would be closed at $250; overall profits would then be $2,750 or 68.75%.

For the investor or portfolio manager analyzing the risks of a trading policy, the comparison of 50% profit/loss versus a 100/75% profit/loss has to be analyzed and quantified based on a comparison between the desired 25% net profit versus 68.75%. As an element of risk management, is it possible to accomplish 68.75% profits, and, more to the point, can you expect a 100% return in three out of four trades?

This study of risk and management of profits and losses serves as a basis for how the trades themselves have to be managed. A prudent portfolio manager understands this, even if that manager does not adhere to the standards consistently. It often occurs that a specified set of standards is understood to apply in "normal" times, but is modified if unusual opportunities are presented, or if market conditions are perceived to be exceptionally risky. However, even the most experienced managers are not going to be able to recognize these exceptional times, nor to know the equally important timing of when to revert to "normal."

For these reasons, traders need a hypothesis that can be applied consistently to determine when entry and exit will conform to a predetermined level of likely profitable results. The reliance on gut feelings, reading the market, or other nonscientific methods for timing of trades has never panned out to consistent profitable management of the portfolio. In fact, speculation itself has proven highly unreliable, with a tendency among speculators to believe they will somehow know exactly when to close positions—in spite of the reality that the majority hold on for too long and end up losing. One study cited a famous case: Isaac Newton speculated in the South Sea Bubble in 1720, first gaining a profit of about 50% but ultimately losing £20,000. Of this experience, Newton said, "I can calculate the motions of the heavenly bodies, but not the madness of people."[4]

The Hypothesis—Relative Correlation

The premise in the hypothesis is based on the observation that the significance and value of candlestick indicators are not universal. They are reliable in varying degrees. Some lead to reversal 80% of the time. However, a broader assumption is that the true value of a candlestick signal is based on its interaction with other signals (other candlesticks, traditional technical price patterns, volume indicators, moving averages, and momentum oscillators). It is also based on proximity to the trading range borders of resistance and support.

So this hypothesis, which is termed *relative correlation,* is at the core of candlestick analysis. Some observations that will be demonstrated in coming chapters are as follows:

- **Likelihood of reversal.** When a reversal signal appears at the point of resistance or support, the likelihood of an actual reversal is greater than elsewhere.
- **Significance of moves outside of trading range.** When a reversal signal appears at a point where price has moved above resistance or below support, reversal is significantly greater than elsewhere.
- **Strength of preceding trend and price gaps.** When a reversal signal appears at a point where price has moved above resistance or below support following an especially strong uptrend or downtrend *and* when that move above resistance or support includes price gaps, reversal is a near certainty notably compared with any other point in the trading range.
- **Price range border flips.** When a flip has occurred (prior resistance converting to new support, or prior support converting to new resistance), the new price range is far stronger than elsewhere, especially when confirmed by continuation signals.

As a general observation, a short list of strong candlestick patterns with exceptionally high likelihood of reversal serves as the core of a charting strategy. However, to use candlestick patterns effectively, the independent confirmation with additional signals is essential.

Confirmation should not be limited to the usual method in which it is used. In this method, finding two signals with the same directional forecast is promising, and finding three or more increases confidence to nearly 100%. However, this assumption is flawed if the principles of relative correlation are not folded into the analysis. The strength and proximity of the signal and confirmation are the keys, not just the type of indicator.

This hypothesis can be summarized:

> *A candlestick indicator serves as an initial forecast of coming price reversal or continuation. However, it is not dependable, even with confirmation, unless and until it is analyzed in conjunction with proximity to the edges of the trading range and the strength of trend and price characteristics in play. At that point, the relative correlation of the candlestick indicator is a variable, and should be quantified before assuming that the indicated forecast direction is likely.*

A problem, even with a focused hypothesis, is in dealing with the variables it presents. For chartists, the complexity of variables in price prediction is a constant concern. Nothing is certain in price direction and prediction, and chartists have to rely on probability rather than on certainty. The apparent relationship between an indicator and confirmation might be coincidence, or it might be directly related. How can you know the difference?

Only through observation of multiple instances in which indicator and reversal are found can you determine whether these occurrences do point to price direction, or are random and of no use. The contention of the relative correlation hypothesis is that signal and confirmation are directly related and can be used to project a likelihood of the next price movement.

In statistics, the initial indicator (for example, a reversal indicator in the form of a candlestick) is called an independent variable. The isolation of indicators that do lead to reversal a majority of the time adds strength to the signal; and for many chartists, this is as far as the analysis goes. However, the flaw in this is in failing to seek confirmation, which is a dependent variable. This is the type of variable that affects the occurrence of the independent type. So a confirmation signal acts as a dependent variable that adds credibility to the initial reversal signal (the independent variable).

When these direct relationships are expanded to include only the strongest candlesticks, and further when they are located in proximity to resistance or support, the ability to predict price movement is improved vastly. Furthermore, when that variable is itself quite strong, the likelihood of accurate prediction is further enhanced. For example, a particular candlestick might meet the criteria defined in its pattern, but minimally. Another instance of the same indicator might be quite strong. These variations in strength are found in the length of trading range within a single session, for example. An indicator consisting of a small range followed by a larger range demonstrates this relative strength. The larger the range of that second session, the stronger the signal tends to be; this is not a universal fact, but a reasonable observation. It may be applied to judge the strength or weakness of both the initial signal and its confirmation (independent and dependent variable).

These events (initial signal and confirmation) refer back to one aspect of the relative correlation discussed in the hypothesis. A valid hypothesis should be based on observation of relationships and the assumption of their meaning (followed by a series of tests to validate or disprove the belief). It should never be based on what a trader believes to be true. So a chartist who rejects candlesticks in all cases has a flawed belief that rejects the value without proof. By the same argument, a true believer in candlesticks may believe enthusiastically in the predictive power of the signal, but may fail to understand the distinction between proving a belief and hoping that belief is true. The only way to manage the variables and conclude accurately what they reveal is to test the belief with actual charting and see whether or not the outcomes conform to the assumptions developed through the variables.

Identifying the Errors of Popular Charting Beliefs

For a chartist to maintain objectivity, it is also necessary to keep open the possibility that the belief is incomplete or even wrong. The faith in charting as a method for accurately forecasting the next movement in price direction is not absolute. The hypothesis rests with the idea that highly reliable indicators (based on many observations) will aid in predicting the next change in price movement, as long as the proximity of the indicator (close to or through resistance or support) and independent confirmation do improve timing of trades above the random event (for example, a 50% chance of being right about a price reversal).

This brings up an essential attribute of empirical research and observation. It is far too easy for a chartist, desiring a reliable system for improving timing of trades, to easily accept what works and just as easily overlook or reject what does not.

To approach the subject with as much objectivity as possible, the hypothesis itself has to accomplish two goals. First, it must clearly state the belief as a possibility, subject to proof. Second, the process of testing that hypothesis has to give equal possibility to the chance that it can be proven to be false. A completely objective approach you can apply to determining the outcome should allow for either possibility—proof or disproof of the hypothesis. A persistent flaw suffered by chartists is the overly fast conclusions reached about a particular concept. For example, ask the question: Do candlesticks accurately predict reversal? If the reaction is an absolute yes or no response, then the truth is that the person responding is not open minded. It does not matter whether the answer is positive or negative because that answer is an absolute.

One important element of the hypothesis based on relative correlation is that there cannot be a simple answer. The hypothesis states the belief that candlesticks work only if and when they contain the elements of confirmation and proximity. Without these, the hypothesis contends, the candlestick's significance is dubious. Like any other indicator, the candlestick has to be located appropriately and confirmed strongly. A chartist who enthusiastically believes in candlestick analysis is likely to lack the ability to accept the possibility that the belief is false. A chartist who rejects candlestick analysis in all instances is also unable to accept the possibility that their dismissal of candlestick analysis is false.

Many chartists are committed to specific ideas. Candlesticks work all of the time or not at all. Price gaps always (or never) forecast retracement or reversal. Violations of reversal or support usually lead to reversal.

These absolute beliefs are at the very least questionable, and in a realistic analysis, can be proven to provide only a small vision of a larger probability—not fact or proof, but probability of how specific signals do, indeed, provide effective forecasts of what is likely (but never certain) to occur. And if a trader accepts candlestick analysis as an exercise in probability, then the timing of trades is also likely to be improved well above the random 50% success/failure rate.

Requirements for Proof of What Works

In seeking proof (or disproof) of the hypothesis, certain characteristics have to be applied. The idea that a truly workable and reliable system can be used is exciting to any chartist. Most technical analysts struggle endlessly to discover that "system" that accomplishes exactly what the hypothesis claims, but they go wrong somewhere along the way. A common error chartists make is believing that they have discovered a highly reliable system, and as a result they increase the dollar value of capital placed at risk. In those instances of poor timing, a single big loss thus offsets a preceding series of smaller net gains. Another flaw is the belief that candlestick signals (especially those with strong likelihood of accuracy) are so reliable that little or no confirmation is required. This is a violation of what may be called the First Commandment of the chartist: You do not enter a trade based on a signal unless and until you find confirmation.

The first form of proof required in studying the hypothesis is based on the human tendency to confuse an empirical belief and a normative one. Does the belief of the predictive value of candlesticks grow out of a hypothesis (but require research, testing, and proof)? Or is the belief based on the chartist's desire for the hypothesis to be true? Anyone who claims that "candlesticks should work and allow me to time my trades with near perfection" is expressing a normative belief—that just because something *should* work, it must be true.

So a distinction between how something works (empirical) versus how something should work (normative) is a profound one, and any trader who has spoken to chartists has without doubt encountered the "normative trader" who has decided to adopt specific beliefs, and who operates on those beliefs, even to the extent of rejecting the idea that proof or disproof has value.

Overcoming built-in bias is difficult even for the most fair-minded chartist. Everyone approaches a study such as this with bias, so to maintain objectivity, you need to apply a few tests. First among these is that a concept (such as the belief that candlesticks work as predictive tools) must be transmissible. This means that the case must be made in a way that others can apply the same tests and arrive at the same conclusions. Part of this process is sharing of the process involved in analyzing the questions, as well as what conclusions were reached. A conclusion that is not transmissible (for example, the belief that candlesticks are predictive, but without documentation of the process involved) is not reliable, and anyone expressing that conclusion should not expect its acceptance unless or until it has been made transmissible. This not only provides proof for the conclusion; it also overcomes the natural assumption that bias has entered into the analysis.

A second concept is that conclusions should be cumulative. This means that an initial finding is expanded by the findings of others. It does not matter how strongly one chartist presents evidence of success if no one else is able to replicate the experience. A true body of knowledge comes into existence only when an idea is put forth and can be replicated and even expanded upon by others. For example, candlesticks were first developed in the mid-eighteenth century in Japan, to track rice futures. The most successful trader, Munehisa Homna, enjoyed such good results with candlesticks that he was dubbed "The God of the markets." Many traders built upon this initial success, and in 1989, Steve Nison published *Japanese Candlestick Charting Techniques* and for the first time introduced candlesticks outside of Japan.

Today, anyone analyzing charts and using candlesticks is enjoying the cumulative studies of Munehisa Homna, Steve Nison, and many others who have contributed to the science of candlestick analysis.

In analysis of the candlestick indicator, traders seek results that demonstrate a direct relationship between different signals. For example, the confirmation derived from two or more candlesticks in close proximity, or between candlesticks and other signals (moving averages, volume indicators, or momentum oscillators, for example), creates a form of empirical generalization, which is somewhat like confirmation but on a level separate from the timing of trades. These results add to the belief in candlesticks containing predictive value (and by the same rule, they take away from the belief that candlesticks offer nothing of value). They are called generalizations because they are logical even though they contain evidence that varies in value. For example, a trader might observe that "when you see a strong reversal signal, the price trend is most likely to turn around within a few sessions." This is not a very strong statement because it is overly general and assumes too much. However, the statement becomes empirical when expressed as: "when you see a strong reversal signal with confirmation, occurring at the top of an uptrend or the bottom of a downtrend, and gapping through resistance or support, the price trend is most likely to turn around within a few sessions." This is a stronger case and conclusion because, with the empirical generalizations in play, the belief is supported and qualified.

Reversal of a trend, as one example, is supported when empirical statements are qualified for the requisite conditions (proximity to resistance or support, price gaps, equally strong confirmation). Unlike the less-realistic belief that a "good" system will ensure 100% success, an empirical system has to be based on probability. The goal of 100% is entirely unrealistic even with the best signals, confirmation, and proximity. However, based on probability, it will reside in a likely outcome better than 50% (random) but less than 100% (certain). This is the core of probability; it is not the random outcome nor the certain outcome you expect to experience, but an improvement of timing at some level better than random (but still less than certain).

This is the entire crux of how candlestick signals have to be understood. They do not provide better outcomes in trades, but they can provide better probability of profitable outcomes based on the identified attributes the signal needs to contain.

The elements surrounding the candlestick signal (strength of the signal itself, confirmation, proximity) lead to conclusions that chartists invariably employ. A deductive conclusion is not possible in chart analysis because charts never contain proof, and no signals—candlesticks or others—provide certainty or evidence of outcomes. Thus, chartists rely on inductive reasoning, which is an inference derived from observation and from combining a set of observed facts and assumptions. For example, a strong candlestick reversal signal, occurring as price gaps above resistance or below support, which is confirmed by volume and momentum indicators after an especially strong trend, provides exceptionally strong inductive conclusions that the price will soon reverse and move in the opposite direction. Inductive reasoning is never going to offer certainty, but because the goal in charting is to improve the instances of successful outcomes, inductive reasoning is not only the best a chartist can expect, but also can provide very strong probabilities of success—as long as the observed facts and assumptions are accurate and employed objectively.

All of these reasoning standards belong within the broader science of critical thinking (or critical theory). Empirical evidence is a disciplined approach to what can be observed on a price chart. However, many difficulties aside from the stock's price pattern have to be understood as well. For example, if you love Coca-Cola but hate Pepsi, will you look at the charts of the two companies differently? (Also note the use of words like *love* and *hate* rather than *like* or *dislike.*) Will you tend to distrust indicators for Pepsi because you prefer a different product? Or can you look at both charts objectively and apply the same empirical standards to both? Under the concept of critical thinking, a chartist should be able to apply analysis to every chart regardless of any personal bias for or against the products the company produces and sells.

One of the greatest difficulties for all chartists is maintaining objectivity in spite of personal biases. Whether the product at issue is a soft drink, fast food, or computer products, every trader is subject to the consequences of his or her experiences with a range of products or with a particular brand.

The application of a scientific theory to charting techniques is necessary because so many opinions dominate the market of technical analysis. The majority of theories are based on noncritical thinking, a complete acceptance or rejection of ideas without the research needed to honestly support them. This is less of a personal criticism to those who adopt a set of beliefs, and more a commentary on human nature. Traders tend to be very analytical in the methods used to study price patterns and in how indicators such as candlesticks are employed. However, many also tend to be less interested in the discipline of the scientific method. In fact, many traders have not gone to the extent of articulating a hypothesis and then testing it; they may simply believe in the power of candlesticks based on personal experience.

If a trader has stumbled upon an effective method for how and when candlesticks and confirmation are applied, he or she may easily have discovered the "proof" that is arrived at with a more methodical system of testing and research. Or it could be that those same traders are vulnerable to acting on assumptions that are *usually* true but not *always* true. For example, given the right circumstances, a particular signal, confirmed independently, and placed well, will lead to the expected price movement most of the time. However, this does not mean that the conclusions reached are supportable with a set of tests and standards. It could mean that the trader employing the system has accomplished success without moving through the hypothesis and related steps.

The next chapter examines the power of pattern recognition as a further expansion of the principles based on hypothesis. The goal is to demonstrate that what often is attributed to intuition or even to experience is actually a form of understanding in line with the same ideas expressed here—that a hypothesis of how and when candlestick signals provide valuable information can be formalized and understood to improve timing and profits.

2

Traditional Analysis—The Power of Pattern Recognition

One key to effective charting is found in the type of price pattern itself. Ease of recognition makes it possible to spot signals, especially reversals. The same rule applies to traditional price patterns as to candlesticks: The most compelling signals should be emphasized, as they provide the best experience of forecasting coming direction.

This means that, like candlestick indicators (so-called *Eastern* indicators), traditional price patterns (*Western* indicators) are subject to the same qualifications:

- **Strong signals.** A short list of exceptionally strong signals should be emphasized over less-common ones, especially when those less-common signals are subject to varying interpretations.
- **Proximity to trading range borders.** The most effective traditional signals are found close to or right at resistance or support.
- **Breakouts.** The strongest-possible reversals based on traditional price patterns are found at the point that price breaks above resistance or below support.

These are forms of relative correlation that have as much influence as candlestick signals, especially when one form confirms the other (Western signals accompanying candlesticks or vice versa).

So relying upon a very limited set of technical signals makes sense, sharing the attributes of proximity, ease of recognition, and strength. To the last point (strength), a base concept in technical analysis is that whenever a signal tests resistance or support without breaking through permanently, it serves as a strong forecast that the price is likely to move in the opposite direction. However, it is also true of all signals, including Western and Eastern, that a reverse movement does not mean that a new secondary trend has developed. So a bullish reversal might only return price into range as a form of short-term trend or retracement, even as a current bear trend is under way; and a bearish reversal may likewise represent an adjustment or retracement back into range.

This understanding—that bullish does not mean bull trend and bearish does not always mean bear trend—is too often poorly understood. There may be a tendency for chartists to assume that reversal is the beginning of a permanent or long-term secondary trend, but in fact, that reversal can be very short term while a prevailing trend remains in effect.

Because the duration of a reversal response cannot be known with certainty in the moment, once a reversal does occur, chartists need to closely monitor subsequent price patterns to determine whether a new trend may, in fact, move all the way to the opposite trading range border. Failing to break above resistance, will price decline and break through support? Or failing to break through support, will price rise and then break through resistance?

A reversal occurring at the point of resistance or support does not necessarily lead to a new trend that will in turn violate the opposite side of the range. The reversal itself may only serve as a temporary trend or retracement to maintain price within the range.

Charts and Directional Identification

Isolating a few high-value indicators helps in the task of technical analysis, which may include dozens of possible signals. Just as candlesticks are limited to only those ten producing the highest frequency of successful prediction (see Chapter 3, "Candlestick Patterns—Recognizing Evolving Strength or Weakness"), a similar limited number of Western technical price signals are used in this book.

These do not include volume or momentum indicators, which are not intended as direct price signals. These topics (see Chapters 10 and 11, "Volume Indicators—Confirmation of Price" and "Momentum Indicators—The Exhaustion Point," respectively) further enable traders to quantify the strength or weakness of reversal trends on the chart.

Price indicators are also analyzed in greater detail in Chapter 9, "Moving Averages—Finding Statistical Correlation," where the key identification of the price trend is emphasized; this includes an explanation of why price momentum (as measured by these signals) is not necessarily the same as trend momentum.

The identification of resistance and support (see Chapter 8, "Support and Resistance—Key Price Points in the Trend") is a key technical base for all other signals, both Western and Eastern. For this reason, resistance and support are not defined as indicators for purposes of this analysis, but as the key points of proximity for all other technical signals. Ten key Western signals emphasized here are:

1. Double tops
2. Double bottoms
3. Price gaps
4. Ascending triangles
5. Descending triangles
6. Symmetrical triangles
7. Rising wedges
8. Falling wedges
9. Trendlines
10. Channel lines

You might be very familiar with these ten Western signals. However, the context of how these are employed within a system of relative correlation (and relying on confirmation as well as proximity) serves as an expanded methodology for chart analysis. When combined with strong candlestick reversals (as well as volume and momentum signals), these signals can become an integral part of a powerful system for timing of trades. So although the following descriptions and illustrations are partly a review of basic technical signals, they also introduce ways in which these signals integrate within an advanced method of relative correlation.

The following sections give examples of each of these.

Double Tops and Bottoms

These consist of two sessions with price spikes next to or close to one another, which touch or move through a top or bottom. This occurrence, representing a failure in the direction of the spike, is followed in most instances by a move in the opposite direction.

For example, IBM's chart is shown in Figure 2.1, and shows two double tops, both occurring at the top of the trend and the point of resistance. These provide initial signals of a coming reversal, due not only to the formation, but also to the placement.

The double tops both appeared at the peak of uptrends, but they forecast reversal and quite often that is precisely what occurs. In this case, strong downtrends followed. The first downtrend is visible on this chart, falling 18 points from $188 to nearly $170. It could be estimated that these reversal points start out looking like resistance, but they are too short term to establish that. The second downtrend is revealed on an extended chart, shown in Figure 2.2.

Figure 2.1 Double tops, four months

Figure 2.2 Double tops, six months

The second downtrend fell nine points from the double top, even though price did break through resistance as it fell. These were most like retracements rather than failed uptrends, due to their short-term nature.

Just as double tops forecast downtrends, double bottoms often occur at the bottom of the trend and forecast reversal to a new uptrend. Figure 2.3 shows an example of this on the chart of Exxon Mobil.

Figure 2.3 Double bottoms, four months

The levels for support and resistance are difficult to spot on this chart, but it appears that the $92.75 price level may develop into a newly set support. The chart expands further in Figure 2.4 to demonstrate the reliability of the double bottom.

Figure 2.4 Double bottoms, six months

In this expanded chart, it becomes clear that the second double bottom marked the starting point for a new and extended uptrend, which is marked on the chart. The reliability of double tops and double bottoms makes both signals useful in analysis; however, this is only one of many signals, and chartists should look for additional confirmation at the point of these indicators.

Price Gaps

Gaps occur often, including "hidden" gaps. In these, daily trading ranges overlap, but a gap occurs between one day's close and the next day's open. Most important among gaps are repetitive or runaway gaps, a series of gapping prices accompanying a strong price move. If this occurs as price moves through resistance on the top or support on the bottom of the current trend, reversal is a very strong possibility.

For example, on the chart of 3M shown in Figure 2.5, several substantial gaps are pointed out. These exclude minor gaps, which occur frequently on most charts.

Chart courtesy of StockCharts.com

Figure 2.5 Price gaps, four months

The gaps on this chart identify potential price turning points. However, you may note that the price does not always turn just because a large gap appears. This further emphasizes the need for confirmation. A strong signal such as a gap needs to be confirmed before acting on an apparent signal ending a trend. Gaps also may be lagging rather than leading indicators. For example, the third and fourth gaps occurring between black candlesticks occur after the downtrend has started, and at that point you would have no way of knowing whether the trend would continue to come to a halt. For this, you need additional forecast indicators.

Figure 2.6 sets up a dynamic trading range starting with the gap at the bottom of the trend. This is not a visible gap, but it is significant. The price difference between the close of the black session and the open of the white session is more than 2.5 points. The long, lower shadow on that white session also reveals a likely decline in momentum among sellers.

Figure 2.6 Price gaps, six months

The growing resistance uptrend is interrupted only once by a brief retracement, and by the end of the charted period, no apparent end to the trend is visible. Price gaps are very common, and they become significant only in some specific cases. These include runaway gaps, a series of repetitive gapping sessions with price moving in one direction. This indicates a strong trend, but the greater the gaps, the more likely the trend will quickly end and reverse. Another significant gapping price move occurs at the top as the gap moves price through resistance, or at the bottom as the gap moves price down through support. These gapping breakouts are most likely to reverse, so when these occur, proximity becomes the most important aspect to the pattern.

Triangles

A triangle is a narrowing range over time, which may be ascending, descending, or symmetrical. An ascending triangle consists of a flat resistance line and rising support, and is bullish. For example, an ascending triangle is found on the chart of Boeing in Figure 2.7.

Chart courtesy of StockCharts.com

Figure 2.7 Ascending triangle, four months

The Boeing (BA) chart contains a strong ascending triangle, which is a bullish forecast; however, the price declines after the triangle closed the range. To see whether or not the bullish forecast materialized, you need to study the extended Boeing chart. This is shown in Figure 2.8.

Chart courtesy of StockCharts.com

Figure 2.8 Ascending triangle, six months

The price did decline, at least long enough to establish a new support level. The delayed reaction to the ascending triangle is not unusual (for this or for any other signal). However, in this instance, the final bullish trend did materialize and it took price up to the range set in the previous December.

The opposite signal, a descending triangle, has a flat support line and a declining resistance line, and is bearish. For example, on Johnson & Johnson's chart, a descending triangle marks such a decline, as shown in Figure 2.9.

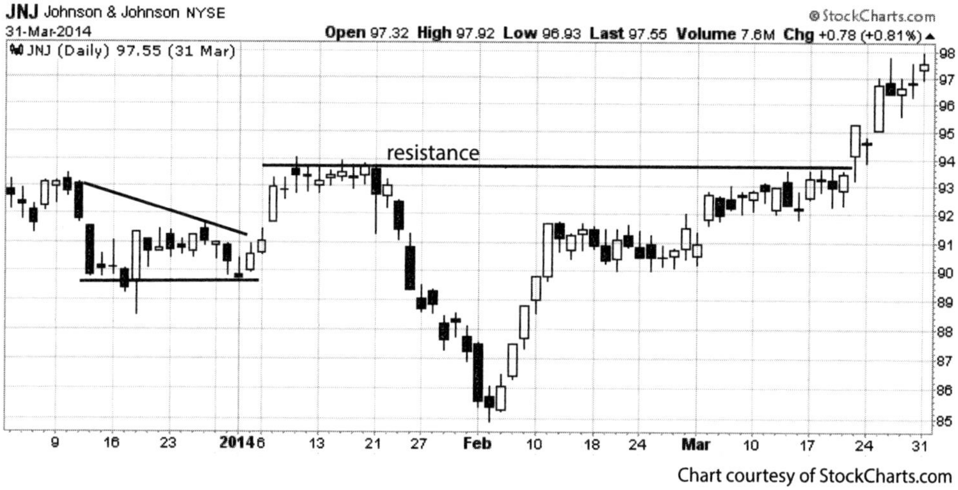

Figure 2.9 Descending triangle, four months

In this case, the descending triangle extended over three weeks; but the question for the chartist remains: Did it lead to a bearish trend? Like the previous example, price rose for a short period of time and established a new line of resistance, and then declined. This point of resistance held all the way through to mid-March, before price broke through above that level. So although the descending triangle did lead to a short-term bearish move, what happened next? The extended chart is shown in Figure 2.10.

It turned out that the downtrend occurred, but only in the short term. The long-term trend remained bullish as price broke through the newly set resistance and remained above that level for the remainder of the period charted.

A symmetrical triangle (also called a coil) is quite different than ascending and descending triangles, as it may be either bullish or bearish. It consists of a declining resistance line and a rising support line. For example, the chart of American Express reveals this formation, as shown in Figure 2.11.

Figure 2.10 Descending triangle, six months

Figure 2.11 Symmetrical triangle, four months

Price jumped well above the narrowing range set by the symmetrical triangle, but then fell rapidly. So in this instance, it would seem that the triangle led to a bearish trend. This is a difficult chart to read due to the volatile price movement for the remainder of the chart. The extended chart provides a little more insight, as shown in Figure 2.12.

Figure 2.12 Symmetrical triangle, six months

Once price settled down, it set up a new line of support, which then flipped to resistance. At the end of the chart, price broke through this line and continued upward. So how should the symmetrical triangle be interpreted? Considering the time that passed between its formation and the latest chart pattern, it is inconclusive. This points out the difficulty in interpreting signals that may be either bullish or bearish. In fact, this type of signal may be of little value unless it is used as a confirmation indicator for other, more-specific signals.

Wedges

The triangle can be a strong signal, especially the ascending or descending variety. The symmetrical triangle is not useful except as a confirmation pattern. In comparison, a wedge may be rising or falling. A rising wedge consists of rising resistance and support as the breadth of the range narrows, and is a bearish signal. For example, on the Visa (V) chart, a rising wedge developed, as shown in Figure 2.13.

The reaction to this rising wedge appears to be clearly bearish, as expected. However, the larger question of what happens next also has to be addressed. The extended chart shown in Figure 2.14 provides additional insight to the outcome of this signal.

This is an interesting formation. The price declined as expected and then formed a second rising wedge, another bearish signal for Visa (V). This demonstrates how many charts move into repetitive patterns that, although not reliable for future indicators, are useful as long as the signals can also be confirmed.

Figure 2.13 Rising wedge, four months

Figure 2.14 Rising wedge, six months

A falling wedge consists of falling resistance and support with a narrowing breadth of trading, and is a bullish signal. For example, a brief falling wedge was spotted on the chart of United Technologies (UTX), shown in Figure 2.15.

The response (after a brief decline) was a strong uptrend. Notice how the decline included a gap-taking price below support. When this occurs, a reversal is more likely than at any other point in the range. To see what happened next, refer to Figure 2.16.

Figure 2.15 Falling wedge, four months

Figure 2.16 Falling wedge, six months

The price did evolve into an uptrend with rising support. The momentary decline immediately after the wedge closed in actually confirmed the uptrend. The attempted drive downward failed, which strengthened the uptrend revealed on the remainder of the period.

In addition to the very distinct triangles and wedge formations, simple lines drawn along rising or falling levels of resistance or support aid in identifying when trends are likely to end, and also mark movement if and when the breadth of trading remains the same. So trendlines and channel lines are useful tools for chartists; when used as an aid in identifying relative correlation with additional indicators and confirmation, these lines define the likely points of reversal.

Trendlines and Channel Lines

These are lines drawn to indicate consistency of a current trend, and the line itself continues until it runs into the price. At that point, reversal is likely.

A trendline is a single line drawn above resistance when price is falling or below support when price is rising. The trendline should closely track the changing border of the range and will not cease until price reverses and interrupts the line.

For example, trendlines have been highlighted on the chart of Goldman Sachs, shown in Figure 2.17, one for an uptrend and another for a downtrend.

Figure 2.17 Trendlines, four months

The uptrend moves to a point where resistance appears, and is then followed by a strong downtrend to a support area. Both of these trendlines clearly identify the dynamic price range and make them clearer. To see where the range evolves next, see Figure 2.18.

Figure 2.18 Trendlines, six months

The overall trend continues downward, but notice how the angle of the decline is less severe with each subsequent trendline. The first one is quite steep, the second one is moderate, and the final trendline is very mild. For long-term forecasting, this may reveal a declining bearish trend and potential leveling out and reversal in the future.

A channel line is an expansion of the trendline. It involves a line drawn above resistance and another below support. It provides a visual summary when the breadth of trading is consistent even as prices rise or fall. When price reverses and interrupts the channel, it often acts as a signal of a trend ending or retracing.

For example, the chart of Chevron highlights a declining channel line. Note that the breadth between resistance and support remains approximately the same even as the price level declines. This is shown in Figure 2.19.

The 10-point decline in the trading range occurred even as breadth of trading remained at 4.5 points. This is significant; a big decline such as this often is accompanied by volatility and changes in the breadth of trading. So the consistency of the range implies low price volatility even as the decline evolved. This continued beyond the initial chart, as shown in Figure 2.20.

The price trended upward, culminating in a surge in the second half of April. At this point, another downtrend took over, this time with a narrow breadth of trading; the channel lines covered only 2.5 points as price began trending downward.

Figure 2.19 Channel lines, four months

Figure 2.20 Channel lines, six months

This visual charting tool is valuable in charting because it not only tracks a bullish or bearish trend, but also identifies level of volatility. The channel lines reflect a consistent trend, just as triangles and wedges summarize an evolving change in breadth of trading. Placed in a context beyond the initial meaning of the price pattern, in other words as part of relative correlation to what occurs on a price chart, the Western indicators may be leading signals or lagging signals. When further reviewed in proximity to support or resistance, and when enhanced by candlesticks, volume, or momentum indicators, these signals improve the ability of chartists to better forecast price movement.

Testing the Pattern

Every chartist contends with the problem of properly reading what the pattern reveals. A reversal might be merely a retracement, a breakout could be establishing a new trading range, or an exceptionally strong Western or Eastern reversal could fail. All of these possible events point to the need to test patterns.

In the preceding examples of well-known technical signals, patterns were tested by observation. A series of trendlines with less-severe angles to each implies that the momentum for each is declining. This can be confirmed by checking momentum and other signals, with the goal of determining whether the current trend is gaining or losing strength.

The purpose in signal identification is not only to identify likely reversal or continuation. For chartists who limit their analysis to just finding indicators, a great opportunity is lost. The greater purpose is to use indicators as a context for examining proximity (to resistance or support) and to examine confirmation. Proximity is a key to understanding strength or weakness of a signal; when a strong reversal occurs just as price moves through the borders of the trading range, it is the relative correlation of proximity that makes the signal exceptionally strong.

Some forms of confirmation are stronger (or weaker) than others. A reversal occurring at resistance or support gets a chartist's attention, but the type of confirmation is equally important. For example, finding a corresponding candlestick that leads to reversal only half of the time is of only limited value. Although a 50/50 outcome is not compelling, there is a degree of confirmation when that signal occurs at the same placement with another signal. However, it is always preferable to find stronger confirmation in one of many forms.

Strong confirmation may consist of a candlestick that reverses over 80% of the time, or a momentum oscillator whose index has moved strongly into overbought range (for breakouts above resistance) or oversold range (for breakouts below support). When you find gapping price action moving price through these borders, and confirmation is equally strong, the likelihood of reversal increases to *nearly* a certainty. This might be a bold claim based on the knowledge that there is no such thing as 100% certainty; however, when you combine exceptionally strong price patterns with equally exceptionally strong confirmation, the probability of reversal is greatly increased.

For example, gapping price movement through resistance, culminating in a double top, and confirmed by a bearish engulfing candlestick pattern (with an 82% likelihood of reversal, as explained in Chapter 3), and further confirmed by Relative Strength Index (RSI, a momentum oscillator), you have the ultimate combination of reversal and confirmation. These are found in price movement, Western signals, Eastern signals, and momentum. This type of exceptional strength in reversal and confirmation, added to the proximity factor of price moving through resistance, is the epitome of relative correlation.

For example, the chart of Buffalo Wild Wings (BWLD) contains a strong set of reversal and confirmation signals with the proximity making reversal most likely. This is shown in Figure 2.21.

Figure 2.21 Strong reversal confirmation, four months

The signals include a breakout above resistance, which, as the chart shows, did not last. This occurred at a point of a bearish engulfing pattern (which leads to reversal 82% of the time), which also formed a double top. Although Relative Strength Index (RSI) did not move above the 70 index value, it was trending toward the overbought level. The relative correlation of multiple signals at a breakout above resistance makes reversal highly likely.

To see what did occur next, examine Figure 2.22.

Figure 2.22 Strong reversal confirmation, six months

The decline anticipated by the multiple signals on the previous chart materialized and became a 20-point downtrend over the ensuing month. In this situation—when all of the signals point to the same confirming likelihood and the proximity is through resistance (or support)—making a trade at that moment will be well timed in a majority of instances, even for a stock as volatile as BWLD.

Bringing Order to the Pattern: Measuring the Trading Range

The hypothesis of relative correlation can be displayed on price charts, but every trader knows that conforming examples and exceptions can both be found. So how do you measure the concept?

For a hypothesis to be provably valid, it has to be testable. Every trader can test the concept daily by seeking those confirmation and proximity factors on charts. However, this does not provide a consistent measurement of how and when the trading range acts and how it is likely to reverse. For this, you need to apply tests to the empirical data, to decide how strongly the hypothesis applies and how well it enables you to improve the timing of trades.

Measurement creates a direct connection between the hypothesis and actual outcomes, and may help to better understand how a concept operates in a world containing degrees of randomness and chaos. Part of the hypothesis claims that given the proximity of a reversal (to resistance or support) and the strength and degree of confirmation, reversal is more likely to occur. Thus, applying this to trading, you *should* be able to improve your timing to create more profits, more consistently. However, this is part of the hypothesis and not proof. To develop this into a system in which the hypothesis can be proved to contain reliable attributes, you need to measure that one aspect to the chart that defines trends and reversal—the trading range.

In looking at a variety of different trading ranges, it becomes clear that no two are alike. Some remain very narrow even while prices change dynamically. The price levels rise or fall, but the breadth of trading is remarkably consistent. For other stocks, the range moves in the short term within a series of triangles or wedges, or jumps the breadth lines with large gapping price changes. This more volatile breadth of trading makes all forms of prediction more difficult, and in some cases nearly impossible. In this case, measurement might be so elusive that you will not want to apply the relative correlation hypothesis. In other words, the hypothesis itself cannot be assumed to apply universally. As part of the measurement requirement, some specific attributes have to be present as a starting point:

- **Consistency of the trading range.** The trading range has to be consistent over time, whether trending up or down. The predictability of the range and its breadth of trading are not at all unusual but are not fully appreciated until compared with a highly volatile chart that cannot be as safely studied and for which a forecast is more difficult.

- **Recognition of forecasting patterns.** Patterns have to emerge in some form. As obvious as this might seem, chartists may be frustrated upon discovering that some charts (or specific time ranges within a chart) seem truly random, with prices evolving sideways and without any apparent trend. This is simply the real world; some stocks need that period of consolidation after conclusion of a trend and before a new trend begins.
- **Continuation patterns.** Just as reversal trends can be sought within the multiple attributes of relative correlation, continuation trends are just as important. For example, if the breadth of trading moves to resistance or support and then breaks through with a continuation pattern and confirmation, this makes it likely that the price trend will continue moving in the current direction. In other words, just as reversal is most likely when reversal signals appear at the proximity of resistance or support, the same is true for continuation. A trend is likely to continue through resistance or support when that continuation signal is confirmed.

These "rules of thumb" constitute the definition of how you measure the trading range and how well the hypothesis does or does not apply. The important observation here is that this hypothesis does not apply in every case. Chartists know that nearly every chart will contain something of interest, even in hindsight; they also know that some charts are so erratic, and some trading ranges are so unpredictable or even nonexistent, that the hypothesis cannot be applied.

For example, the chart of U.S. Steel (X) is shown in Figure 2.23. The breadth of trading does not change much over time, but the trend is quite erratic. Three short-term trends are identified, each in the form of a rising wedge. This is a bearish signal, but after the first and third occurrence, prices rose. The middle wedge concluded with a large downward price gap and a volume spike, good confirmation for a coming downtrend. But the previous uptrend was short and mild, so there was not that much to reverse. The downtrend that did follow was also quite weak. So on this chart with its unpredictable price pattern, the relative correlation ideal may not apply. The chart does not lend itself to confident price forecasting.

Chart courtesy of StockCharts.com

Figure 2.23 Volatile trading range, four months

Expanding this chart to see what occurs next is interesting because price seems to evolve into a more predictable pattern. This is shown in Figure 2.24.

Although the volatility is likely to still be a problem for this chart, the added two months represented a clear channel of trading. Even with past volatility, this is reassuring to the chartist. All that is required is to track this chart as it continues, seeking either a continuation or reversal signal. If that were to occur sharply above or below the channel (which also defines dynamic resistance and support), and if that signal could be confirmed, confidence may be greater for timing of a trade.

One attribute to this chart that may frustrate the effort to forecast future prices is the consistency of the momentum oscillator RSI. Throughout the entire period, the index remained between 70 and 30. As frustrating as this is, this points to yet another opportunity within the hypothesis of relative confirmation. When a new signal does emerge, if it is accompanied by a move in RSI above 70 or below 30, it would be compelling. This could provide either a reversal or a confirmation signal, depending on the direction of the initial signal and the momentum index. However, momentum oscillators normally accompany reversal signals as symptoms of exhaustion to the existing trend.

Chart courtesy of StockCharts.com

Figure 2.24 Volatile trading range, six months

This is an example of how the initial hypothesis of relative correlation can be expanded and applied to a chart that historically was difficult to read, but which then fell into a more predictable pattern. This happens often, just as a chart that was historically accurate may move into a period of higher volatility and lower predictability. Someone taking the initial hypothesis beyond its initial expression might do so in many ways. For example, a trade might suggest that the concepts of proximity and confirmation could raise profitable timing experiences to 75%, meaning a trade will be profitable three out of four times.

Before attempting to measure this assumption, however, the trader would need to add in some qualifying "rules" to this expanded idea. First, once rules have been set for when and why to enter and exit, those rules have to be followed consistently. If they are not, then the assumed 75% profit level will not be possible. In fact, the failure to follow set goals and rules may account for a large percentage of failed trades experienced by everyone.

Another qualifying rule is that the hypothesis has to be tested on charts meeting the attributes of consistency and pattern recognition. The hypothesis is only as good as the charts studied, so if you try to apply it to a volatile chart, it will not work.

Finally, every trader has to define "acceptable profits" as part of the process. For many, the aggressive assignment of a rate of return may be too inflexible; it may also exclude the identification of a bail-out point in the case of losses. When traders proceed without a measurement in mind and clearly defined, one likely outcome is to take extremely small profits and at the same time experience much larger losses. Overall, this is not a winning combination, if only because it is a process without definition and without the means for measurement.

The trading range defines predictability of every chart. A clearly identified resistance and support level and a clearly visible breadth of trading are the starting points. A trend will be fairly uninteresting on such a chart, at least until the price levels begin to diverge from the established norm. So violations of resistance or support, large price gaps, specific candlestick reversal signals, big volume spikes, and other changes in the course of price movement define the likely changes in the trading range as well—expansion, contraction, or breakout.

Accuracy in Prediction

Pattern recognition, in the minds of some traders, is the easy part. In fact, however, when you combine pattern recognition with correct interpretation and action, it becomes evident that traders should seek reliable and accurate patterns.

One method for ensuring the accuracy of a prediction based on observed signals is to use the *test and retest* method. When you find recurring patterns, is the outcome the same or similar? It makes sense that an initial test is validated only if the outcome can be duplicated. In charting, no two outcomes are likely to be identical, but what adds value is when the same results (in varying degrees of price movement) occur after a strong signal. That signal, when it comes to proximity to resistance or support, and when clearly and strongly confirmed, is expected to lead to an outcome such as reversal. The number of points of movement cannot be known for several reasons. First, a five-point move for a $20 stock is more substantial than a five-point move for a $100 stock. Second, the move itself is going to be affected by the duration of the preceding trend, overall market sentiment, competition within a sector, timing of the price move to earnings, and numerous other factors.

What can be predicted based on observed signals is how well specific signals work together. The hypothesis claims that gapping price movement through resistance or support has a good chance of reversal; in fact, probability is overwhelming when confirmed by momentum oscillators, volume, and other price signals. The degree of move in a reversal may not be known, but the reversal itself approaches "certainty" better than other methods of forecasting. Referring back to Figure 2.22 for Buffalo Wild Wings, all of the required elements were present for a strong and immediate reversal. However, the point move could not be known.

In this case, you need to settle for the testing and retesting of direction, but not for the number of points of movement expected to occur. This remains unknown and unpredictable. So many factors come into play during a trend or, for that matter, at any time, so that predictions of the number of points of movement are most difficult. This is why, from the technical point of view, accuracy gained by testing and retesting the reversal pattern makes sense; however, attempting to identify a target price is usually a matter of guesswork. Although analysts like to set target prices one year out for companies they analyze, the price level is elusive and one year is far away.

A second method for testing the accuracy of prediction is an alternative method, in which the same price movement is measured, but different signals are employed. For example, in observing that prices tend to reverse when a bearish engulfing candlestick appears along with a double top as price breaks out above resistance, you have two strong signals, both likely to lead to reversal. But given the same violation above resistance, what happens when you combine a big price gap and a volume spike? Here, you observe two different signals, but reversal also occurs. But which of the two sets of measures (bearish engulfing and double top, versus price gap and volume spike) leads to reversal more? This method of testing may result in compelling outcomes, although it is a limited system. The answer is that one set will reverse more than the other for some companies, but not for all. The alternative method of employing different measures for the same expectation of price reversal is one of many valid tests, but it still does not prove that any one combination of indicators is foolproof.

Validating the Pattern

One of the greatest obstacles chartists face is in validating a legitimate pattern. The failure of validity comes in several forms:

- **Ignoring contradictory patterns.** If you identify a reversal signal, the tendency is to seek confirmation of reversal in the same direction. But what happens if you find contradictory patterns, such as strong continuation signals, or an opposite signal (bear when you expect bull, or vice versa)? If you ignore these contradictions, making a trade based on selective information may lead to ill-timed entry (or exit).
- **Spotting reversal without a trend.** A reversal signal must have a trend to reverse. So, for example, if you spot a bear reversal signal during a downtrend, that cannot be treated as a reversal. At the very least, it is a continuation signal; it might also be no signal at all, just an arrangement of shapes that does not spell reversal at all.
- **Misreading the signal.** A key attribute to signals is that not every signal means a trend is ending or about to reverse. A bullish signal does not mean a long-term bearish trend is about to end, even with excellent proximity and confirmation. It could be nothing more than a momentary shift, a retracement, or an aberration. This is why even proximity to resistance or support is not enough; you also need equally strong confirmation before you can consider a signal to be valid.

Validity can lead to two conclusions. You validate the hypothesis when you discover a high level of reliability in discovered signals with proximity to resistance or support, and with strong confirmation. You can also validate the failure of the hypothesis under specific circumstances. These circumstances may include an earnings surprise, options expiration dates, ex-dividend dates, economic news, merger rumors, or lower guidance for the coming year, to name a few. So it is possible that the hypothesis has to be expanded with a set of qualifiers. These include the absence of mitigating events or impending announcements, deadlines, or dates. The failure of the hypothesis may be converted to more-effective interpretation when these qualifying factors are also taken into consideration.

The *face validity* of the hypothesis is straightforward. If you measure what is expected to occur (for example, trend reversal) based on the attributes of proximity and confirmation, you are testing the face validity of the hypothesis. This is the most obvious and easily proven or disproven form of validity. However, once you add in the mitigating and qualifying factors that may affect the hypothesis, you need to expand face validity to a higher level, that of content validity. In other words, the hypothesis may be considered effective, *if* earnings, dividends, rumors, and news all are within expectations. Given this, or adjusting the hypothesis to allow for the *if* factor, leads to content validity.

The application of validity may take on even more complex forms. Applying construct validity is one example. In this system, you study one set of assumptions (such as price reversal signals) and then study related attributes. This is what confirmation is all about on one level; however, in the process of validation, you might discover that some forms of confirmation are more reliable or less reliable than others. In this case, you conclude that simply finding confirmation is not the end of the process. You need to apply the idea of construct validity to determine whether some indicators provide more predictable confirmation than others.

An example of construct validity applies to the use of candlestick indicators. Many reversal indicators lead to reversal only 50% of the time. When analysis is limited to this fact, it is clear than a 50/50 likelihood is of absolutely no use. It is just too random. However, those same indicators can be used as one form of confirmation for other signals. The question then becomes more interesting: Does a 50/50 candlestick signal provide any value as a confirmation indicator?

Most chartists will agree that finding a 50/50 confirmation signal does not take anything away from the original signal, and may add some value. However, it would not be prudent to rely on that as a sole confirmation indicator. Such signals may work well as second or third forms of confirmation, but they do not provide a compelling argument for confirmation on their own merits.

The problem with low-value indicators is one of reliability, without doubt. Another example of this is a common gap, the kind that occurs often in most charts. Can it be considered a form of confirmation? Probably not, especially by itself. So indicators like the 50/50 candlestick and the common gap are not expected to provide a cause and effect between themselves and the reversal signal. Their correlation is either weak or nonexistent. This relationship (or more accurately, lack of relationship) between two indicators is called discriminate construct validity; it disproves the value of weak indicators for confirmation.

When you discover that application of a set of reversal indicators and confirmation produces similar outcomes, this becomes another method for proving validity. This interim association adds validity not just to the particular signals used, but to the overall hypothesis as well. If the hypothesis applied only for a very small number of signals, then it could not be applied and tested over a range of charting conditions. So interim association should demonstrate that given a set of likely reversal indicators (Western technical signals, Eastern candlesticks, volume, or confirmation), the outcome should have a high expectation of success, given the elements of the hypothesis. The use of ten of the strongest technical signals as well as ten highly reliable candlesticks (Chapter 3) makes the interim association stronger than it would be if applied to random sets of indicators, including those with low reliability such as 50%.

Measuring the Trend

A distinction has to be made between measuring the trading range and measuring the trend.

To measure the trend, you need to examine the assumptions used in exercise of the hypothesis. For example, in dealing with a number of signals (which may also be called variables), do you assign the same value to each? Most traders do assume equal value to all forms of reversal, whereas others recognize that a larger trading range in a single candlestick is likely to be more compelling than a very narrow range, or a large upper or lower shadow is likely to be more meaningful (in how it is interpreted) than little or no shadow.

If you assume that all reversal signals contain the same value (which might also be an unconscious assumption), you are applying a nominal measurement to the hypothesis. But is it realistic? The differences in sizes of price gaps, daily trading range, and candlestick shadows are likely to be interpreted differently. In Western analysis, a double top or bottom with extremely long shadows is likely to be a stronger reversal signal than a set of relatively small shadows.

A higher analytical level of measurement, called ordinal measurement, assumes different levels of strength based on these visual attributes. It's a matter of extremes. In candlestick analysis, great importance is given to either a doji (a session opening and closing at the same price) or a long candlestick. The very short or very long distance between opening and closing price is viewed as significant, an ordinal measurement. These dichotomous measurements (recognition of two levels only) are one approach to measuring the strength of a signal. However, this does not mean that the sizes and shapes in between have no value; they are just less extreme varieties of measurement.

In extreme price patterns like long candlesticks, the practice of assigning different levels of importance based on the degree of the interval (or, interval measurement) is an effective method for qualifying the hypothesis. A trader might observe, for example, that a reversal signal that includes an exceptionally long candlestick pointing to the reversal direction is going to be a stronger reversal signal than one with the same patterns but a smaller distance between opening and closing price. Is this a valid measurement? Can it be proved? Yes, through observation. If the candlestick science tells you that reversal accompanying long candlesticks is stronger than one with smaller price ranges, then this suggestion can be tested and retested to validate it.

At this point, an important overall qualifier has to be mentioned. A *long* candlestick is not transferable between charts, but has to be defined as a comparison to other, more typical lengths of candlesticks for the same company, and displayed on the same chart scale. A four-point move for a stock with ten-point scaling will not seem especially long, even when that day is much longer than the more typical one-point and two-point moves. A four-point move on a chart scaled in one-point increments will be much longer in comparison, due to the scaling. So in the analysis of charts, interval measurement has to take into account the scaling of the chart.

This chapter demonstrated how ten Western indicators are applied in charting to identify likely points of reversal. This is part of the process of relative correlation. Pattern recognition is the starting point, and from there you can move on to candlestick analysis. The use of Western and Eastern patterns together makes the hypothesis especially useful, notably for confirmation. The next chapter describes ten of the strongest candlestick indicators and shows how they appear on the stock chart, in the context of proximity to the trading range.

3

Candlestick Patterns—Recognizing Evolving Strength or Weakness

In the last chapter, ten traditional Western signals were presented. The purpose was to demonstrate how specific signals are stronger when found in close proximity to resistance or support, and especially so when the pattern takes price through those levels. Reversal is also forecast more specifically when the signals are strongly confirmed with independent signals.

This chapter expands on the concept by providing the same levels of insight for ten frequently successful candlestick indicators. The term *successful* means the percentage of times the indicator leads to predicted price movement. The ten signals include both bull and bear, and both reversal and continuation price patterns.

Candlestick Comprehension

Although candlestick charts are popular and widely used, the intricate details of signals and what they show are not always well understood. Most traders have some knowledge of the candlestick concept, but not enough to make informed timing decisions. Even those who do have a deeper awareness of what specific signals reveal do not necessarily know how to decide whether a signal is strong or weak. This is important because some candlesticks are accurate only 50% of the time. This makes such indicators useless by themselves (although they may be of limited use as forms of confirmation, but only when accompanied by other confirming indicators).

As a starting point, knowing which candlesticks are accurate more times than not is essential in deciding which ones to look for. This chapter describes ten of the highest-performing candlesticks out of the dozens that exist; only those appearing between 71% and 100% of the time are included.

When these ten high-ranking candlesticks are confirmed by other indicators, their power is vastly increased. In addition, when you seek indicators and confirmation at resistance or support (especially moving through those levels), the overall reliability is further raised. This combination of signals, with confirmation and proximity in play, demonstrates the effectiveness of charting based on relative correlation.

A few key reminders about candlestick limitations:

1. **A perfect pattern formation will not always be located.** Interpreting candlestick patterns contains a degree of intuition. If you are familiar with the signal rhythm and the volatility tendency to a particular stock, you are more suited to knowing where and when to look for reversals. This intuitive observation leaves room for a degree of interpretation when you find a pattern close to one of the strong reversals, but not quite complete.

   Candlestick indicators reflect a tendency in the price based on buyer and seller pressure, movement within a single day, price gaps, and much more. So a signal that almost conforms to the perfect pattern may be considered acceptable, as long as confirmation and proximity also work. If you wait for the perfect candlestick formation, you might never find it, and you will miss many opportunities to trade entry or exit based on patterns that are close to perfect.

2. **The meaning and importance of specific patterns are not well understood.** Many traders use candlestick charts as the default type and have a rudimentary understanding of how they work. However, it may be of limited value to think of candlesticks as just an alternative expression of the older OHLC (open, high, low close) chart. The candlestick provides much more information in a highly visual manner, and the use of specific signals can be proven to help improve timing of trades. This claim is based on a study of stock charts in all types of markets and a ranking of how often each candlestick pattern appeared and performed (in other words, leading to the type of price movement the pattern predicts). This work was performed by Thomas Bulkowski and fully documented in his book, *Encyclopedia of Candlestick Charts*. More information about these ratings follows later in this chapter.

   The point in focusing on specific patterns is that many of them truly do predict price movement accurately and work a majority of the time. It is a mistake to rely solely on the Western form of technical signals, which were described in the last chapter. These Western signals are powerful predictive tools on their own, given proximity and confirmation. They work within the hypothesis of relative correlation. However, when these are combined with Eastern indicators (candlesticks), they are much more powerful and accurate in forecasting price moves.

3. **Even the strongest patterns and confirmation do not guarantee perfect timing of trades.** There are no 100% outcomes. If you could devise a system to be perfect in timing of entry and exit in all cases, you would use that system. However, there is no such thing, which is why the careful application of relative correlation is crucial. In addition, even when all of the signals are strong and specific, a degree of caution has to be applied. Even the best signals, strongest confirmation, and perfect proximity do not work all of the time. This book claims that you can approach 100% accuracy, but you will never reach that elusive goal because the random nature of short-term price movement defies even the best combination of signals.

   Because you can never escape the possibility of an ill-timed trade, you need a policy for risk mitigation. For most traders, this will consist of one of two possible systems. The easiest is to enter all trades with approximately the same dollar value, regardless of the strength in signals. This ensures that in those cases where the signals fail, the loss will not be catastrophic. The second system is to rank the strength of the combination (signal, proximity, confirmation) and determine an appropriate investment level as a result. For example, a value of 1.00 indicates a typical set of signals, including initial signal, proximity to resistance and support, and at least one confirming signal. If the initial signal is confirmed by two or more other signals, the value could be increased to 1.25. An exceptionally strong pattern might raise the value again, to 1.50. If the signal is rare, such as a momentum oscillator moving far into the overbought or oversold range, the value could increase to 1.75. And in cases where all of these conditions exist along with an earnings surprise and a highly exaggerated price response, the value may be increased to 2.00. In this case, the investment dollar value would be twice that of signals rated 1.00. The problem with this rating system is going to be in testing whether or not the stronger signals do actually lead to accurate forecasts more of the time. This is likely to vary based on the stocks selected, overall market conditions, and combination of signals used (Western price signals, Eastern price signals, momentum, and volume).

   Even when you develop what you consider a reliable ranking system to assign value, the variable will remain. You cannot know whether the price response will be immediate or deferred, or even whether or not it will take place. Some reversals, for example, occur immediately, whereas other reactions are delayed several days or weeks. Another variable is degree of movement. A reversal might occur as expected, but how many points of price movement will occur? How quickly? And in what time frame?

4. **Contradiction is just as valuable as confirmation.** In the search for confirmation, what should occur when it is not found? The best course is to take no action, and the same general rule applies when you find contradictory signals. The difficulty here is being able to spot these contradictions. Human nature may add a blind spot to the trader's analytical nature. So the search for confirmation may include failure to recognize a contradictory signal. However, when an initial signal is contradicted (and especially if the contradiction is confirmed), it is powerful information, and adds insight to what the initial signal means.

   A signal first viewed as a reversal might be invalidated when stronger contradictory signals are found. So traders who are able to spot these paradoxical situations are also able to either take no action until the price picture is clearer, or take an opposite action when conditions justify it. For example, an initial bullish signal might be contradicted by a bearish one, and that bearish signal confirmed. Proximity also comes into the picture. Although you expect reversal to be most likely at resistance and support, continuation is also a possibility. So price gapping through resistance on the top or support on the bottom at the same time a reversal signal occurs is a strong indication of what might happen next. However, the breakout might hold, and a new trading range might come into play. Those contradictory signals can lead you to forecasting price movement in a direction opposed to what the initial signal predicted.

5. **One of the biggest obstacles is skepticism and a closed mind.** Traders tend to be analytical. They like charts and patterns, and they believe in the predictability of price movement. However, it becomes quite easy to reject strategies that disagree with an adopted set of ideas. For example, if you are a true believer in Western analysis and the power of price gaps, double tops and bottoms, and signals gained with breakouts above resistance or below support, it might be very difficult to accept an expanded idea of how else analysis can be performed. Some traders see candlesticks as either signals only in the moment and without lasting value, or as lacking any real forecasting value at all. History contradicts this. You only have to consider the history of candlesticks to appreciate their value.

   In eighteenth-century Japan, candlesticks were developed as a means for tracking and forecasting the value of rice futures. The most successful trader was Munehisa Homna, also known by the name Sakata. He was so successful that he was nicknamed "the god of the markets." The key to this early success of candlesticks was not only that they could be used to accurately forecast price movements, but that repetitive patterns and price tendencies were recognized. Although this was applied to successful trading in rice futures, modern chartists recognize that the same probabilities are applied to stock price movement. In spite of widespread belief in either the random walk hypothesis (RWH) or the efficient market hypothesis (EMH), the facts are difficult to dispute. The market is neither random nor efficient.

Candlestick analysis demonstrates that price movement is predictable when the elements are present (signal, confirmation, proximity) and when that price movement is studied on a broader level than just price movement. This means combining price with volume, moving averages, and momentum, adding to the value of forecasting price direction. Just as Sakata combined price movements with weather forecasts and crop yields (appropriate for futures contracts), today's stock chartist needs to analyze charts using as much information as possible—overall market conditions, economic influences, timing of earnings and dividends, competitive position within a company's sector, and, of course, the related signals beyond price that appear on a stock chart. It is not only that shapes develop into signals, but the question of whether these signals are significant or random. If they are random, then candlestick indicators have to be questioned; however, if it can be demonstrated that specific combinations of patterns do lead to predictable price movement (reversal or continuation), then the value of candlestick indicators cannot be ignored.

A Review of the Candlestick and Its Attributes

For every trader, the candlestick represents the most visual summary of daily price movement—open, close, high, low, and direction of movement. When a series of daily candlesticks is displayed on the chart, you can immediately spot the trend, daily breadth of trading, and levels of volatility.

The basic candlestick contains specific attributes worth remembering. For those traders who use candlestick charts but are not familiar with the attributes, this section is a summary of the basics. For those traders more familiar with candlesticks, this is a review.

The complete candlestick and its attributes are shown in Figure 3.1.

The white candlestick appears when price moves higher during the session, and the black candlestick appears when price moves down. The range from high to low is expressed in the form of the rectangle, known as the real body. The opening price is at the bottom (on a white candlestick) or the top (on a black). The closing price is at the top (on a white candlestick) or the bottom (on a black).

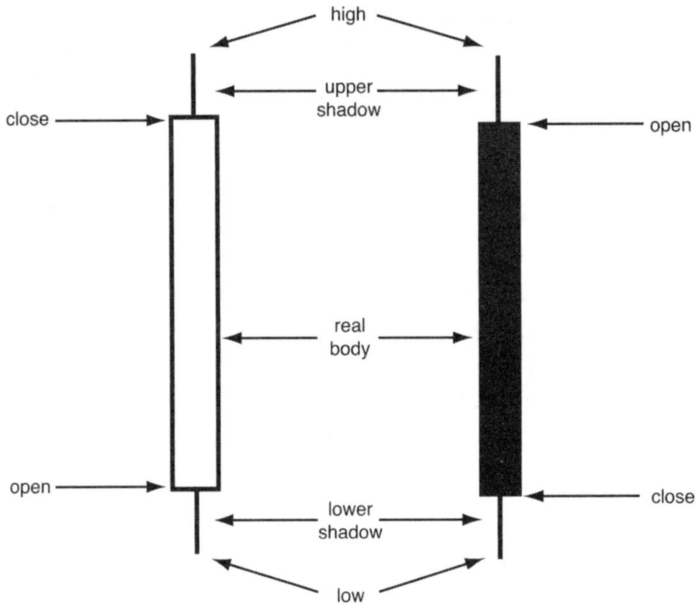

Figure 3.1 Candlestick attributes

The rectangle immediately reveals the range from open to close, as well as the direction of movement. Beyond this are upper and lower shadows. These are the day's range of trading from high (top of upper shadow) to low (bottom of lower shadow). The longer these shadows are, the greater the volatility for a specific day.

Most traders immediately understand that several attributes of the candlestick provide useful data on a day's trading. The longer the candlestick is, the greater the breadth of trading. The longer the upper or lower shadow, the more failed price movement occurred in the indicated direction. So a very long upper shadow reveals a failure among buyers to move price higher, and a very long lower shadow displays the failure among sellers to move price lower. These two factors—size of the real body and length of the shadow—define a lot of what a candlestick's significance is within a single session. When the collective candlestick movements for an entire chart are studied together, trends develop in terms of volatility, volume, and momentum. When candlestick signals are combined with Western indicators, the power of trend development, confirmation, and proximity is augmented.

So the candlestick is not singularly important within one session. In fact, it is difficult to judge attributes like volatility without also comparing the length of today's real body with the lengths of preceding sessions. The value of candlesticks is found in the development of patterns over time, and precise relationships from one session to another form actual forecasting signals that traders can use to predict reversal or continuation of a trend.

The Ten Candlesticks and Their Attributes

There are dozens of different candlesticks, in bull or bear formation, extending from a single session to multiple sessions, and some whose meaning depends on where it appears on the chart. These include the hammer and hanging man, which are identical signals, but are found at either the bottom of a downtrend (hammer, a bullish reversal) or the top of an uptrend (hanging man, a bearish reversal). Another of these is the spinning top, a doji (a horizontal line indicating the same opening and closing price) with exceptionally long upper and lower shadows. This takes on the appearance of a lowercase letter *t* and its significance depends on what else is going on around that session.

Beyond these conditional signals, many lead to predicted movement only about 50% of the time. This makes these signals largely useless as predictive tools, but they may add a qualified level of confirmation to another signal. However, because they are only 50/50, they do not provide enough confirmation on their own.

Many other signals are successful between 50% and 70% of the time. This is better than a random outcome assumed at 50/50, but it still is not as strong as most chartists would like. For this reason, only ten signals are used in this book, all of which have led to predicted outcomes more than 70% of the time.

These ten indicators are summarized in Table 3.1.

Table 3.1 Ten Candlesticks with High Performance Rankings

	Performance Ranking Percentage	
	Bullish	**Bearish**
Three black crows		79%
Three stars in the south	100%	
Three-line strike (bullish)	83%	
Three-line strike (bearish)		84%
Three white soldiers	84%	
Identical three crows		72%
Bearish engulfing		82%
Morning star	78%	
Bearish belt hold		71%
Mat hold	78%	

Source: Thomas Bulkowski, *Encyclopedia of Candlestick Charts*[1]

The study undertaken by Bulkowski involved a program-generated analysis of thousands of charts over ten years, so it contains quantitative value. This included five million candle lines for more than 100 candlestick patterns. The database was the S&P 500 stocks for a ten-year period. Bulkowski arrived at what he termed *performance rankings,* the percentage of time a pattern appearing in a chart leads to what has been predicted. He also developed a theoretical definition of a signal as bullish, bearish, reversal, continuation, or indecision.[2]

Six Basic Candlestick Formations

There are only six possible formations of candlesticks, and all patterns (over 100 in total) are developed from combinations of these six.

The six formations are summarized in Figure 3.2.

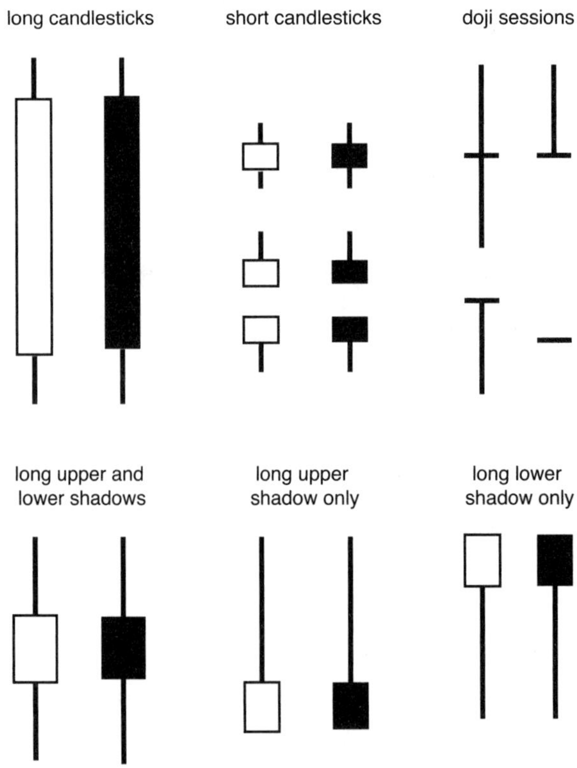

Figure 3.2 Six basic candlestick formations

The six formations are the following:

1. **Long candlesticks.** The long session may be white (upward-moving) or black (downward-moving). It indicates exceptionally strong interest during the session. A longer than usual breadth of trading in a single session often accompanies reversals, so these play a key role in pattern analysis.

   A variation of the long candlestick is the marubozu. This is a long candlestick with little or no shadows. The word in Japanese means "with little hair," and it describes the long candlestick of this type. Either white or black marubozu sessions may have no shadows on either side, or extremely small shadows on one side or the other. Because of little or no shadow involved, the marubozu is interpreted as extremely strong in the indicated direction. There was little or no effort beyond opening and closing prices, so the bullish (white) or bearish (black) tendency is stronger than a candlestick of the same size with a much larger shadow.

2. **Short candlesticks.** A variety of short white or black candlesticks may have shadows on both sides, or upper or lower shadows only. They play a role in several important indicators. For example, single-session short candlesticks are found in hanging man, hammer, inverted hammer, inside and outside patterns, morning and evening star, and squeeze alert, to name a few.

   The short real body may indicate a very small interest level during the session, or a struggle between buyers and sellers with a very narrow breadth between what each side is willing to give to the other. As a result, short candlesticks often are seen during periods of sideways movement, when neither side holds a clear advantage or control, and a consolidating period is under way until one side or the other makes a strong move.

3. **Doji sessions.** The doji (in Japanese, "mistake") is a session with little or no real body; thus, the rectangle is replaced by a horizontal line. This may be accompanied by shadows on both sides, upper or lower only, or none at all. Each of these takes on a particular meaning within specific patterns, such as the harami cross, doji star, abandoned baby, or tri-star.

   Other doji sessions provide one-session indicators that may be bullish (dragonfly doji), bearish (gravestone doji), or indecisive (long-legged doji). However, this signal may also move prices in the direction opposite the indicated one, so these are among the most perplexing of all candlestick signals.

4. **Long upper and lower shadows.** When a session contains both upper and lower shadows, it can be difficult to interpret. It signifies that buyers and sellers were

both unable to move prices in the desired direction. The value of such a signal often is found in what else is occurring before and after the session with both types of shadows. However, lacking a specific price forecast, the shadows often mean little or nothing. The study of price charts reveals that shadows on both sides are common.

5. **Long upper shadows only.** This can also have several meanings, but it tends to be more bearish than bullish. A long upper shadow is a sign that buyers moved price higher during the session but were unable to hold onto those price gains. Price retreated back to its close.
6. **Long lower shadows only.** The long lower shadow tends to be bullish. It occurs when sellers moved price lower than the open-close range but were unable to maintain the lower price levels.

The true meaning of all six formations is not precise or consistent. The "rules" are really generalizations and many exceptions will be found. Traders are more likely to focus on specific patterns, confirmation, and proximity than on the attributes of a single session.

Examples of Ten Candlesticks

This section examines the ten candlesticks listed earlier and demonstrates how they appear on actual stock charts. Emphasis here is to show how the proximity factor works. Later in the book, various forms of confirmation (for candlesticks as well as the last chapter's Western signals) make relative correlation work well.

These ten candlestick signals are not necessarily the ten best-performing signals. They are high performing with the combination of high frequency, meaning they are not difficult to find. Using a highly reliable candlestick indicator that rarely appears is frustrating because so much of timing for trades involves the liquidity of information.

With this in mind, the following sections present the "pure" or "perfect" form of each indicator, then show the same indicator on a stock chart, and finally show an expanded chart showing what occurred after the appearance of the indicator.

Three Black Crows Pattern

The three black crows is a bearish reversal signal that leads to actual reversal 79% of the time that it appears. For this "rule" to apply, you would expect to find the signal at the top of a current uptrend. Upon recognizing it, you would want to take immediate action to close out a long position or to open a short position. The position may involve shares of stock, exchange-traded funds, or options. The three black crows candlestick is shown in Figure 3.3.

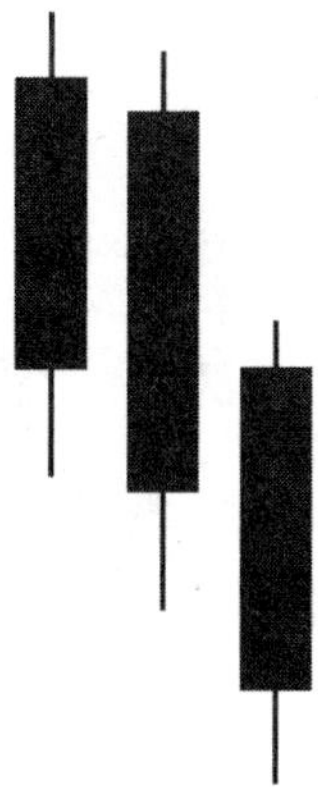

Figure 3.3 Three black crows pattern

The attributes of three black crows are quite specific. It consists of three consecutive sessions. Each session opens within the range of the previous real body and closes lower. Thus, each session starts with a lower high and ends with a lower low.

The pattern is found frequently on stock charts, although perfect placement at the top of an uptrend is not always the case. It may show up once a downtrend has already begun, and acts as confirmation that the uptrend has ended. However, a problem with this pattern is that once it appears, the downtrend may be well under way already, so some price movement has occurred and an opportunity to maximize profits is lost, at least partially.

An example of this pattern is found in the chart of Home Depot (HD), as shown in Figure 3.4.

This chart revealed two of the patterns, both with similar shapes and proximity. Resistance curved upward and then declined, and the three black crows appeared in both cases after the downturn had already begun. Even so, the decline in the first appearance was a full seven points from the appearance of the three black crows to the bottom of the downtrend. The second instance looked nearly identical to the first in terms of resistance shape and delayed appearance, but its outcome could not be seen on this chart. To see what happened next, check Figure 3.5.

Figure 3.4 Three black crows, Home Depot, four months

Figure 3.5 Three black crows, Home Depot, six months

Not only did the second indicator act very much like the first, but a third indicator also showed up after the initial period. This third one acted just like the previous two, occurring shortly after the uptrend peaked, and then confirming the downtrend with a deferral of a few days.

Three Stars in the South Pattern

The three stars in the south is a bullish reversal indicator. Its performance ranking is listed at 100%, although this only indicates that in the testing performed, all instances led to a bullish reversal. This does not mean a 100% outcome should be expected; it only means that in the sampling, very few instances of this pattern were found and all of those led to reversal. Any trader willing to settle for 80% or 90% reliability on a candlestick signal will see performance in the profit column, and should be willing to accept occasional losses.

The pattern is shown in Figure 3.6.

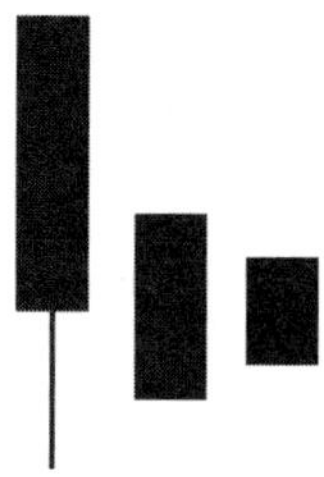

Figure 3.6 Three stars in the south pattern

The pattern has two attributes, making it somewhat unusual and hard to find. First is a black session, followed by another opening within the range of the first and closing lower. The third session is also black and opens and closes within the range of the second day. The pattern is unusual because it consists of three black sessions, but is a bullish reversal.

The chart of Intel (INTC) included an example that is not perfect, but is close. It is shown in Figure 3.7.

The signal occurred at support and broke through, so the reversal was expected. This is perfect proximity for a reversal to succeed. The question here is whether or not the bullish trend continued. The continuation of this chart is shown in Figure 3.8.

The price trend continued above $25.75 per share where a new support level was established. This is a common development, in which a rising support trend levels out and sets a new, higher support after a strong bullish reversal. The fact that the three stars in the south occurred right at support and tried to break through makes the subsequent uptrend especially strong.

Figure 3.7 Three stars in the south, Intel, four months

Figure 3.8 Three stars in the south, Intel, six months

Three-Line Strike Bull Pattern

The three-line strike is a continuation pattern, and it does lead to continuation 83% of the time. This means you expect to find it during a trend, and for the trend to then continue. The bull version of the three-line strike pattern is shown in Figure 3.9.

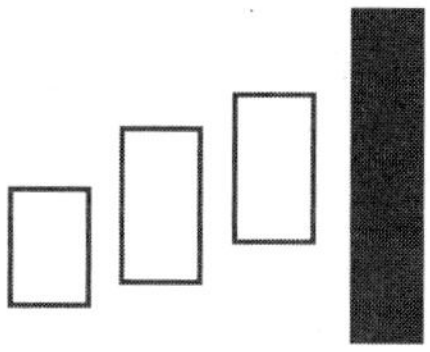

Figure 3.9 Three-line strike bull pattern

This is another unusual candlestick, as it begins with a series of white sessions, but ends with a long black candle. Although they are black, the daily price trend rises. It culminates with a longer white session that engulfs all or part of the previous sessions. Figure 3.10 provides an example of this continuation pattern on the Wal-Mart (WMT) chart.

Figure 3.10 Three-line strike bull, Wal-Mart, four months

What is interesting about this is a proximity issue. When price moves above resistance, you expect a better-than-average chance of reversal. However, in this case, a bullish continuation pattern is found at the point of the breakout. If you were able to locate confirmation for a bullish move, this could mean that the breakout will hold and a new, higher trading range will be established.

Figure 3.11 shows what happened next on the WMT chart.

The price move did hold as predicted by the three-line strike pattern. In fact, the resistance level flipped and became new support. This adds strength to the new trading range; a flip is a strong indication that there will not be a reversal in the near future.

Figure 3.11 Three-line strike bull, Wal-Mart, six months

Three-Line Strike Bear Pattern

The bear version of the three-line strike has the same format as the bull version, but with opposite coloration and movement. It succeeds 84% of the time. The downward trend revealed in the black sessions ends with an engulfing white candlestick, unusual in a bearish indicator. However, it does imply continuation of the bear trend. Figure 3.12 shows how this pattern appears.

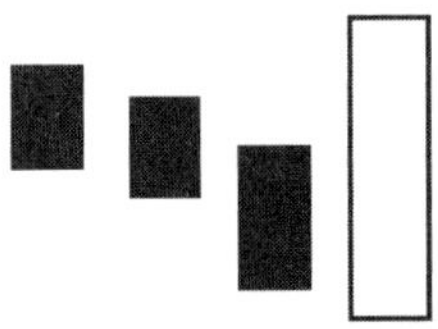

Figure 3.12 Three-line strike bear pattern

The move reveals that the downtrend is expected to continue. An example of this pattern is shown in the chart of 3M (see Figure 3.13).

The preceding downtrend was not a very strong trend; in fact, it is not clear whether this should continue or not. Then the three-line strike continuation signal appeared, forecasting a continued downward path. This took place and, in fact, took price down 14 points.

The next move was not clear based on this chart. To see what happened next, check Figure 3.14.

Figure 3.13 Three-line strike bear, 3M, four months

Figure 3.14 Three-line strike bear, 3M, six months

This demonstrates the uncertainty of how long a trend will last even after a continuation signal is found. This downtrend lasted only three weeks, but during that time price did fall substantially. Then the reversal to a new bull trend took over. The move below support revealed the high likelihood of reversal; this was another example of how reversal is most likely at the point of support (or resistance).

In an interesting later development, the bull trend continued until it broke through resistance and at that point a three-line strike bull provided another continuation forecast for the bull move. It appeared to continue above the established level of resistance.

Three White Soldiers Pattern

The three white soldiers appears often on price charts, but like its related three black crows, by the time you spot this reversal, it could be too late to capitalize on the uptrend. So this often serves as confirmation of a previously identified bullish reversal; it may also fail, but the success frequency is still high at 84%.

The three white crows pattern is summarized in Figure 3.15.

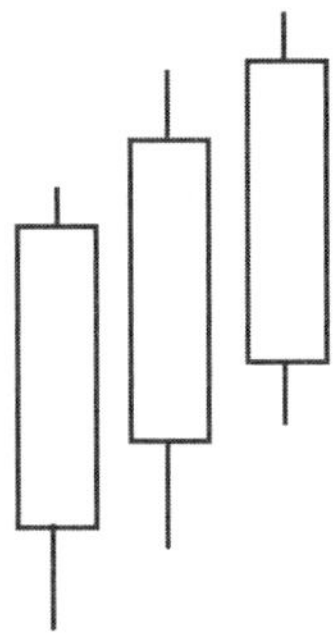

Figure 3.15 Three white soldiers pattern

The pattern consists of three sessions. Each one opens higher than the previous open and within the borders of the previous real body; it then closes higher than the previous close. This is a series of higher lows and higher highs.

An example of this pattern is seen on the chart of Cummins (CMI), shown in Figure 3.16. The downtrend stopped at the double bottom and then moved strongly upward beginning with a long white session. The three white soldiers appeared just as the price level moved above resistance. After this, resistance flipped and reverted to support.

The next phase of this trend is found in Figure 3.17.

The newly set support level held as the price continued moving upward. In this example, three white soldiers did not initiate the bullish reversal but confirmed it. Because it moved price above resistance, the outcome was uncertain at that point. It could have served as a failed signal and then a reversal, due to the proximity and breakout above resistance. However, it turned out to be a strong continuation of the uptrend.

Figure 3.16 Three white soldiers, Cummins, four months

Figure 3.17 Three white soldiers, Cummins, six months

Identical Three Crows Pattern

The identical three crows pattern results in reversal 72% of the time. The pattern consists of three black sessions. The ideal version opens at the same price as the previous day's close, as shown in Figure 3.18.

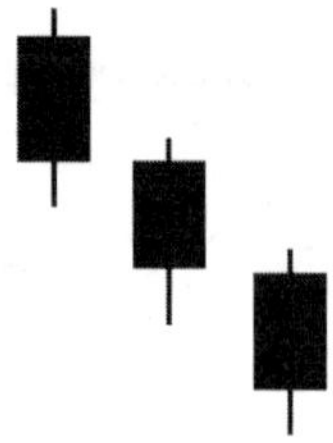

Figure 3.18 Identical three crows pattern

The exact conformity to this requirement is difficult to find. However, the chart of American Express (AXP) shown in Figure 3.19 identified resistance, a failed breakout, and a three-session pattern that almost accomplishes the identical three crows pattern. The question for traders is whether or not this is close enough to act on as a bearish reversal. The example is a hybrid of identical black crows and three black crows, so it should be a reliable bearish reversal signal. Of greater concern is the fact that the previous brief uptrend had largely reversed back to nearly the point of resistance before the identical black crows appeared. However, because this is a reaction to a breakout, the likelihood of a bearish move is strong.

Chart courtesy of StockCharts.com

Figure 3.19 Identical three crows, American Express, four months

Figure 3.20 shows what happened next on the AXP chart.

Chart courtesy of StockCharts.com

Figure 3.20 Identical three crows, American Express, six months

The price did fall seven points. However, it quickly recovered and began trending upward. As with previous examples, this demonstrates that reversal is rarely permanent, and might last only a few weeks or even a few days. Once a trade is entered in response to a reversal such as this, you need to continue monitoring the price pattern and looking for yet another reversal moving in the opposite direction.

Bearish Engulfing Pattern

The bearish engulfing pattern is found often on price charts, so it is a strong reversal signal with an 82% rate of success leading to reversal. The pattern is shown in Figure 3.21.

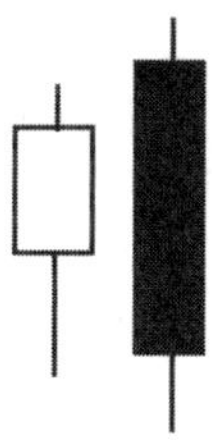

Figure 3.21 Bearish engulfing pattern

This is easily spotted on the price chart, but it should appear at the correct spot to meet the definition of a bearish reversal signal. This means it should be located in an uptrend, in which case it forecasts a coming reversal.

An interesting example of the bearish engulfing pattern is found on the chart of J.P. Morgan Chase, shown in Figure 3.22.

Figure 3.22 Bearish engulfing, J.P. Morgan Chase, four months

The first bearish engulfing on this chart is identified as a failed signal because the price trend moves in a bullish direction. However, there is not much of a downtrend to reverse, so this could also be interpreted as a nonsignal. For a reversal to be considered valid, there must be a trend in place. There does not appear to be a downtrend here.

The second is a double signal, which is very unusual. Because the engulfing is such a strong signal by itself, a double engulfing is exceptionally strong. Prices did decline as forecast by four points in about ten days.

The third instance, like the second one, appears at the peak of the uptrend and at resistance. It leads to a short-term downtrend of less than one week, and then prices move upward once again. However, this series of signals is even more interesting when viewed on an expanded chart. This is shown in Figure 3.23.

The breakout occurring at the end of the previous chart failed, and in dramatic fashion. The reversal was strongly confirmed by a double bearish engulfing and a gap in between. After a weak short-term upward move, yet another bearish engulfing appeared, forecasting yet another decline. The decline followed, moving price down another three points.

The bearish engulfing is a strong signal with a high performance rating, and you will find many of them on stock charts. If located at proximity to resistance and additionally confirmed with other signals, it is one of the best and most easily spotted bearish reversals.

Figure 3.23 Bearish engulfing, J.P. Morgan Chase, six months

Morning Star Pattern

The morning star is a bullish reversal. The "star" refers to the doji separated from the other two sessions by gaps. This is a transitional pattern consisting of a down day, downside gap, the doji, upside gap, and an up day. This is summarized in Figure 3.24.

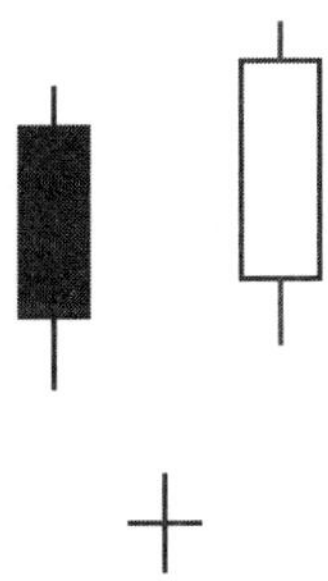

Figure 3.24 Morning star pattern

An example of the morning star is shown in the chart of Cisco Systems (CSCO) in Figure 3.25.

This contains two very distinct morning stars, both with proximity to support, as the formation dips below and then rebounds above. However, the conclusion of the chart is inconclusive because it does not reveal whether the predicted bullish move occurred. To see what did occur, refer to Figure 3.26.

Figure 3.25 Morning star, Cisco Systems, four months

Figure 3.26 Morning star, Cisco Systems, six months

As it turned out, the double morning star accurately predicted a bullish move, with resistance rising as the trend progressed. The breakout near the end of the period included a very large upside gap. Normally, when price gaps above resistance, you expect to see a downside reversal. In this case, however, it appears that rising resistance flipped and became rising support. If this trend did continue, it would demonstrate that the initial double morning star was accurate. This was inconclusive for the month of June that followed. Prices remained in a narrow breadth between $24 and $25 per share.

Bearish Belt Hold Pattern

The belt hold is a signal that contradicts the established trend. A bearish belt hold consists of rising sessions of either color and followed by a black session that contradicts what appeared to be a strong continuation of the uptrend. The preceding sessions are expected to be primarily white, but black sessions can also be included in the mix. The pattern is shown in Figure 3.27.

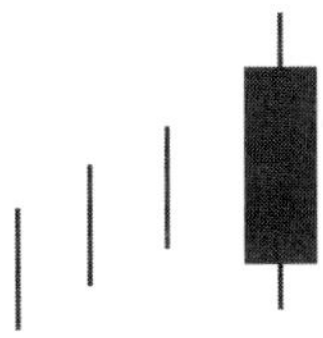

Figure 3.27 Bearish belt hold pattern

The chart of Unitedhealth Group, shown in Figure 3.28, includes an example of a strong bearish belt hold. This appears exactly where you would expect to see it, after a strong uptrend. In this example, the proximity supported the strong bearish change, as the pattern moved price above resistance. The upper shadow of the black session further demonstrated the inability of buyers to move price higher.

Chart courtesy of StockCharts.com

Figure 3.28 Bearish belt hold, Unitedhealth Group, four months

Because this pattern showed up near the end of the charted period, the next step cannot be known. However, Figure 3.29 shows an extension of the chart and subsequent price action.

Figure 3.29 Bearish belt hold, Unitedhealth Group, six months

The pattern was followed by two weeks of indecision characterized by the sideways movement of price. However, it then did move into a downtrend as predicted. Price declined seven points before settling into yet another sideways movement and then a gradual uptrend.

Mat Hold Pattern

The mat hold is a bullish continuation pattern with a complex series. It begins with a white session and then is followed by an upside gap and three sessions moving down. These are either all black or contain a middle white session. The final, fifth session once again takes over to the upside and predicts continuation to the upside. This is shown in Figure 3.30.

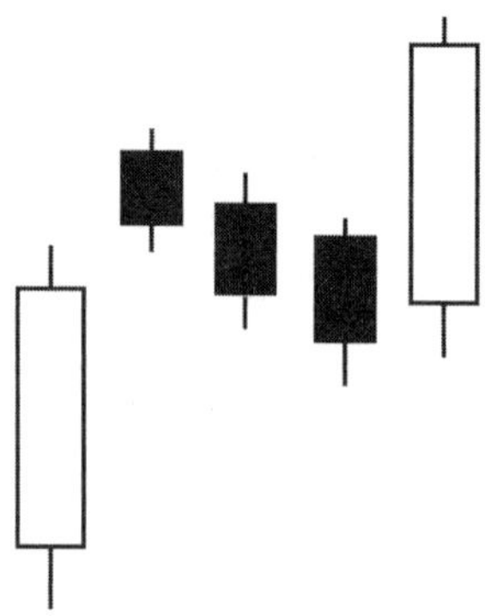

Figure 3.30 Mat hold pattern

An example of the mat hold is found on the chart of IBM. This is shown in Figure 3.31.

Figure 3.31 Mat hold, IBM, four months

The location of the mat hold makes it difficult to determine whether there is actually an uptrend to be continued. Prior to this charted period, the price pattern was just as volatile as what is shown. In the preceding period of October 15 to November 30, price moved from $170 to $185. In the two weeks from November 15 to December 1, price declined back to about $177, where Figure 3.31 takes over. So if the first segment of the prior period is considered an uptrend, followed by an adjustment, then the mat hold does provide a good signal for continuation. In fact, it does continue with slightly rising resistance.

The trend concludes with a move above resistance, normally indicating a coming correction. The next phase of this trend is shown in Figure 3.32.

The move above resistance settled into a falling wedge, which is yet another bullish indicator. So it appears that IBM would be likely to continue moving higher. The month of June (beyond the period charted) saw price decline another two points to approximately $180.50, so the outcome of the falling wedge was inconclusive at that point. However, for the period charted, the original mat hold was a solid bullish continuation signal.

Figure 3.32 Mat hold, IBM, six months

Pitfalls: Scaling and False Signals

This section examines several of the realities of candlestick charts that may mislead rather than enlighten the trader. Some attributes of scaling, true range, and blending distort the real picture of how the price trend works.

Scaling—the number of points and distance between price points—is set automatically by the trading range in the selected period. So if you choose a six-month period and one company's price moves 150 points during that time, scaling will have to be set at 150 or 160 points for the entire range to show up on that chart. But if the range from high to low was only 25 points, the scaling will be set much closer.

This becomes a problem because volatility is visual, but it is also relative. So you cannot compare the degree of movement in two different companies that are scaled at different levels. The movement within the chart will rely on the scaling and cannot be compared with a different company. For example, the chart of Netflix (NTFX) required ten-point scaling, as shown in Figure 3.33.

The first highlighted area contained a very large upward gap and spanned 50 points; the second downward highlight moved price 100 points. Considering that the price range on this chart is between $300 and $460, these moves represent volatility within the period, but it is not the number of points the price moved that defined that volatility. It is the degree of movement. The second example, price moving down 100 points, took place over three weeks and represented more than a 20% drop in price.

Chart courtesy of StockCharts.com

Figure 3.33 10-point scaling, Netflix

In comparison, the chart of Boeing in the same time period had a 2.5-point scaling system in place, but the degrees of price movement were just as dramatic as the Netflix example. The Boeing chart is shown in Figure 3.34.

Chart courtesy of StockCharts.com

Figure 3.34 2.5-point scaling, Boeing

The 20-point drop is approximately the same degree of volatility on this stock as the previous Netflix 100-point drop. The Boeing drop is a nearly 18% decline in the price level, even though one-fourth of the number of points were involved. The second move, about 5% from one point to the other, is quite different from the Netflix example, but both stocks displayed similar levels of volatility.

So scaling has to be taken into consideration when quantifying volatility. Comparing two companies on the basis of the number of points of movement is inaccurate as long as the scaling is not identical. Volatility is a relative matter within the chart itself, and between an established breadth of trading in one period versus the price move in a subsequent period.

A second form of potential misleading information is found in the analysis of true range. This is a method used by some chartists in which the actual session-to-session price movement is adjusted. The opening price from one day is compared with the closing price of the next day. For example, the chart of McDonald's (MCD) shows how true range can be applied. This is shown in Figure 3.35.

Chart courtesy of StockCharts.com

Figure 3.35 True range, McDonald's

True range can be applied to any two consecutive days. Five examples were selected here, circled on the chart and listed here in sequence:

1. $93.75 to $94.50; and $94.40 to $93.25; true range: 0.50 points
2. $91.50 to $92.75; and $93.00 to $91.50; true range: 0.00 points
3. $93.50 to $94.40; and $94.25 to $93.25; true range: 0.25 points
4. $96.75 to $96.25; and $96.25 to $97.25; true range: 0.50 points
5. $100.25 to $99.50; and $99.40 to $100.75; true range: 0.50 points

The point here is that two days can be adjusted so that the interim volatility disappears. The intention is to better analyze actual price movement by removing that volatility, but in fact the practice of adjusting to find true range may ignore the importance of price movement from open to close, not to mention the extended trading ranges reflected in upper and lower shadows. These day-to-day changes may provide important signals that can disappear when true range is employed.

True range may be useful in some applications, but it distorts the reality of how prices move. In theory, any two days can be manipulated to make the volatility appear less important or, if selected to augment gaps and trading range, volatility can be exaggerated beyond each day's change.

A final practice of concern is called blending. Like true range, blending adjusts the change from one open to another close, but extends over several days. For example, on the chart of Travelers (TRV), in Figure 3.36, four examples of blending are provided. These drastically reduce the volatility of the series by comparing the opening price of the first session with the closing price of the last session.

Chart courtesy of StockCharts.com

Figure 3.36 Blending

The four blended sessions are as follows:

1. $86.75 to $86.50; $87.10 to $88.00; $88.05 to $87.50; $87.50 to $87.00; and $87.40 to $86.00; blended 1.75 points

2. $80.25 to $81.25; $81.80 to $82.10; $81.25 to $81.20; $81.25 to $81.50; and $80.35 to $80.20; blended 0.05 points

3. $83.00 to $83.40; $83.50 to $84.00; $84.25 to $83.55; $83.25 to $83.25; and $83.75 to $83.00; blended 0.00 points

4. $86.75 to $86.20; $85.90 to $86.10; $86.15 to $86.20; and $86.25 to $87.75; blended 1.00 points

In these cases, the levels of price movement within the blended period are collectively very small, even though some significant changes did occur. Whether these movements represent reversal signals, retracements, or random movement does not matter. The problem with blending is that it distorts the price trend by making even a fairly volatile short-term trend appear as little or no movement.

The problem with calculations of true range or blending is that they do not always yield an accurate picture of the chart pattern. You can make any volatile situation appear much less volatile, or exaggerate mild volatility by blending an evolving series of price changes into one dramatic jump in price. In either case, the calculation of true yield and blending may not provide useful insight, but is just as likely to distort signals and even make them disappear.

The next chapter addresses reversal signals and how to spot them, including the danger of acting without strong confirmation or contending with failed reversal signals.

4

Reversal Signals—Spotting the Turning Point

Reversals are the types of signals that traders look for most often. They come in many forms and the key to acting on them consists of three parts: recognition, proximity, and confirmation.

Not all reversals are equal. Chapter 3, "Candlestick Patterns—Recognizing Evolving Strength or Weakness," documented the extensive study by Bulkowski that identified the frequency of successful reversal for specific signals. The high level of confidence in the ten selected signals is a primary reason for picking these, and for focusing on them in this book. The same is true for the selected Western technical signals in Chapter 2, "Traditional Analysis—The Power of Pattern Recognition." In both cases (Eastern signals and Western signals), the ten selected signals are by no means exhaustive. There are dozens of signals of both types, but the ones picked tend to offer the strongest and most easily recognized indication that reversal is more likely than not, if confirmed. So as part of pattern recognition, you also need to be aware of the strength in a signal.

Proximity is a second key part of acting on reversal signals. A weak set of reversals and confirmation keeps confidence low and may move your success rate closer to a random 50/50 outcome, when what you seek is a confirmation level approaching 100%. By ensuring that proximity works as it should for the maximum strength in a reversal signal, you are able to improve the profitable timing of trades over the otherwise random profit-to-loss ratio.

Confirmation also varies in terms of strength. Many candlesticks that have acted as expected only 50% of the time or close to it appear useless—and they are useless by themselves. But they may also provide *additional* confirmation to a reversal signal, with one important qualification: The 50/50 candlestick cannot be the only confirmation you find. It has to be used in the role of secondary confirmation. It makes sense that a high-frequency profitable reversal will also make a stronger form of confirmation. Signals cannot be absolutely assigned as initial reversal signals and confirmation. They cross-confirm one another. So the stronger the confirmation between two or more signals, the higher your chances for improved trade timing.

Even with the likely outcome approaching 100% confidence, you will never reach the 100% level. You can only strive for it and recognize that some signals—even when strongly confirmed and with the maximum proximity—will fail. This chapter concludes with a description of a signal's relative strength or weakness.

Recognition

Even experienced traders may overlook the subtle differences between strong and weak reversal signals. Chart analysis is an inexact science, so traders have to rely on several closely associated attributes of relative correlation. These include:

- **A study of strength and weakness in specific signals.** The ten candlestick signals introduced in Chapter 3 are among the most reliable, and the seven reversals in this group may provide a starting point for identifying exceptionally strong reversal. The ten Western technical indicators found in Chapter 2 have not been assigned degrees of reliability. However, by the same argument as that for candlesticks, these are among the most reliable price patterns and, when confirmed, they work with other signals (candlesticks, volume, and momentum) to identify strength to the signal.
- **Comparative analysis based on proximity.** Observing how signals behave at different points in the price trend is revealing. For example, a bearish reversal found within a bear trend is not much use. It implies a reversal, so you would give such a signal more value when found in a bull trend. Furthermore, the strength is likely to be greater when preceded by other strong indicators, such as repetitive price gaps, long candlesticks, confirming bear signals, volume spikes, and momentum oscillators moving into overbought conditions. The strength of an indicator is likely to be quite different in strong proximity than it will be when appearing in less-likely price locations. When you find a reversal signal in a trend already moving in the implied direction, it may serve as a continuation signal, but this is a weak compromise. Some specific signals are acknowledged as confirmation. But a reversal signal appearing in the wrong trend is not necessarily a signal of continuation; rather, it is a lack of signal and cannot be used reliably.
- **Heeding the strength of reversal and confirmation signals.** You may find strong reversal signals accompanied by relatively weak confirmation signals. Preferably, the confirmation signal should be as strong as the initial reversal. This is not always possible, but it is an ideal setting for reversal forecasting, and such a

condition—strong reversal and strong confirmation—will approach 100% more than strong reversal with weak confirmation. This might seem obvious; even so, it is a point easily overlooked. The object of this comment is to remind traders that confirming signals have to be quantified just as initial reversals should be—and forgetting to critically analyze confirmation signals increases the chance of failure in the set of signals.

Some examples follow. First is the problem with a reversal with weakness in proximity in the trading range, as seen on the chart of Disney (DIS), shown in Figure 4.1.

Figure 4.1 Weak signals—price gap and three black crows, four months

The initial upside gap led to a ten-point rise in price. However, in that moment it would be difficult to recognize the breakout, or to know whether or not the trend would continue upward or reverse. The three preceding sessions could be interpreted as a double bottom (albeit a weak one) and then a session with a long lower shadow, which indicates a likely bullish move. But these signals are weak and would require stronger confirmation before acting on the seemingly bullish signs.

The next highlighted signal, three black crows, is bearish, but proximity is also very weak. You expect to see this signal after a strong uptrend, but in this case, the prior uptrend ended over two weeks prior, so whether or not this signal forecasts a strong downtrend is unknown.

More information about what happened next is found in the expanded chart. Figure 4.2 reveals the subsequent price action.

Figure 4.2 Weak signals—price gap and three black crows, six months

The expanded chart reveals an indecisive price pattern, moving sideways in a five-point breadth of trading. The bearish three black crows was a failed signal, which might have been anticipated based on its weak proximity. However, toward the end of the charted period, another bearish signal appeared, the identical three crows. This is somewhat different from the three black crows based on the closing price of one session residing near the opening price of the next one. However, as in the previous instance, there is no strong uptrend to reverse. This is also a weak signal and could not be relied upon to signal a new downtrend. In fact, price then continued upward through the end of May. In the period after the one shown, price held and trended upward into early July. So both the three black crows and the identical three crows were weak signals, and both failed.

This example reveals that proximity is all-important in the judgment you make concerning signals. Traders may easily fall into the belief that a strong candlestick signal (and both of these are among the list of ten strong reversal signals) is infallible. It is not. More than any other factor, proximity has to be correct for these signals to work. A strong uptrend that ends with one of these reversals is most likely to succeed in forecasting reversal. Equally likely, when proximity is weak, confidence should also be low. Proximity reveals the truth about reversals: There must be a trend to reverse before a signal gains meaning, and a weak trend equals a weak signal.

Proximity

The proximity of a signal matters greatly and perhaps more than any other attribute of a reversal signal. So when you understand that a particular signal leads to reversal most of the time it is seen, this has to be further qualified. It is more accurate to state that a strong signal is likely to lead to reversal when it appears at the proximity you would expect. Thus, a bearish reversal is most accurate at the top of an uptrend, and a bullish reversal at the bottom of a downtrend.

This is an issue often overlooked in discussions of candlestick signals, as well as of Western indicators. A tendency might be to treat a strong signal based on its historical reliability, rather than qualifying it as proximity-based. For example, the chart of Procter & Gamble (PG) revealed a strong bearish signal, but its proximity was entirely wrong. This is shown in Figure 4.3.

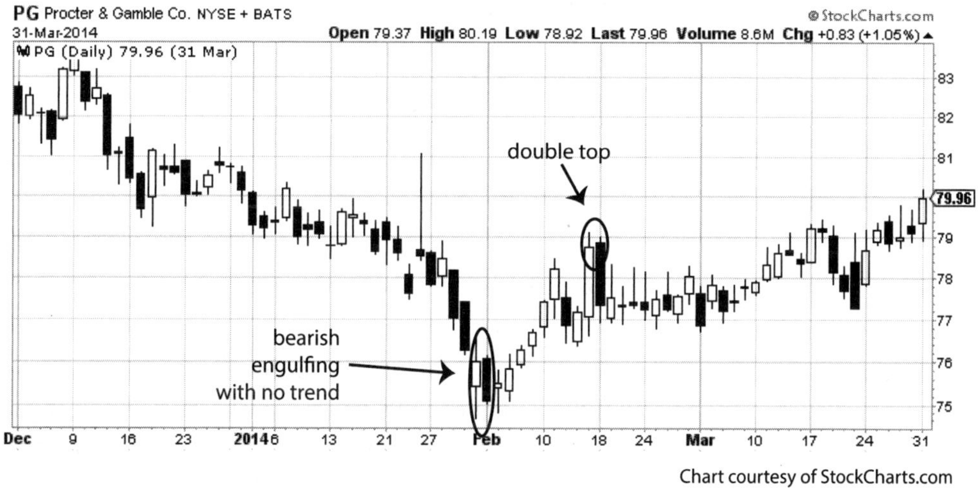

Figure 4.3 Weak signals—bearish engulfing and double top, four months

The bearish engulfing showed up at the bottom of a downtrend, when the correct proximity would be at the top of an uptrend. Traders responding to this signal by considering it a bearish continuation are in error because the proximity does not change the reversal automatically. To consider this as a continuation, you would expect to see additional patterns confirming that belief.

The second signal was a double top, but it was weak for two reasons. First, the upper shadows were quite small, whereas in a strong double top you would prefer to see longer upper shadows, indicating lost momentum among buyers. Second, the preceding uptrend was only four points over two weeks, not much of an uptrend to reverse. The trend continued upward in spite of both bearish signals, the engulfing, and double tops. The problem with both of these was that proximity just was not correct.

What happened after this is equally interesting in terms of the issue of proximity. Figure 4.4 continues the time period beyond what was shown initially.

Figure 4.4 Weak signals bearish engulfing and double top, six months

In this longer time span, the poor proximity of the first two signals continued. Finding two rising wedges in close proximity would normally be strongly bearish, but in spite of that, the price trend continued upward. As of this point, there were four bearish signals, but all occurred with weak proximity in what appears to be a strong bullish trend. The first of the two rising wedge signals occurred without any uptrend to reverse. The second rising wedge moved only 3.5 points from the starting point of $78 per share at the beginning of March. This also represented a very weak uptrend when considering whether or not to act on a double bearish signal.

As it turned out, none of the bearish reversals on this chart led to a bearish move, and the cause is assigned to poor proximity. The lesson in this for any trader relying on chart patterns is that the appearance of a reversal signal has little or no meaning if it shows up in the wrong location within the trading range. In all of these instances, uptrends either did not exist or were very minor. So in terms of reversal, the proximity was not there.

The same rule applies to continuation patterns. You need to find signals with proximity and confirmation before accepting the implied continuation in a signal. For example, the chart of Nike (NKE) exhibited two interesting patterns with bullish continuation patterns, and both failed. The chart is shown in Figure 4.5.

Figure 4.5 Weak signals—ascending triangle, four months

The ascending triangle is supposed to serve as a bullish continuation signal. However, these appeared twice and both times led to a price decline. In both instances, the uptrends were not particularly strong. Even with a continuation signal, they did not necessarily have the momentum to continue. It appears more apparent that the price trend reached a plateau at the point of resistance.

A great problem with continuation signals refers back to proximity. For confirmation to offer a strong signal, there should be room to continue before resistance will be reached. Otherwise, the high likelihood of reversal at the resistance price may offset what otherwise appeared as a continuation forecast.

This chart continued to contradict the continuation assumption, as shown in Figure 4.6.

The continuation simply never occurred, and this longer time period reveals the same proximity problem in the opposite direction. The three-line strike is a bearish continuation pattern, but it appeared after six weeks of sideways movement. There was no specific downtrend to be continued. So contrary to continuing a downtrend, price then trended upward.

Figure 4.6 Weak signals ascending triangle, six months

This chart presents a problem for chartists who expect signals to work, but who do not pay close attention to the proximity factor. Two bullish continuation signals appeared at the wrong place and were followed by strong downtrends. Then, a bearish continuation appeared, also at the wrong place, and led to an uptrend. It might seem that when continuation patterns appear in the wrong proximity, they act as reversal signals. This could be a flawed assumption, however. Just as a reversal signal does not constitute continuation when proximity is flawed, by the same argument a poorly placed continuation signal should not be translated to serve as a reversal indicator.

Confirmation

The problem of acting on weak signals affects the quality of confirmation as well as brings a reversal signal into doubt. For example, the chart of Caterpillar (CAT) contains two strong reversal signals, both bearish engulfing. But even though they confirvm one another, should you expect a reversal? The chart is shown in Figure 4.7.

The problem here is that the bearish engulfing signal is exceptionally strong, when found in the right proximity (namely after a strong uptrend and at or near resistance). When you find two of these signals close together, it can be exceptionally strong because the second one confirms the first.

None of that matters, however, if the other attributes are not in place. If you assume that resistance is at about $97 per share (a level established for less than two weeks), neither of the engulfing patterns move price through resistance. That is only one of the two big problems. The second problem is the lack of a strong uptrend to reverse. With previous resistance trending between $90 and $92 per share, there is not much of a move at all on this chart.

Chart courtesy of StockCharts.com

Figure 4.7 Weak signals—bearish engulfing, four months

The problem with a weak uptrend and no move through resistance is that the bearish reversal does not have much of a price trend to reverse. Thus, the weakness in proximity equates with a weakness in confirmation. If this pattern had been preceded by a stronger uptrend, and recent sessions had moved above resistance, this double bearish engulfing would have been exceptionally strong. The bearish engulfing is reliable 82% of the time it is found. This means that when it appears, a downtrend will follow 82% of the time—but there is a condition to this rule. For the engulfing to be applicable and to act as expected, there must be a strong trend to reverse, and the signal has to appear in the right proximity. Neither of these applies here, so in this case, the signal does not act as a reversal, and confirmation has nothing to confirm.

To see where this chart goes next, check Figure 4.8.

The weakness of the previous uptrend was not reassuring and, as this expanded chart reveals, not likely to turn around any time soon. The reversal signals you discover and confirm are always strongest when the preceding uptrend is strong as well. This is a statistical certainty; a few basic rules apply to charts, including:

1. Trends never continue forever.
2. Weak trends flatten out or reverse weakly; strong trends tend to reverse strongly.
3. Even with the uncertainty of price movement, the trend and the signal reveal the *likely* next step.

Chart courtesy of StockCharts.com

Figure 4.8 Weak signals—bearish engulfing, six months

In this expanded chart, all of these rules can be applied. Even though the stock reveals an overall uptrend, it is slow and flattens out often, so there is no reason to expect a sudden or dramatic reversal. The trend is weak, so any reversal should be expected to also be weak.

The lack of bearish reversal is further confirmed by the newly emerged support line, which itself trended slightly higher for the last two months of the period charted. Failing the emergence of a new bearish signal with confirmation, this makes any reversal unlikely. A reversal is likely to be just as weak as the established trend. Resistance is slightly more volatile than support during these last two months, but the price breadth of resistance was only about five points. To set up a strong bearish reversal, you would expect to see a clear breakout above that level with price gaps, volume spikes, and clear reversal signals in the price pattern. This does not appear anywhere on the current chart, and after this period, price continued trending upward, to a range between $107 and $111 by early July. This means all of the bearish signals earlier in the chart failed, and for logical reasons: weak uptrend, poor proximity, and no specific challenge to resistance at any point in the chart. In fact, the gradually upward-trending resistance can be traced for most of the chart, as shown in Figure 4.8. It is bullish but slow, so it makes no sense to seek a bearish reversal signal unless and until the bullish trend accelerates.

Failed Signals

It may be profound to observe that strong trends lead to equally strong reversals, and that weak trends do not. As statistical realities, these facts can be demonstrated repeatedly on stock charts. Just as proximity to resistance and support defines the strength of reversal, and just as reversal is possible only when a trend exists, another reality comes into play: Signals fail more often than not because signals themselves are weak. So finding a signal that meets the minimum criteria in terms of shape and size may not be enough to act, even with confirmation that is equally minimal.

Signals are most likely to fail in that condition. A lack of proximity, after a slow or weak trend, and then followed by weak reversals and confirmation does not add up to a high level of confidence.

What constitutes a weak signal? The obvious answer is dramatic visual attributes. Long shadows are powerful, for example, as long as they show up where they count the most. So when you find a bullish reversal at the bottom of a downtrend, an unusually long lower shadow reveals a loss of momentum among sellers. This is itself a strong signal that the downtrend is ending and a new uptrend is about to begin. The same applies to a long upper shadow on a session at the top of an uptrend, when you will seek a bearish reversal.

Signals themselves vary in levels of strength, apart from whether a previous trend is fast or slow, strong or weak. For example, a strong white soldiers or black crows pattern will consist of several important attributes, including two primary ones: strong price ranges in all three sessions, and openings within the range of the previous day accompanied by closings well beyond the previous day's range, not just barely beyond. A signal that just barely meets the pattern criteria is, by definition, weaker.

Strong and weak versions of the white soldiers and black crows patterns are shown in Figure 4.9.

The consistency of opening and closing prices based on the criteria (opening within range and closing beyond) is easily spotted in the strong variety of each. And in the weak variety, the sizes of the sessions are inconsistent and the opening and closing of each session a weak conformity to the criteria for the patterns.

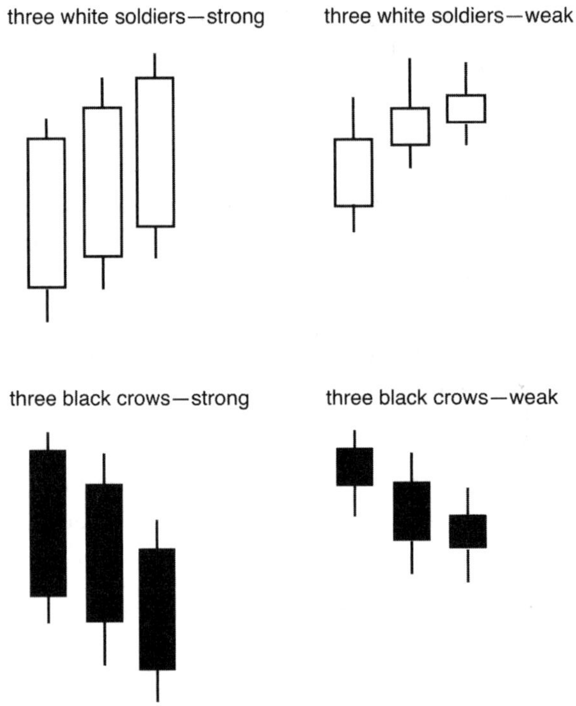

Figure 4.9 Strong and weak signals

The emphasis on reversal signals makes a majority of technicians focus on this event. That is logical because many traders are not sure what to do with continuation itself. The problem becomes one of how long continuation will continue, and on whether or not continuation is reliable. Finding a reversal signal that appears in the wrong proximity or within a trend moving in the wrong direction does not create strong continuation. For that, you need to seek specific continuation patterns. These are examined in the next chapter.

5

Continuation Signals—The Mid-Trend Signs

The focus of most traders on reversal signals is understandable. The point of reversal is where a majority of trades will occur. Continuation only forecasts that no action should be taken. However, some attributes of continuation should be remembered, including:

- **A reversal signal does not act as continuation.** Some arguments about indicators, especially candlesticks, include the point that when a reversal signal appears in the wrong place, it acts as a continuation signal. For example, a bearish signal appearing during a bear trend fits this category. However, it is not as simple as relabeling a reversal signal to conform to conditions. When you find a reversal signal in the wrong place, it is more likely to provide you with a false signal. The nature of a signal—reversal or continuation—is not necessarily transferable.
- **Continuation has to be confirmed just like reversal.** A common mistake is to forget the importance of confirmation when a continuation signal appears. This is an easy mistake to make, as though the trend itself confirms the continuation. However, just as reversal signals require independent confirmation, so does continuation. What does it imply when a continuation signal is not confirmed? It could be a false signal if you do not find confirmation, and a failed continuation signal itself may be a reversal if confirmation is not located.
- **Signals vary in reliability just like reversal signals.** The observation that some signals lead to reversal most of the time can be applied equally to continuation. So for those high-frequency and high-reliability signals, continuation becomes a high possibility. This explains partially why continuation signals are confusing to some traders and why they are easily ignored. Even a highly reliably confirmation signal can elicit a response of "so what?" The fact that the current trend is continuing does not need confirmation because traders assume that to be the case until reversal signals appear and are confirmed. There is logic in this belief.

So continuation signals only strengthen when you might assume, but they also reduce the potential for reversal to occur with little or no warning. A strong continuation is worthwhile if only because it tells you to not take profits and close a position at the moment.

- **A continuation signal may fail.** Like all signals, nothing is 100%. A continuation signal may fail just as a reversal signal may fail. So spotting continuation does not mean diligence can be suspended, and it does not guarantee that a reversal will not occur. One of the chronic problems in charting is identifying duration of a forecast. A continuation signal of high reliability may lead to a trend continuing for another month, or only for a matter of days. This is a problem with reversals as well, and a turn in the trend can be immediate or delayed for a considerable period of time. It is reasonable to say that even when confidence is high in what a signal reveals, proximity is right, and confirmation is strong, you still don't know *when* the event (reversal or continuation) is going to occur. It often is the case that finding a reliable signal is the easy part, but timing remains elusive and uncertain.

Retracement Versus Reversal

A retracement—a temporary countermove within a trend—is not always easily spotted. It often is the case that a clear difference can be assumed in one way: A reversal includes a signal and confirmation, whereas a retracement often lacks any signal whatsoever.

Retracement often is expected once price moves to a new high or new low (as measured within a period of time or within the current trend). However, retracement may also occur within a trend and is simply a statistical probability. Nothing moves in the same direction forever, and a countermove of three or four sessions often is nothing other than an adjustment in the speed and degree of price movement.

Being able to tell the difference between retracement and reversal is not always an easy matter. However, this is one moment in which a continuation signal is of great value. If you find a continuation signal and then price moves in the opposite direction, this could indicate that a retracement is under way. However, confirmation of the continuation signal is the only way to increase confidence in this theory.

Another distinction can be made based on proximity. Reversal is most likely at resistance or support, but this is not exclusive. When you find strong reversal and confirmation signals at these levels, confidence should be high. However, when price moves counter to an established trend and the price is not at or close to resistance or support, is it reversal or retracement? Reversal can occur anywhere in the price range, so the lack of reversal proximity is not conclusive. However, when a price countermove occurs elsewhere, it also increases the likelihood that you are witnessing a retracement.

Some ways to distinguish between reversals and retracement include:

- **Lack of reversal and confirmation.** The most important factor of all is whether or not a reversal signal is found. If price changes direction but you do not see any reversal signals, there is a strong possibility that it is a retracement.
- **Appearance of indecision candlesticks.** An indecision candlestick is one appearing at the top or bottom of a trend, but whose direction either depends on the circumstances, or is just not clear. Narrow-range days like the spinning top and long-legged doji are typical. Both are also expected to reveal long upper and lower shadows, betraying a struggle on both sides to move price, but failing to do so. When these appear at the point of price reversal, it is a clue that a retracement is under way but not always a reversal.
- **Momentum of the trend.** The retracement is expected to appear after a very strong move. So when price reverses after price trends strongly upward or downward, it could be a retracement. This is especially likely when the price has not trended close to resistance or support. This strong momentum can also be confirmed with momentum oscillators. If you spot a move into overbought or oversold territory, a price directional change is more likely to be a retracement.
- **Fibonacci signals appear.** A Fibonacci retracement (based on the Fibonacci sequence) is an identified percentage adjustment in the current trend. So when price moves counter to the trend, look for these percentages (the percentage is based on levels of a trend that retrace within a few sessions). The most important among these are 23.6% (any value in the sequence divided by the value three places higher), 38.2% (any value divided by the value two places higher), and 61.8% (any value divided by the next value). So when a retracement appears, look for it to offset these percentages of the existing trend before the retracement ends. Although this is not a precise method, it provides several stopping points where a retracement is likely to conclude.

There are occasions in which a continuation signal will be followed closely by retracement. For example, the chart of Microsoft (MSFT) displays an uptrend, a three-line strike, a brief retracement, and then a resumption of the uptrend. This is shown in Figure 5.1.

Figure 5.1 Continuation—three-line strike bullish, four months

The initial uptrend was not long in duration or particularly strong. And in this condition, the appearance of a continuation signal will not always be compelling. However, the three-line strike is exceptionally strong, and the retracement set up a longer-term and stronger uptrend. From here, the trend was seen to continue, as demonstrated in Figure 5.2.

Figure 5.2 Continuation—three-line strike bullish, six months

The uptrend not only continued but flipped prior resistance into new support. When this occurs, the new support level is likely to be strong and to hold as the new trading range continues to emerge.

A similar pattern was found in the chart of Chevron (CVX), shown in Figure 5.3.

Figure 5.3 Continuation—three-line strike bearish, four months

In this bearish example, a downtrend included the bearish continuation signal, but moved upward before the continuation occurred. The beginning downtrend appears brief, but prior to the period shown, the price level was as high as $123 per share in August and September. The continuation continued until price gapped and then moved sideways. To see what happened beyond this period, see Figure 5.4.

The bear trend clearly ended at the point of the downside gap. After this, a bullish trend took over and is shown in the upward-trending channel lines. The chart concluded with a falling wedge, a bearish signal.

Retracement occurred at two key points in this chart. First was the upward retracement that took place from the last ten days of December through the first three weeks of January (followed by the downtrend continuation). The second retracement was found in the second week of April at the conclusion of the channel lines pattern and before the falling wedge. This retracement marked a point of continuation and was confirmed by the wedge pattern.

Figure 5.4 Continuation—three-line strike bearish, six months

Strength and Weakness—Candlestick Signals

Beyond the sometimes highly visible retracement patterns, you will also find signals like the three-line strike at the proximity of resistance and support. A continuation pattern at these points contradicts the previously noted attribute of reversals. A reversal occurring at resistance or support indicates high confidence that price will turn and move in the opposite direction. However, by the same argument, when you find a continuation pattern in the same proximity, is it just as strong in favor of a breakout from the established range?

This is a difficult question to address. Any breakout above resistance or below support is likely to reverse back into range, and the occurrence of a continuation signal is not enough by itself to contradict the likely reversal. However, other factors—absence of a specific reversal signal or reversal confirmation—strengthen the likely continuation of the trend through resistance or support and establishment of a new trading range.

This will be most likely to occur when you find continuation confirmation in additional signals, and when you also discover resistance/support or support/resistance flips. At times, however, a continuation signal appears complete with confirmation, but there is a delayed reaction on the chart, perhaps even an extended countermove. One example of this is seen in the chart of Exxon Mobil (XOM), shown in Figure 5.5.

The mat hold is a bullish continuation signal and on this chart, two appeared in close proximity. This is not only unusual, but exceptionally strong, with the second signal confirming the first. You would have expected the price to continue strongly to the upside, but instead it trended down for an entire month.

Figure 5.5 Continuation—mat hold, four months

After this extended downtrend, the anticipated uptrend did emerge and continued through to the end of the period. However, the high levels of the first trend were not reached. Figure 5.6 reveals the next step in this chart.

Figure 5.6 Continuation—mat hold, six months

The uptrend continued for two months before leveling out. However, the new high of $103 was reached by the first week in July (beyond the period shown), so in a long-term perspective, the mat hold that appeared in December (and again in January) did correct an extended continuation trend over coming months.

This is a good example of the uncertainty of timing even with strong signals. In this case, continuation did not occur immediately after the signals were found but moved in the opposite direction before the trend took off. However, once this occurred, the resumption of the uptrend was strong as well as long-lasting.

Strength and Weakness—Western Signals

Candlestick continuation signals may be found in many forms, including three-line strikes and mat holds. However, several Western technical signals also provide convincing evidence of likely continuation in a trend. The candlestick and Western signals confirm one another, in addition to other forms of confirmation, notably in momentum oscillators.

Among the strong Western continuation signals is the ascending triangle. This may extend from a few days to many weeks. The idea is that with flat resistance and rising support, as the breadth of trading narrows, a breakout above resistance is likely to occur. For example, the chart of Coca-Cola (KO) shown in Figure 5.7 displays an interesting ascending triangle, complete with a downside gap and retracement pattern lasting three sessions. After this, rising support once again appeared. The rising support itself represents short-term uptrend movement, and the triangle formation became a bullish continuation pattern.

This continuation pattern should lead to an uptrend breaking through resistance. Even with the interrupted rising support, does this actually occur? Figure 5.8 demonstrates that the ascending triangle did accurately predict a new, higher trading range.

A strong uptrend with a price gap led to establishment of a new support level. The next question is whether or not the new trading range would hold. After the period shown, price did continue higher and by early July was above $42 per share. So at that point, it is clear that the predicted continuation seen in the initial ascending triangle was an accurate forecast for a new uptrend.

Figure 5.7 Continuation—ascending triangle (bullish), four months

Figure 5.8 Continuation—ascending triangle (bullish), six months

The opposite pattern, a descending triangle, is bearish. The chart for Goldman Sachs (GS) included a descending triangle, as shown in Figure 5.9.

Figure 5.9 Continuation—descending triangle (bearish), four months

The triangle predicted continuation of the downtrend that began at the start of the year. However, the next question is whether or not a downtrend did continue. Figure 5.10 shows that a downtrend did emerge with resistance at the same price as the prior support level. That support (established at the bottom of the descending triangle) reverted to resistance, making it especially strong. Subsequently, price did evolve above resistance in June, but by July, it had fallen back close to this resistance level.

Figure 5.10 Continuation—descending triangle (bearish), six months

The third triangle is symmetrical. Because it consists of falling resistance and rising support, it may be either bullish or bearish. Because either is a continuation pattern, the nature of the symmetrical triangle relies on what type of trend preceded it. A good example is found in the chart of Walt Disney (DIS), shown in Figure 5.11.

Chart courtesy of StockCharts.com

Figure 5.11 Continuation—symmetrical triangle (bullish), four months

This is a bullish example. The month of December was bullish, and then price declined and formed the symmetrical pattern. The trend did continue and the charted period concluded with yet another symmetrical triangle. Although the second triangle was another bullish continuation signal, what happened next? Figure 5.12 reveals a sideways price movement.

The price did evolve higher in the period after that shown, so the continuation occurred, but on a delayed basis. The symmetrical triangle is not as clear a signal as the ascending or descending triangle because it often is not strong enough to provide a clear signal. In the Disney example, the first symmetrical triangle was quite strong and contained clear attributes to make it a good continuation signal (sharp decline in resistance accompanied by sharp rise in support). However, the second symmetrical triangle was not as strong, with more moderate movement on both sides and of shorter duration. The fact that the next uptrend was delayed by two months makes this second signal much weaker. Given the time span it required to work, it might even be considered as a failed signal. However, a true "failed" signal would tend to be followed by a price decline. In this case, price held at a three-point breadth until the new uptrend did eventually appear.

Chart courtesy of StockCharts.com

Figure 5.12 Continuation—symmetrical triangle (bullish), six months

The bearish symmetrical triangle is equally challenging and not as strong as other triangle formations. A bearish example is found in the chart of Pfizer (PFE), shown in Figure 5.13.

Chart courtesy of StockCharts.com

Figure 5.13 Continuation—symmetrical triangle (bearish), four months

The first of these did lead to a very brief decline, but after that, price rose, making the first symmetrical triangle a failed signal. However, the second example on this chart had a much steeper angle. However, its weakness is that there is little in the way of a downtrend to be continued. So in that respect, this one is also of limited value. The chart contains a lot of volatility, but the entire chart range is only three points; so the patterns are valid, but movement was actually quite modest in terms of price change.

Where did this lead? Figure 5.14 shows an interesting evolution in the price. A third symmetrical triangle appeared below the previous one and in this instance there was a valid downtrend to be continued.

Figure 5.14 Continuation—symmetrical triangle (bearish), six months

It did continue downward, in fact, and took the price range down significantly (however, even this greater trading range represented only four points overall). The symmetrical triangle is probably not always as reliable as ascending or descending triangles, but in the right placement, it can provide strong bullish or bearish signals. However, as with all continuation signals, the larger question is: How long will the continuation last?

Because continuation is far less certain than reversal, it also comes with problems. The extent of continuation is uncertain in each case, and traders seek reversal at some point. The continuation signal only tells you that a reversal is not likely to occur, at least not in the moment. However, you cannot know whether a reversal will be found next week or next month.

The continuation pattern reveals information about the price trend, but is easily misread. The implication of this signal, especially with strong confirmation, is that the price trend has a long way to go. But this is not always true. A dynamic resistance or support complicates the matter because with that moving range, proximity is moving as well. So identifying a reversal signal in proximity to resistance or support is itself a moving target. In these circumstances, continuation does reveal that it is not yet time for a reversal. However, the reversal could appear at any time.

One signal that the continuation is concluding would be a leveling out of the trading range. As resistance stops rising or support stops falling, price tends to settle down into a sideways range, often with a narrow breadth. This is a condition in which a reversal signal is likely to emerge. Look for price testing resistance or support with price gaps and strong reversal signals. In this condition, once price has settled into a set breadth and price range, continuation would be difficult to interpret, but reversal is more easily spotted.

The next chapter explores ways in which candlesticks and Western indicators can be used to confirm one another. The introduction of confirmation into this discussion demonstrates that individual signals are good starting points, but once those signals can be confirmed, they take on strength and their forecast next move gains strength.

6

Combining West and East—Candlesticks and the Technical Signs

The process of building up to confirmation for any form of signals includes a necessary set of building blocks. In coming chapters, a variety of combinations (candlesticks, Western price patterns, volume indicators, and momentum oscillators) will be documented. All of this will be provided in the context of relative correlation—the likelihood of an expected outcome based on (a) strength and speed of the current trend, (b) correct placement of the indicator (bullish reversal after a bear trend, or bearish reversal after a bull trend), and (c) proximity to resistance or support.

This chapter begins the process of identifying confirmation with a series of comparisons between candlestick signals and Western technical indicators.

Combinations in Different Time Spans

The first example of the two-part confirmation involves a strong uptrend culminating in a gapping mover above resistance, a developing rising wedge (a bearish signal) as an initial reversal signal, and confirmation in the form of three black crows. The chart for Visa (V) is provided in Figure 6.1, in which these developments are highlighted.

The elements are all in place to increase confidence in the likelihood of a downtrend as the next price direction. The beginning of the chart consists of a strong uptrend, and then a strong move above the range and assumed resistance. Next, a rising wedge develops over two months, so that you would expect to see a downtrend as the wedge narrows. Confirmation of this is seen in a very strong three black crows formation.

Whether or not this actually forms into a reversal cannot be known on this chart alone. For the next evolution in this pattern, see Figure 6.2, which extends the charted period.

The rising wedge reversal and three black crows confirmation did lead to the expected downtrend; in fact, price returned to the low levels seen at the beginning of the charted period.

Figure 6.1 Combinations—three black crows and rising wedge, four months

Figure 6.2 Combinations—three black crows and rising wedge, six months

This is a good example of simple two-part reversal and confirmation. Confidence was high because placement and proximity were exactly what you would expect: a reversal after a strong uptrend, and confirmation at the conclusion of the extended initial bearish signal. In later chapters, when these high-confidence signals are expanded with the addition of volume and momentum signals, the theory of relative correlation will be further tested. The argument in favor of high confidence in this example is based on only two signals. When examined in the context of even more confirmation, the confidence level may approach 100% in some cases.

Continuation Combination Patterns

The principle of relative correlation applies to continuation signals as well as to reversals. However, placement is quite different. You expect to find continuation signals at midrange and in one of two proximity cases: when the trend is not close to resistance or support, or when it is and you use the continuation signal to increase confidence in a successful breakout and establishment of a new trading range.

The "continuation" should consist of a clearly understood continuation signal, versus a reversal signal appearing at an unexpected place. The point has been raised before, but is worth repeating: In spite of the belief by some, reversal and continuation signals are not necessarily transferable. So a specific signal is most likely to be one or the other. When you find a reversal signal in the wrong place, the rationale that it is actually a continuation signal is a dangerous assumption. A more prudent assumption is that signals should not be transferred between reversal or continuation, but should be assumed to maintain their characteristics. This does not mean that transfer is impossible, but the reliance on that concept is questionable. Under the principle of relative correlation, transfer between reversal and continuation is a weak hypothesis. If you do rely on the concept, you may also want to find exceptionally strong multiple confirmations before proceeding with a new trade.

An example of a continuation pattern with confirmation is seen in the three-month chart of The Travelers (TRV), shown in Figure 6.3.

The ascending triangle is a bullish continuation signal. However, because it is close to a rising wedge in shape (a rising wedge is a bearish reversal), exceptionally strong confirmation should be found before relying on the ascending triangle.

If the resistance level of the triangle were to rise even slightly, it would change the nature of this signal. The big difference is that continuation is represented in the rising support, versus a sideways resistance level, which makes this a bullish signal. In the rising wedge, both resistance and support trend upward but breadth of trading narrows. This is a potential flaw in Western technical analysis. The difference is slight, but the impact is potentially significant. So whether working with a rising wedge as bearish reversal, or with an ascending triangle as bullish continuation, the key to accurate interpretation has to be strong confirmation. An additional method for distinguishing between the wedge and triangle is in how steep a slope the pattern represents. The greater the slope, the stronger the signal. When the slope is very low, caution is advised.

Chart courtesy of StockCharts.com

Figure 6.3 Combinations—three-line strike and ascending triangle, two continuation patterns, four months

This chart provides very strong confirmation in the form of a three-line strike—and not just one, but two of these in close proximity. The three-line strike is not very common or easy to find, so locating two of them like this increases confidence in an otherwise questionable pattern such as the ascending triangle. In this chart, the ascending triangle is not especially strong because its slope is small, so you have to rely on strong confirmation, such as the double three-line strike.

The next step in the chart's pattern reveals whether or not the continuation signal was accurate. Figure 6.4 shows what happened next.

The ascending triangle and three-line strike double confirmation were accurate. The next step was an extended uptrend. One possible criticism of this as a continuation signal could be that the initial uptrend was brief, lasting less than two weeks. However, in a pattern like the ascending triangle, which extends at times for several weeks (in this case, for six weeks), the rising support represents part of the uptrend. So, in fact, the uptrend being confirmed extended from mid-February to the end of March, a much longer period. The continuation signal occurred during the uptrend itself.

Because continuation is more difficult to interpret than reversal, a strong level of confirmation is desirable; in this case, the confirmation is very strong. A trader holding positions would react to this by taking no action, or by increasing holdings (assuming confidence was high).

Chart courtesy of StockCharts.com

Figure 6.4 Combinations—three-line strike and ascending triangle, two continuation patterns, six months

Bullish and Bearish Combinations Together

Yet another form of confirmation takes the form of reversal in one direction, followed by reversal in the other direction. Of course, confirmation is essential for this back-and-forth price pattern to be managed with confidence. As with all signal types, the strength or weakness of placement, proximity, and confirmation tell the entire story.

The chart of Unitedhealth Group provides an initial bullish set of signals and confirmation, as shown in Figure 6.5.

The long-term rising resistance improves confidence of a likely continuation, but the upward-moving price gaps present a problem. Because it moves price above resistance, does it mean the expanding resistance will continue and perhaps even move higher? This is a proximity and placement problem. The long-term uptrend will eventually exhaust, and the placement of these gaps is the right place for a reversal. Proximity at a resistance breakout also increases the likelihood for a bearish reversal. But is this enough to make that determination? Not yet. It could represent a growing bullish trend and setting up of a new, higher trading range, or it could be the first signal of a bearish reversal. To make this decision, more information is needed.

Figure 6.5 Combinations—bullish price gaps and bearish multiple signals, four months

Figure 6.6 answers the questions by presenting strong bearish reversal in the form of an engulfing pattern, followed quickly by identical black crows. Both of these are reliable most of the time (bearish engulfing reverses 82% of the time it is seen, and identical three crows reverses 72%). So based on these two signals appearing close together, confidence is high for a bearish reversal.

Figure 6.6 Combinations—bullish price gaps and bearish multiple signals, six months

The bearish engulfing showed up at the peak of the uptrend and confirmed the gapping price action moving through resistance. At this point, closing out long positions or entering short positions would be clearly justified, just based on proximity and the strength of the engulfing pattern. The identical three crows decided the question, but by this point, the downtrend was already well under way and, as it turned out, it was not long lasting.

The last leg of this chart revealed a price decline of eight points, followed by an offsetting bullish trend in the form of the upward-moving price channels. So, the initial signal in the form of bullish price gaps presented a problem because price moved through resistance, the proximity location where reversal is most likely. The bearish response occurred quickly but did not last long. And, finally, after a considerable drop in price range, a new bullish trend was set up by a very narrow channel of only three points.

Another example reveals that bearish continuation signals should lead to a continued downtrend, ultimately concluding with bullish reversal and then a bullish continuation signal. The chart of Procter & Gamble (PG) provides a good example of such a trend, as shown in Figure 6.7.

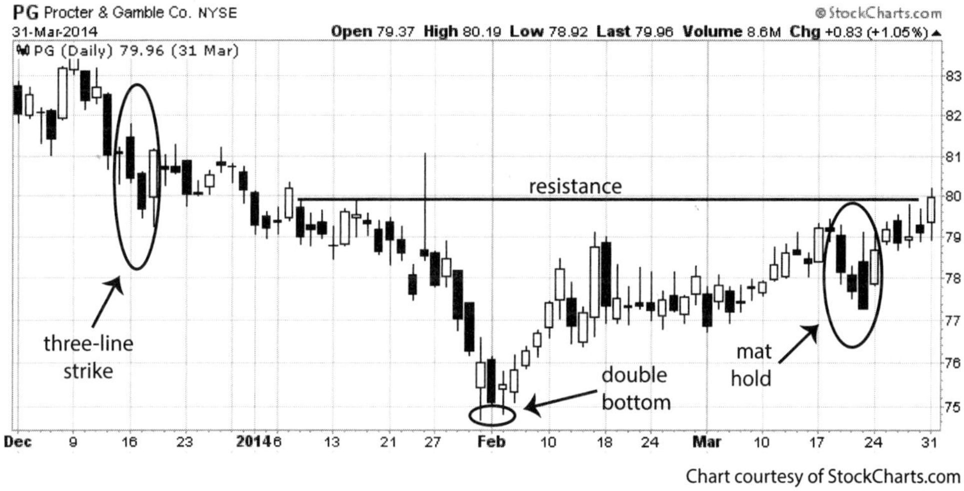

Figure 6.7 Combinations—bearish and bullish signals, four months

The three-line strike is a bearish continuation signal, which, as the chart reveals, does lead to a continued downtrend. Because this shows up at mid-trend, continuation is appropriate in this proximity. The only question that remains is how long continuation will last.

It appears to end with the very clear double bottom. The uptrend follows and is confirmed by the continuation mat hold. The end of the chart includes the last session closing just above resistance. Based on the strong continuation in the form of the mat hold, does this proximity mean the uptrend is over, or that it will continue? As with all continuation signals, the next challenge is in identifying how the trend will last. Figure 6.8 shows what occurs next on this chart.

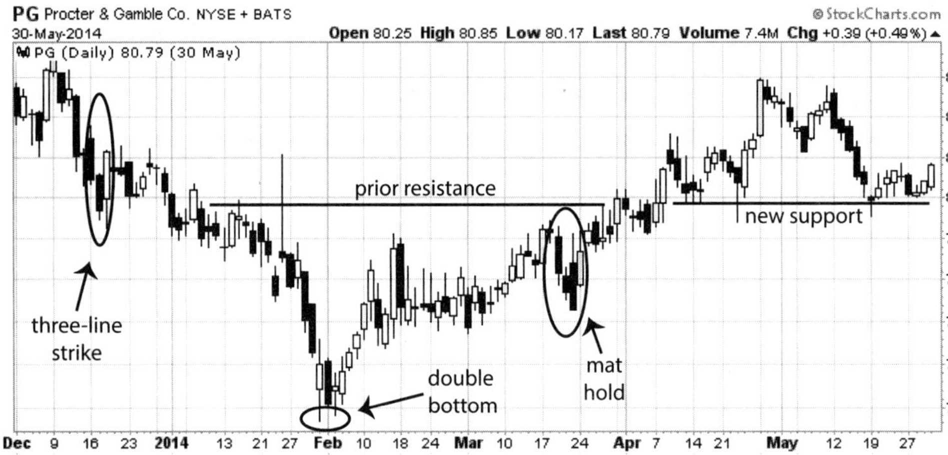

Chart courtesy of StockCharts.com

Figure 6.8 Combinations—bearish and bullish signals, six months

Two important developments strongly confirm the bullish trend for Procter & Gamble. First, the uptrend does continue as forecast. Second, and equally strong in confirming the trend, a new support level is set at the price representing resistance in the prior segment of the chart. The resistance flip makes the new support level exceptionally strong. In the following period (not shown on this chart), price dipped to as low as $78.50 per share, but in July, it rebounded sharply and above the new support level.

Another example of bullish and bearish signals found on the same chart is found in the case of Home Depot, shown in Figure 6.9.

This is a busy chart with a lot of information. First, price breaks through support, and this proximity makes reversal very likely. As expected, the price does revert to the upside with a double bottom and is confirmed by a three white soldiers indicator. This predicts a strong return back into range.

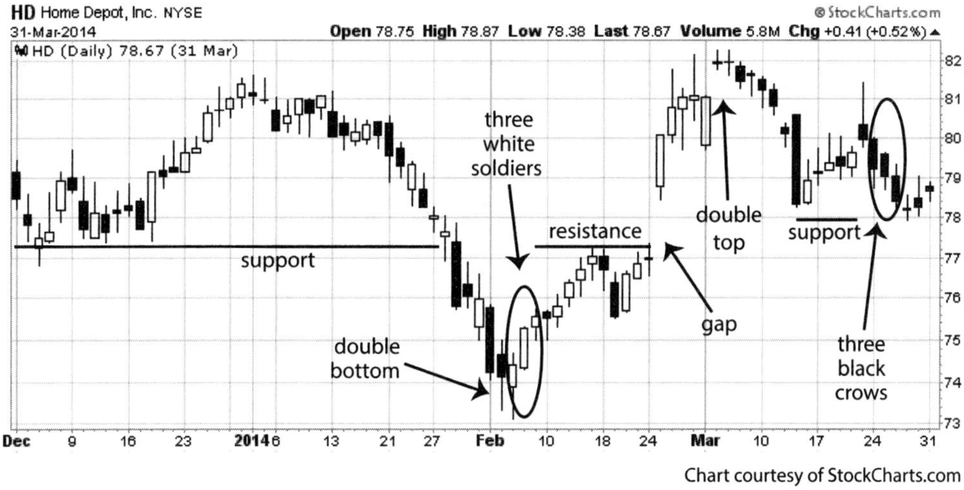

Figure 6.9 Combinations—bullish and bearish signals, four months

A short-term and contradictory resistance level forms but is quickly broken as price continues moving upward. In fact, the gap through that level is quite wide, indicating that the prior trading range has been reset, at least for the moment. The double top signals the end of the uptrend and a new reversal to a downtrend. But given the support level set by mid-March, the ability of the downtrend to continue is questionable. Then, a new three black crows pattern appears after a very brief uptrend. Given the volatility of this chart, this indicates that the short-term support level will not prevent the downtrend from continuing.

The next step is revealed in the expanded chart, shown in Figure 6.10.

This expanded chart is just as busy as the previous one. The three black crows accurately forecast a further price decline. A new resistance and support level were then set with strength. This is displayed by the shadows moving below support and above resistance, but not able to close outside of the newly established range. This trading range held throughout June (after the period shown) and went through a brief uptrend above $80 in early July, to then return back into the established trading range.

In spite of the volatility in this chart, the strong signals and clearly set resistance and support levels made the chart quite predictable. This demonstrates that with proper identification of reversal or continuation signals, and confirmation for each, even volatile price patterns can be managed and new direction anticipated with reasonable confidence.

Figure 6.10 Combinations—bullish and bearish signals, six months

The two types of reversal and continuation signals presented here—candlestick and Western—reveal that both types accomplish the same level of forecasting and confirmation. The all-important proximity is a key to every reversal signal, which is why emphasis on resistance and support is a crucial attribute of relative correlation. A review of the preceding examples demonstrates that reversal forecasts are strongest at the levels of resistance and support, especially when they break through, and that continuation indicators appearing at the same proximity make it likely that the price will continue moving in the breakout direction.

This one factor—continuation at proximity to resistance or support—is probably the strongest counterargument to the likely reversal at the same proximity. As price breaks through the current range, a reversal signal gives high confidence for realization of that outcome, and strong confirmation moves confidence close to 100%. But when a continuation pattern appears and (a) is confirmed with other continuation signals or (b) lacks a clear reversal signal to contradict it, then continuation confidence also approaches 100% confidence.

The likely continuation of an existing trend based on patterns and confirmation brings to light a key benefit of the continuation signal. It is not merely a forecast that you should take no action. Rather, it bolsters the argument that a breakout is going to succeed. A strong form of confirmation in this proximity is a resistance/support flip or a support/resistance flip. The flip becomes a strong indication that the newly established level will hold; the duration, however, cannot be known. Continuation trend duration cannot be predicted, so a cautious trader will continue to monitor the trading range looking for new breakout signals, and will also seek new reversal signals and confirmation to mark the end of the trend.

The next chapter delves further into the nature of confirmation. Just as an initial signal can fail, a confirming signal may also fail. For this reason, the stronger the signal or the more signals located, the higher the confidence level will be about reversal or continuation.

7

Confirmation—An Essential Second Part of a Signal

Confirmation comes in many shapes and sizes. Any signal (Western or Eastern, price, volume, or momentum) can provide either an initial signal or a confirming signal. Any variation among these indicators is possible, and under the hypothesis of relative correlation, the type of signal and confirmation is not as critical as the strength of the confirmation itself. The greater this strength, the higher confidence levels will move.

The hypothesis of relative correlation has been applied in previous chapters to the nature of reversal and continuation indicators. This chapter examines the same hypothesis as it relates to continuation. Here, you find some interesting observations about the nature of confirmation and how it varies based on several factors. Proximity, of course, affects the strength of confirmation in the same way it affects the initial signal. The strength or weakness of both the initial signal and its confirmation is equally significant, but here you find a different type of correlation—the strength of one signal is related directly to the strength of the other. Finally, the speed and strength of the preceding trend also affect the strength or weakness of reversal or continuation signals; they also influence the speed and strength of the resulting trend reversal or continuation.

These are worthy observations and represent a logical expansion of the hypothesis itself. Relative correlation references not only signals, but also the overall patterns of trends and price volatility of the stock. So, it is not enough to identify a confirmation signal and accept its validity to improve confidence in the forecast. Relative correlation integrates the entire price pattern, both before and after the signal, to define the likelihood of the anticipated outcome.

Relative Correlation and Inertia

The initial hypothesis of relative correlation related to reversal and continuation signals has been demonstrated to be valid. The likelihood of forecast outcomes is a function of placement within a trend and proximity to resistance or support. A reversal signal in the wrong placement cannot reliably be assumed to act as a continuation signal, and a continuation signal in the wrong placement is not likely to serve as a reversal signal. The two types are not dependably interchangeable. This observation is profound given the reality that many chartists assume that any type of signal may work as either reversal or continuation. This is a dangerous assumption that may easily lead to ill-timed trades and inaccurate levels of confidence in timing.

Proximity means that reversal occurring at resistance or support is a stronger signal than a reversal located at midrange. When reversal occurs as price moves through these borders, especially with gapping price movement, confidence is much greater and, if confirmed, may approach 100%. For continuation, the opposite indication may be observed (assuming, of course, that an initial continuation signal is also confirmed). When a continuation signal is in close proximity to resistance or support, a successful breakout is more likely than when the same signal appears elsewhere in the trading range. Timing trades at or close to resistance or support (and especially after an initial breakout) is always problematic because the breakout itself adds a degree of uncertainty to the next step. Even with strong signals, the pattern is unreliable because of the violation of the trading range. However, this is where the strength or weakness of confirmation makes all the difference in the level of confidence in either reversal or continuation.

The hypothesis has to be adjusted to add three additional assumptions. The first:

> *Strong reversal signals are likely to be accompanied by equally strong confirmation signals* ***if and when*** *the preceding trend was strong (meaning clear in direction and long in duration) and if and when proximity is maximized (reversal and confirmation appearing at or trending through resistance or support). When these conditions are present, reversal confidence is at its highest possible level, meaning a retreat from the previous trend and price movement in the opposite direction. A strong reversal is also most likely to lead to a strong reversal trend.*

This observation relates specifically to confirmation in the sense that it is of equal strength to the initial reversal signal. A similar hypothesis relates to continuation signals:

> *Strong continuation signals are likely to be accompanied by equally strong confirmation signals. This is especially true when the preceding trend was strong and with maximum proximity (close to or at resistance or support). When these conditions are present, continuation confidence is at its highest possible level, meaning likely breakout above resistance or below support. A strong continuation is also most likely to lead to further movement with strength at least equal to the preceding trend.*

Finally, the hypothesis is expanded to observe the nature of weak reversal or continuation signals:

> *Weak reversal or continuation signals are likely to be accompanied by equally weak confirmation signals or even by contradictory signals. This applies in all levels of proximity and to all levels of trend strength (and most likely when the preceding trend was weak as well). The weakness of signals and confirmation are most likely to be located at midrange and not in close proximity to resistance or support.*

The conclusion to this set of assumptions is that trend strength and duration, initial signal, confirmation, and subsequent price movement are all directly related and tend to behave in a specific manner. This is an application of the theory of inertia—that bodies in motion tend to stay in motion and bodies at rest tend to remain at rest. Applied to stock charts, "inertia" means that the strength or weakness of one attribute will remain consistent for the rest of the attributes (initial trend, reversal or continuation signals, confirmation, and subsequent trend).

For many traders and candlestick analysts, a continuation pattern has limited value. When these signals appear, under this assumption, the patterns "are a time of rest in the market."[1]

This belief overlooks the value of confirmation signals occurring at proximity to support or resistance. In those moments, a strong trend approaching the edges of the trading range is likely to continue through and experience a successful breakout. The continuation signal in this case provides a role far more valuable than marking a time of rest. On the contrary, strong signals followed by strong confirmation at the right proximity increase confidence in the breakout, more than any other factor.

Multiple Confirmation Patterns

The discovery of multiple confirmation signals tends to increase the overall strength of the collective confirmation. This applies to both reversal and continuation signals, given the assumption that placement and proximity are also maximized. In fact, multiple confirmations located after a strong trend of long duration and occurring at resistance or support approach 100% confidence. Most traders know that finding multiple confirmation signals adds to the likely outcome forecast by the initial signal.

Multiple confirmations, however, do not grow an exponential factor in determining the strength of a forecast. Having two very strong confirmation signals adds confidence to the initial indicator, but it does not improve likely outcomes *more* than the individual confirmation signals. So, it is a mistake to assume that one signal increases confidence, but two (or three) signals make the outcome a certainty. The danger in this false assumption is that some traders will increase their risk levels based on what is perceived as a stronger-than-average forecast. Two or more weak signals, or signals with poor proximity, or signals occurring after a weak trend, are just as vulnerable to failure as a single confirmation signal. The key to succeeding with multiple patterns is to seek strong indicators and to resist acting on weak indicators.

An example of multiple confirmations is found in the chart of General Electric (GE). This is shown in Figure 7.1. This includes both a bearish and bullish signal, both confirmed separately.

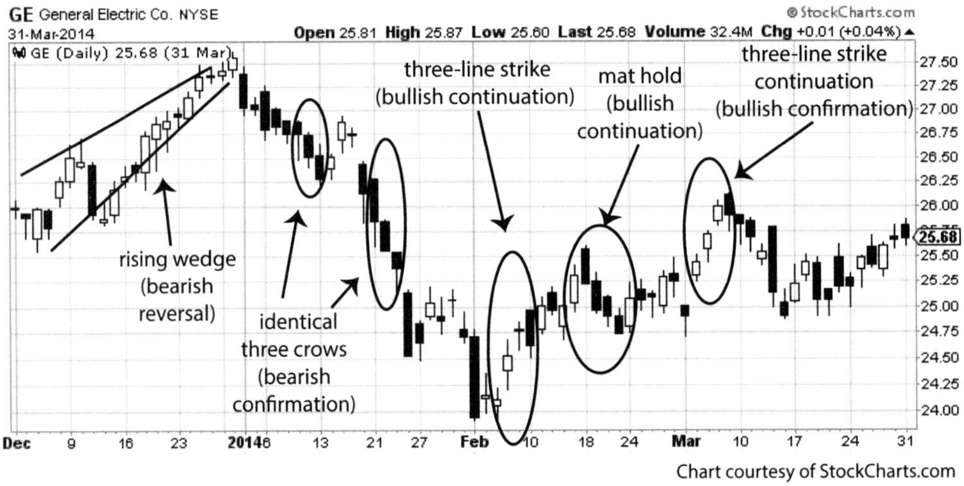

Figure 7.1 Multiple confirmations, four months

The first signal is bearish. The rising wedge starts out the chart and then is confirmed by two separate identical three crows signals. These are strong forms of confirmation for the bearish reversal; however, the second one occurred after the reversal was well under way. It serves one purpose, confirming that the current trend is a downtrend and not just a retracement against the original uptrend.

The second occurs after price bottoms out. The gapping price movement to the upside marked the end of the downtrend but also formed as a three-line strike, a bullish continuation signal. The problem with this as a continuation is that there isn't much of an uptrend to confirm; so a trader might view this with caution until confirmation appears. This did appear in the form of a mat hold, another bullish continuation. This made it clear that a definite uptrend was under way. The second confirmation was found in the form of another three-line strike.

The chart continued to display a strong uptrend as the period extended. This is shown in Figure 7.2.

Chart courtesy of StockCharts.com

Figure 7.2 Multiple confirmations, six months

Both resistance and support formed into a strong upward-moving channel, and the uptrend continued throughout the rest of the chart. Toward the end of the period in late May, the trading breadth settled into a very narrow range, but it was still within the uptrending channel. In this case, strong initial signals (first a bearish reversal and then a bullish continuation) were confirmed by two separate signals, which forecast a coming direction, and the outcome occurred as expected.

Examples of Strong Reversal

A signal is considered "strong" in several different ways. The most obvious is the preceding trend. For a reversal to be strong, the most desirable condition is a strong downtrend. However, some downtrends will be very gradual; in this case, the reversal will not have a strong trend to reverse. However, a second form of strength is found in the reversal signal itself.

For example, the chart of McDonald's (MCD), shown in Figure 7.3, revealed a very gradual downtrend from the beginning of the period charted through to March 10. Although it was a downtrend, it was not a particularly strong one.

Figure 7.3 Strong reversal, four months

However, the reversal in the form of a morning star was exceptionally strong. Note the very long white candlestick in the third session, indicating very clear upward pressure. In fact, this single session took price to a new high since the beginning of the period.

The reversal was clear and bullish. However, price then began sliding downward once again. Even so, it formed a bullish confirmation in the falling wedge that followed immediately. This is one of those patterns typified by falling resistance and support, anticipating more upward movement once the wedge has narrowed. The next step occurred after the period shown, and is summarized in Figure 7.4.

In this case, the reversal and confirmation was based on a subtle downtrend. However, the reversal itself was exceptionally strong and led to an equally strong uptrend. This lasted through mid-May. In this case, the expanded hypothesis is confirmed. A strong reversal and strong confirmation in combination are likely to lead to equally strong price behavior as forecast.

So within the expanded hypothesis, the initial assumption was that a strong trend was likely to reverse just as strongly, given proximity and reversal with confirmation. However, in this variation of that idea, it was the reversal and confirmation strength that led to a strong uptrend. So, the inertia of a previous trend is not the sole factor in accurately forecasting a reversal of equal inertia in the opposite direction. Even a very mild trend (like that on the MCD chart) may lead to strong reversal like the morning star, and then cause a strong offsetting uptrend to follow. In this case, it was the inertia in the reversal signal and not in the trend that predicted a strong uptrend to follow.

Chart courtesy of StockCharts.com

Figure 7.4 Strong reversal, six months

A problem with this variation on the theme of relative correlation in the strength of trends and signals is that it may be difficult to prove that signal strength is as accurate a predictor as trend strength. It may be, or it may not be in some cases. A wise policy is to recognize exceptionally strong reversals as one of several factors likely to lead to strong price movement in the next step. This increases confidence in a way similar to strong trend movement, but the factors are different (signal rather than trend, and signal with confirmation rather than signal alone).

Because trends and signals occur together but are not the same, care should be taken to keep the distinctions in mind. Chart readers take comfort in recognizing a trend as it begins to weaken and leads to likely reversal. This is a visually likely scenario because the typical price chart moves through periods of offsetting short-term and intermediate-term trends. In comparison, a reversal signal will appear, at times suddenly, and contains no historical context to convince a trader that the trend is as likely to reverse. The MCD chart was one example of this issue. The downtrend was long-lasting but quite gradual. The reversal signal appeared without warning and was exceptionally strong (due to the long white candle session). This was immediately confirmed and was followed by an uptrend.

Note the difference in strength between the mild downtrend at the beginning of the chart, and the much stronger uptrend that followed the highlighted signals. This contrast is a symptom of the reversal and confirmation signals' strength. In this case, the signal strength led the reversal and added strength to the uptrend. So the hypothesis allowed for this by recognizing that "strength" is usually derived from the attributes of the preceding trend; however, there are times in which "strength" grows from the convincing pattern in the reversal and confirmation signals.

Examples of Weak Reversal

A weak reversal can be found in many forms. The most obvious is a lack of confirmation. However, weakness may also refer to the size and shape of the reversal pattern itself. In the previous example, a strong bullish reversal for MCD was defined by an exceptionally long white candle session in the third day. Weak reversals may contain relative small trading breadth or minimal conformity to the pattern's attributes.

An example of a chart with multiple weak reversal signals is that of Johnson & Johnson (JNJ), shown in Figure 7.5.

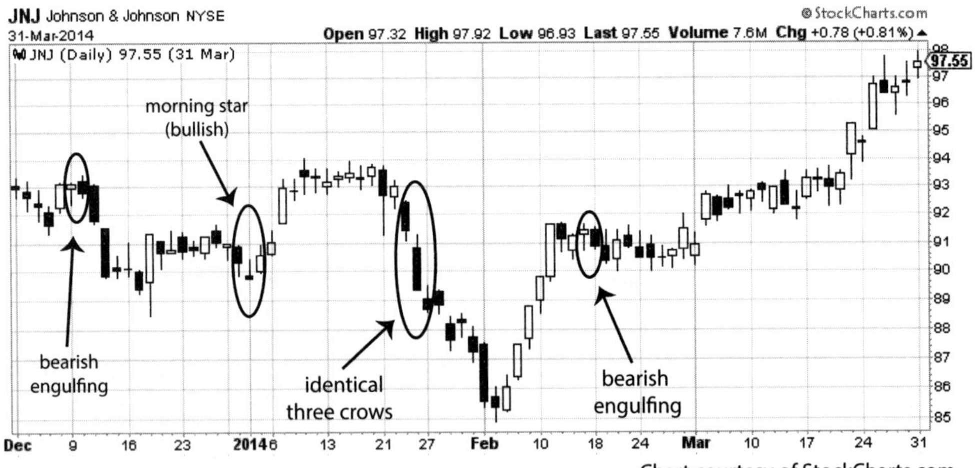

Chart courtesy of StockCharts.com

Figure 7.5 Weak reversal, four months

The first signal was a bearish engulfing, normally a highly reliable signal. However, note that both sessions making up this signal were extremely small in breadth. Second, it is not clear from the chart as shown whether an uptrend had occurred and thus could be reversed. (In fact, a fairly strong uptrend did occur from the beginning of October through the end of November, and the first few sessions of December appeared in context to be the end of that trend. Even so, the bearish engulfing pattern was not strong under any definition.)

This definition should include what subsequently occurred. In this example, the resulting downtrend was quite weak and short-lived. It moved only three points and lasted less than two weeks. There was no clear confirmation signal either.

This led to yet another signal, a bullish one in the form of a morning star. This was another weak signal, especially when compared with other examples, such as the earlier one of MCD. This bullish signal had very little downtrend to reverse, one reliable definition of a weak signal. The resulting uptrend moved only four points in one week and then flattened out. In this short-term trend, there was no confirmation of the initial signal.

The next signal, an identical three crows, occurred well after the new downtrend began, and at the conclusion of this pattern, the price continued downward for only one week, moving less than four points. Again, no confirmation was noted.

The final weak signal was another bearish engulfing. It was as weak as the first one in terms of the size and shape of the sessions. There was no confirmation. This was an obvious failed signal because the price did not react to the downside at all, but trended sideways and then up.

This collection of unusually weak signals involved poor trending prior to the forecast moment, very weak placement and response, and a complete lack of confirmation. Even with confirmation, the overall weakness of these signals makes them unreliable, and confidence would be quite low based on this JNJ chart.

The next phase was even worse. The price continued upward even in the face of relatively strong bearish signals, an initial and confirming rising wedge. This is shown in Figure 7.6.

The relatively strong uptrend defied all of the recent bearish signals. A double rising wedge is unusual and normally would be considered strongly bearish. However, in this case, as with the entire chart, the signals ended up as weak because price moved opposite the direction these signals anticipated. Although the second rising wedge could be called confirmation of the first, several points have to be remembered. First, these patterns followed a failed bearish engulfing, which itself was quite weak. It would be just as easy to label the first rising wedge as confirmation of the bearish engulfing, but both failed. Finally, the rising wedges were also weak, starting out with only a two-point spread and narrowing only slightly to a one-point breadth at best. A strong rising wedge would have more of a point spread to close up, and a greater slope in one or both of the wedge lines.

Figure 7.6 Weak reversal, six months

Overall, this chart exhibited weakness in many forms. It demonstrates conditions in which no action is justified based on either of the trends (which were of short duration and weak), or the signals themselves.

Examples of Strong Continuation

Many traders make the mistake of assuming that a continuation signal, even a strongly confirmed one, means the current trend is "safe" and will continue indefinitely. However, continuation does not provide any guidance about duration; it only means that the current trend will continue. The duration might be three days, a week, or a month. However, strong continuation and confirmation are more likely to lead to greater duration, and weak continuation and confirmation are more likely to lead to trends of shorter duration. This is another observation of inertia in both trends and signal patterns.

An example of strong continuation is found in the chart of Wal-Mart (WMT), in several instances. This is shown in Figure 7.7.

The first bearish continuation signal is the three-line strike. Appearing after the downtrend seen in the very beginning of the chart, this is strongly confirmed by the descending triangle, and a renewed, strong downtrend followed.

The next trend moved in the opposite direction. The reversal was signaled by the three white soldiers and was confirmed immediately by the ascending triangle. In this example, the confirmation appeared across a range of time before and after the initial reversal signal. The big question for traders in this situation is whether the downtrend will continue or a true reversal will occur.

Figure 7.7 Strong continuation, four months

Price broke through the resistance level, which also served as the top of the triangle. A breakout is always troubling because reversal is more likely than anywhere else. However, a continuation signal also makes the breakout more likely to result in a successful move in the same direction. In this case, the breakout was strongly confirmed by two three-line strike continuation signals, a strong forecast of continued upward movement.

The next move in this chart is shown in Figure 7.8. The trending price set up a new level of support at about $75.25 per share. This level was tested at the end of the chart and it held, so the signs for price remaining above this level were strong. In the period after the one shown, the support level was tested twice in six weeks, but it held. So in this chart, the application of continuation signals as confirmation proved to be an effective system for increasing confidence that the trend would continue moving in the same direction.

The observation about reversal proximity applies equally to continuation proximity. When a reversal signal appears at or closer to either resistance or support, a reversal is at its most likely point. But when a continuation signal appears, a breakout and continued movement is at its most likely point. So proximity and the relative correlation of how effectively signals are confirmed works in both situations.

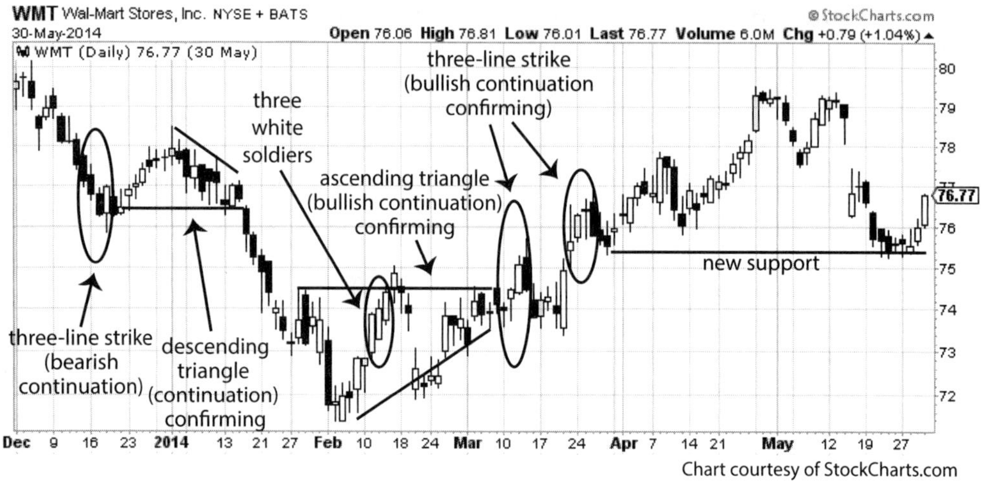

Figure 7.8 Strong continuation, six months

Examples of Weak Continuation

Strong continuation is reassuring to a trader attempting to time trades. But weak continuation works in the opposite manner, as a warning that the trend may not be safe, and that a reversal or sideways movement in price might be coming in the near future.

A case of weak confirmation appeared in the chart of Disney (DIS). This is shown in Figure 7.9. What makes this signal weak are the proximity as well as the price trend, which is sideways rather than upward; after the signals appear, price even began slipping downward, a troubling sign. So even with the continuation forecast by the first three-line strike, and confirmation by the second, the outcome is in doubt.

The next phase in this trend is shown in Figure 7.10. Price did trend lower, but then moved into yet another bullish continuation pattern in the form of an ascending triangle.

Even though the initial signals were weak relative to proximity, the outcome appears to continue in a bullish manner. This is a case of an uncertain continuation pattern leading to success, even though it was slow and gradual. The large price gap that appeared in the beginning of February added to the initial weakness; a trader might have been concerned about a reversal, especially because this gap took price above the resistance level without initial continuation indicators present. From the period of February 10 through March 1, it would be reasonable to expect a reversal, just based on the move above resistance along with a large price gap.

Figure 7.9 Weak continuation, four months

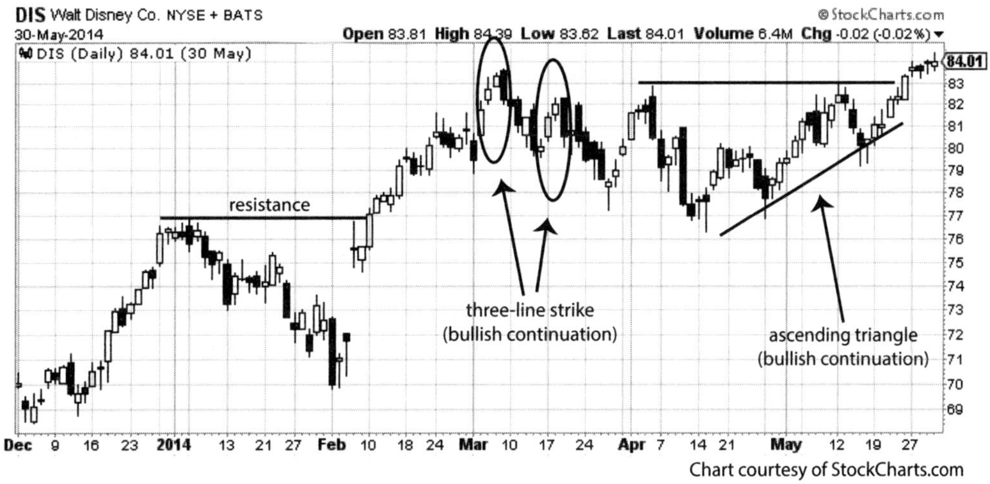

Figure 7.10 Weak continuation, six months

This chart demonstrates that a weak continuation signal does not ensure a failure in the trend. In this situation, the uptrend did continue and it held beyond the period shown. However, the weakness in these signals was a warning to traders to proceed with caution. A weak signal is more likely to fail than a strong signal, and that is the point. Confidence should be low even as the uptrend continued, due to the weak price trend. There was no absence of continuation signals on the chart, but the desirable strength and speed of the trend was not evident.

Maximum Versus Minimum Conditions

Chart analysis requires an ability to make judgments about conditions that more often than not exist in gray areas rather than in black or white. So within a range of signal strengths, you may find indicators with minimum conditions (weak) or with maximum conditions (strong).

A weak indicator does not lead to an assumption of failure, as the last example clearly demonstrated. It may be a symptom of a very slow-moving and gradual trend, as in the case of the Disney chart, where repetitive continuation signals were weak but still confirmed an uptrend. Weakness may also refer to the speed and slope of a trend. A weak trend (slow-moving with a minimal slope) remains a trend and may be subject to confirmation signals, but is less likely to provide strong evidence for either reversal or continuation. Inertia tends to affect all aspects of the trend, signals, and confirmation.

The indicator may be weak itself without regard to the strength or weakness of the trend. A minimal signal barely meets the requirements set forth, such as in the example of JNJ (refer back to Figure 7.6). In that chart, numerous examples of weakness were evident. First, the two bearish engulfing signals contained sessions with very small ranges. A strong bearish reversal is likely to include sessions with much broader ranges, especially in the second session of each. These were also weak in the sense that the trends (both preceding and subsequent) were of short duration and minimal in point movement.

In the same chart, an identical three crows reversal appeared after the downtrend had begun, and the downtrend was brief and did not move very far. And, finally, the chart ended with two bearish rising wedges in close proximity to one another. This would be an exceptionally strong bearish reversal in other conditions. However, these appeared even as price continued trending upward. But what made the rising wedges exceptionally weak was that they met the criteria only minimally. In both, the slope of both wedge lines was small and the breadth quite narrow. In a strong rising wedge, you expect to see a broader price range and more dramatic closing of that breadth as the wedge closes upon itself. The strong version is far more likely to lead to reversal, whereas the weak type such as those on the JNJ chart are more likely to fail.

This raises another issue concerning minimum indicators. Are they indicators at all? There is always a possibility that a pattern forms without having any specific significance. So what appears as a rising wedge might be a simple coincidence of price movement and breadth of trading. Traders tend to accept patterns discovered on a chart as evidence, so a reversal signal is likely to lead to the end of the trend and a new trend going in the opposite direction. However, a weak rising wedge might be easy to create or force, when in reality no wedge is forming at all.

This problem of questionable indicators (or even the misreading of a chart when no indicator actually exists) is a problem every chartist faces. Knowing the difference between a valid indicator and coincidental price movement is not always a simple matter. However, some tools can be used to make these difficult judgments. First, remember that strong signals are more likely to be valid than weak signals. Second, whether discovering reversal or continuation, the strength of the preceding trend affects the strength of the signal and the likelihood of the assumed outcome occurring. Third, proximity is a ruling force in all forecasting. So pay special attention to trend and signal activity at or near resistance and support. And fourth, strong confirmation is more likely to make the signal valid than weak confirmation.

A questionable indicator may present a greater problem than one of relative strength of weakness. In some cases, you will find contradiction rather than confirmation. Traders often do not know how to react to this situation because it is not expected and provides no actionable change leading to well-timed trades. Contradiction is nothing but confusion for many, but there are methods for using contradictory signals to constructively time trades.

Contradiction as a Different Kind of Relative Correlation

Focusing on successful confirmation (whether strong or weak) is only one of the possibilities in chart analysis. What happens, in comparison, when instead of confirmation you discover contradiction?

A signal that indicates a forecast opposite the initial reversal or continuation signal confuses the issue. Contradiction is puzzling because, unlike the expectation of raising confidence, it brings the entire forecast into question. Three points to remember about contradiction are the following:

1. A contradiction in place of confirmation is a direct factor of the initial signal and its strength or weakness. A weak initial signal is more likely to be contradicted than a strong signal.
2. Contradiction does not always mean the initial signal was wrong. It does tend to neutralize that signal, however, meaning the net result between initial signal and contradiction is that no signal has been found.

3. Reversal and continuation signals cannot be reliably transferred, meaning that such signals in the wrong location are likely to provide no usable signals whatsoever.

An example of a contradictory signal can be found in the chart of Nike (NKE), shown in Figure 7.11.

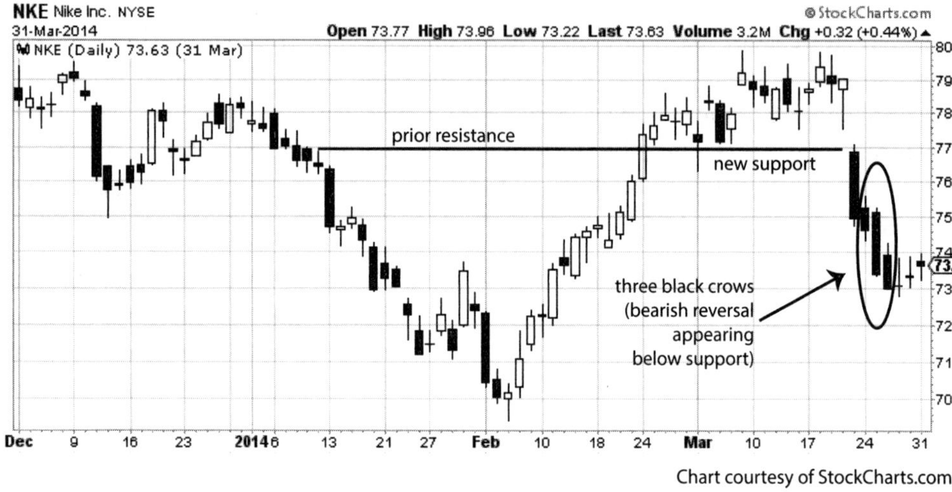

Figure 7.11 Contradictory signals, four months

A flip from resistance to support often may be used as an exceptionally strong reinforcement of a newly established range. So in this case, the new support level would be expected to hold. However, price fell and immediately formed a bearish three black crows pattern. This exceptionally strong bearish pattern contradicts the resistance/support flip. At this point on the chart, traders might believe that a bear trend is now under way.

However, because a contradictory signal occurred, is that assumption safe? Because the resistance/support flip did not forecast price movement accurately, you also may wonder whether the bearish three black crows will usher in a downtrend. The signal does lead to reversal in 79% of all cases, assuming proper trend placement and proximity. However, in having violated support, both of these are imperfect. The uptrend appeared to have ended well before the three black crows appeared—and ideally, this reversal should appear at or near the top of the uptrend, which it did not.

To see what occurred after this initial set of signals, review the chart for Nike shown in Figure 7.12.

Figure 7.12 Contradictory signals, six months

Price stopped its downward move immediately after the three black crows appeared. This was followed by a developing falling wedge, a bullish reversal. However, within that wedge, a new bearish engulfing signal also appeared. The entire pattern continued the contradictory nature of what came before. Price did respond to the falling wedge and began rising, but the uncertainty of what these collective signals reveal makes it unclear which direction will occur next.

The problem with contradictory signals and patterns is in the lack of direction. No clear forecast emerges because you cannot know which signals to believe, bullish or bearish. Both reversal and continuation are confused due to poor placement and proximity. The chaotic nature of random trade direction means that in some cases, no clear signals emerge.

This chart revealed that even the normally reliable order created by resistance and support was not reliable. The levels set were short-term in nature and were quickly violated by subsequent price movement. The resistance/support flip did not create the expected strong support level, and resistance itself was impossible to identify.

The next chapter examines the nature of support and resistance in more detail, to demonstrate how the patterns of the trading range, emerging breadth of trading, and breakouts all confirm continuation and reversal set by other price signals.

8

Support and Resistance—Key Price Points in the Trend

The framework of relative correlation has to be based on well-defined levels of support and resistance. The observed proximity factor reveals that forecasting signals are most reliable when they occur at or close to these borders of the trading range.

Reversal signals are most likely to reverse when they are found in proximity to resistance (bearish reversal) or support (bullish reversal). A reversal signal is reliable only when there is a trend to reverse, and a reversal signal should not be assumed to represent continuation when it appears in the wrong position or proximity. In addition, when the reversal signal appears when price moves through support or resistance with a gap from one session to another, confidence in reversal approaches 100%—assuming the signal is independently confirmed.

Continuation signals are somewhat more elusive because they tell you only to take no action. A reversal indicator is an action point, but a continuation signal is advice to "wait and see" what happens next. However, continuation occurring at proximity to support or resistance is stronger than at any other point in the trading range. If price breaks through above resistance or below support with a continuation signal, the chances for continuation are improved substantially (because these normally are the proximity points where reversal is likely to occur). So the appearance of a continuation signal at this proximity increases confidence that the breakout will succeed.

This chapter examines several formations of resistance and support, including stationary and dynamic patterns, growing or shrinking breadth of trading, proximity, and resistance/support and support/resistance flips.

How Much Time Is Needed to Establish Support or Resistance?

The duration of an identifiable line of support or resistance determines its reliability. Greater duration implies a stronger condition. But this can be a weakness as well. When a line holds for a long period, it may become increasingly vulnerable to breakout—if only because nothing lasts forever, and a long-standing border to the trading range eventually gives way to change.

An extremely short support or resistance level is a problem for traders because it is not necessarily a true level. It could be merely a pause in an otherwise evolving longer-term support or resistance level. A line existing for only five or ten sessions is not reliable, and in a larger perspective often will prove to provide little if any indication of a trading range. It might be transitional rather than a reliable signal of support or resistance.

An example of a chart with short duration trading ranges is found in DuPont (DD). This is shown in Figure 8.1.

Figure 8.1 Short duration, four months

The breadth of trading remained consistent throughout the charted period, but the duration of specific ranges often was far too short to be reliable. A trader attempting to determine the next price direction would have considerable difficulty with this chart due to the short duration of these trading ranges.

An expanded look at the chart reveals some extension of trading range duration, but still not enough to use the range as a solid predictor of the longer-term trend. This is shown in Figure 8.2.

Figure 8.2 Short duration, six months

The short duration trading range is a problem for any trader seeking a reliable and general sense of whether a company's stock is trending higher or lower. The chart for DD seems to trend in both directions over extremely short periods, but this is not useful for predicting even a month ahead.

The opposite kind of chart, one with ranges of long duration, is a more comfortable one for most traders. In tracking a trend, finding reversal or continuation signals has greater meaning because of the duration itself. As a trading range border extends over time, it is more likely to become dynamic, meaning it may evolve in one of two ways. First, the breadth of trading may expand or contract, and second, the direction of price may change as well. This means that support and resistance are rarely fixed over the long term. A study of stock charts shows this to be the case. A majority of stock charts reveals movement in some form, even if only gradual. Other charts are quite volatile, making it difficult to locate and rely upon a clear breadth of trading and trading range.

An example of a long duration trading range is shown in Figure 8.3 on the chart of Caterpillar (CAT). Here, the support line extends over the entire period, and although resistance is broken up by some retracement movement, it also trends higher throughout the period.

Figure 8.3 Long duration, four months

The extended version of this chart reveals that the support line continues even further, nearly the entire six months shown in Figure 8.4.

Figure 8.4 Long duration, six months

This is one example in which a discovered reversal signal would be more significant after a long period, compared with the more uncertain short duration trading range. The double tops highlighted just before the very long-term support level is violated could be a forecast of reversal, but unconfirmed, it is not enough to act on. These tops are not particularly strong, so at best the value of this signal is inconclusive. In fact, the long duration of the trend itself requires very specific and strong reversal signals and confirmation, and this double top by itself is not enough to increase confidence. As it turned out, after the period shown, the late-May decline turned out to be a retracement, and price continued its long-term trend through June and well into July, where price rose to $110 per share, nine points higher than the ending price for the period shown.

The CAT example rose over the long term and was quite reliable, meaning it was dynamic but with low volatility. This is not always the case. Some conditions are so volatile that they cannot be safely traded. If a chart does not reveal a clear trend and a breadth of trading, how can you identify reversal or continuation signals? One of the key attributes needed to identify a valid signal is that an existing trend has to exist. A reversal has to appear after a period of clear uptrend or downtrend. If there is no clear trend, the reversal is not valid. If the signal appears in the wrong place (bullish reversal in an uptrend or bearish reversal in a downtrend), it is not valid either. Assuming that a reversal signal can act as a continuation signal in these wrong placements is not wise.

A continuation signal also appears during a trend. However, like the reversal, such a signal showing up in the wrong placement in the trend cannot be assigned the character of a reversal. So, a bullish continuation found during a bearish trend is not a reliable signal, and a bearish continuation found during a bullish trend is also not reliable.

The attributes of support and resistance contribute to price trends such as triangles and wedges, and they set up proximity of both reversal and continuation signals. The nature of these trading range borders may be stationary or dynamic and may exhibit different breadth of trading attributes (growing or shrinking range, or unchanging price channels).

Stationary and Dynamic Formations

The duration of the trading range should not be confused with the duration of a trend. The previous example of a range with long duration happened to be bullish; however, a long-duration range may also be bullish or flat. What is of greater significance is the breadth of trading itself.

The short duration example of the DuPont chart covered a total of six months. However, the breadth of trading never exceeded two points. The Caterpillar example, with prices ranging twice those of DuPont, never exceeded a breadth of seven points, over a six-month period. Both of these duration-based examples involved trading ranges that were quite narrow. In other situations, more volatile changes may occur. Trading ranges may remain stationary or may display more dynamic characteristics. These attributes refer to whether a stock price remains within a specific price range or moves higher or lower over time. Support and resistance may remain at set prices or may change over time.

An example of a stationary trading range is seen in the chart of Cisco Systems (CSCO), shown in Figure 8.5.

Chart courtesy of StockCharts.com

Figure 8.5 Stationary range, four months

Note that over more than three months, the resistance and support levels remain firmly in place, and trading covered a breadth of only about 1.25 points. This is not a wide breadth even for a stock trading in the $20 to $23 range. With a few moves above or below, the closing price was outside of this range only once during the entire period, in mid-March.

The significance of this small level of movement defines a stationary or low-volatility stock. For a trader, the trend is sideways, and this creates a problem. A signal may occur in either direction above or below the established range, but with no upward or downward trend to reverse; this situation requires a wait-and-see approach. There is no obvious method for determining which direction the stock will move when it does finally break out above or below this range.

The extended chart in Figure 8.6 reveals an upward trend in the stock; however, the ranges at various plateaus continue to move sideways, so that the trend does not allow for any dynamic signals. A reversal signal could appear, but how would it be interpreted?

Figure 8.6 Stationary range, six months

It may be possible to seek a bearish reversal signal based on the overall growing price range. For example, the price gaps toward the end of the chart may be seen as a bearish forecast. However, because the trend is clearly sideways, this is not reliable. In fact, price did continue moving sideways for another month until the end of June, and in July, price began trending upward, although only by about 1.5 points. Considering that the entire six-month history of this series of stationary ranges never exceeded a 3-point breadth of trading, a 1.5-point move is not substantial.

In comparison, a stock chart with a dynamic range is somewhat more interesting, although the support and resistance levels may not be any more revealing than those of the stationary chart. For example, the chart of Merck shown in Figure 8.7 consists of a series of dynamic ranges, defined as price levels trending upward or downward. In this case, most of the chart trends upward, but includes bearish moves as well as retracements. Other than the spikes above or below range, the breadth of trading is never greater than two points.

This chart is not particularly revealing based on the dynamic ranges of price, given the small breadth of trading and unpredictability of what is likely to happen next. The extended chart in Figure 8.8 shows a continuation of the pattern—short-term trends of narrow breadth moving back and forth, with occasional retracements outside of the range.

Figure 8.7 Dynamic range, four months

Figure 8.8 Dynamic range, six months

Although the movement continues an upward bias in the price trend, the narrow breadth makes this version of a dynamic trading range very difficult to forecast. This tendency continued beyond the charted period, making MRK a difficult case. Even with strong and narrow-range support and resistance, recognition of any form of reversal or continuation signal would have to be weak based on the weak trading range and price movement.

Breadth of Trading—Growing or Shrinking Formations and Channels

An analysis of stationary or dynamic movement—defined by price direction with narrow breadth of trading—is among the most difficult charting challenges. There simply is too little in the way of information to rely on any emerging signals. A weak trend or breadth of trading will invariably include weak signals, if any appear at all.

In comparison, a change in breadth of trading is a far more interesting pattern to observe—and to act upon. Whenever the breadth of trading grows or shrinks, it invariably leads to changes (often dramatic changes) in the current trend and in future price movement. The unsettled trading range is a highly visible symptom of price volatility, and volatility presents opportunities to anticipate rapid price moves. That opportunity increases the risk as well, but given the right placement of signals within a trend, proximity to support or resistance, and strength of confirmation, dynamic breadth has great potential for accurate forecasting, and with all of the elements present, confidence in those forecasts may approach 100%.

For example, a growing breadth is one form of dynamic range with great potential for accurately forecasting coming price movement. The chart of Pfizer (PFE) shown in Figure 8.9 included a very strong dynamic uptrend. This formed as an expanding breadth of trading, which culminated with a bearish engulfing indicator, a strong reversal signal. This is one example of how dynamic price movement (volatility) provides equally strong signals.

Chart courtesy of StockCharts.com

Figure 8.9 Dynamic range (growing breadth), four months

The dynamic range expanding to top out with the bearish engulfing did not immediately provide a clear directional response. However, an expanded chart reveals a very specific bearish trend with equally dynamic characteristics. This is shown in Figure 8.10.

Figure 8.10 Dynamic range (growing breadth), six months

Several characteristics of this new downtrend are noteworthy. First, a series of retracements moved price above resistance and below support, in a back-and-forth motion. This whipsaw pattern is typical of dynamic breadth ranges with retracements. A second feature is the recurring gapping price action, revealing a very volatile downtrend.

It bottoms out at a point where two sets of double bottoms appear. These bullish reversal signals are not especially strong, as longer lower shadows would be more convincing. However, these do indicate the end of the downtrend. In fact, in the period after the one shown, price continued sideways for a month before beginning to climb once again. That new reversal trend also developed as a dynamic range and increasing breadth of trading, making that pattern a repetitive one at least for the period studied on this chart.

Another form of dynamic range involves a shrinking range. In this formation, a potential problem arises. A shrinking range is likely to form either a wedge or a triangle. A minimal wedge may be very close in pattern to a triangle, but the two patterns have diametrically opposite meaning. Given how closely these align, great caution has to be exercised in the analysis and interpretation of the shrinking range. It is desirable and tempting to believe that a "perfect" pattern has an exact meaning. But when two patterns are very close in their patterns, interpretation will be difficult, and lacking strong confirmation and proximity, a marginal signal could be misinterpreted.

For example, Figure 8.11 summarizes the two wedge and two triangle formulations that may be very close in shape, but have different meaning.

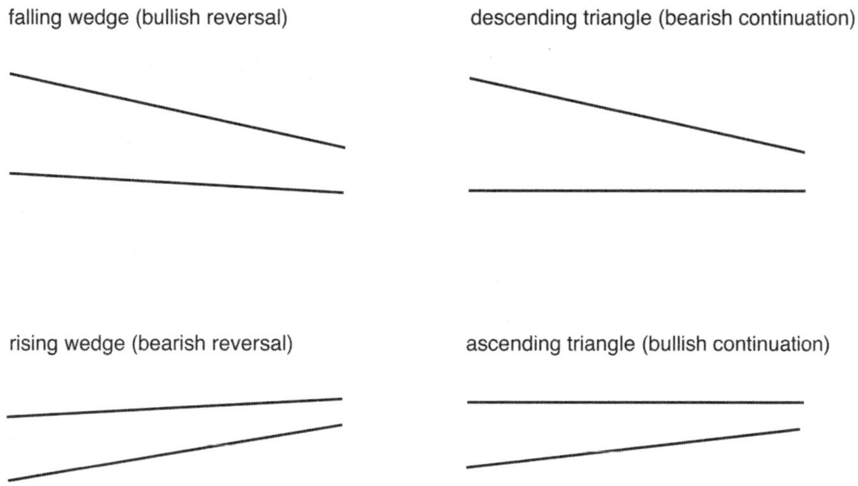

Figure 8.11 Wedges and triangles—potentially confusing signals

The falling wedge with very marginal characteristics may be very close to the descending triangle. However, whereas the falling wedge is a bullish reversal, the descending triangle is a bearish continuation. The dilemma here is that either of these may appear at the same proximity on a chart, after an extended downtrend. Does it mean reversal or continuation? A charge of a fractional point in the support (from a slightly declining price to a flat price) changes the meaning of the pattern.

The same is true for the opposite patterns. The rising wedge is a bearish reversal, and the very closely patterned ascending triangle is a bullish continuation. A fractional decline in the resistance price level changes one to the other. However, it remains very difficult to interpret when the patterns are minimal in degree of slope. A subtle change does not change what the signal reveals; it does add to your difficulty in interpretation.

The solution, as always, is to rely on strong confirmation signals. In addition, extra caution should be exercised whenever dealing with dynamic range with shrinking breadth of trading.

An example of shrinking breadth in a dynamic range pattern is found on the chart of Intel (INTC), shown in Figure 8.12.

Figure 8.12 Dynamic range (shrinking breadth), four months

The wedges formed by these shrinking breadths of trading patterns are quite strong. Compared with a more marginal wedge pattern that may be difficult to interpret, these are quite strong. The first rising wedge leads to a reversal as expected, and the falling wedge that follows also reverses and leads to a new uptrend. The key here is that as long as the degree of slope to the wedge is strong, there is no confusion with the related triangles and their opposite indication.

The next phase in this trend is seen in Figure 8.13, which extends the period studied.

Figure 8.13 Dynamic range (shrinking breadth), six months

This extended chart continues the upward slope of the rising wedge, which then forms into a symmetrical triangle (which may present either a bullish or bearish forecast). In the situation following a long-term rising wedge, the meaning of this signal is not clear.

The period after that shown was quite interesting as well. Price rose substantially over the following six weeks with instances of large upside price gaps (and an extended overbought condition as measured by momentum). This probably means the price was overdue for a correction, but the anticipated reversal in the rising wedge in Figure 8.13 did not materialize immediately.

The volatility and unresponsiveness of the stock to these signals highlights a problem with narrowing wedge patterns in general. Note the difference between the slope and speed of the first two wedges (first rising and then falling). They were steep and fast. The new rising wedge that began in February and continued through to the end of the period was a much weaker indicator that did not lead to a reversal as expected. The conclusion of this analysis is that by itself, a dynamic range with shrinking breadth is not a strong signal. It does reveal the characteristics of support and resistance in one type of price pattern, but it presents numerous problems for accurate timing of trades and anticipated reversal.

Proximity Is Key

Once you focus on proximity of signals to support and resistance, you discover that strong signals occurring in those areas tend to be far more reliable than (a) signals appearing elsewhere in the range or (b) signals that are weaker in their design.

The proximity factor is an excellent starting point for finding strong reversals (meaning a high likelihood of price returning into range) or continuation (meaning a high likelihood of successful breakout). One example of such conditions is found in the chart of Coca-Cola (KO), shown in Figure 8.14.

There is a lot of action on this chart, all based on proximity reversals. The initial rising wedge is a fairly strong one (fast with a steep slope), and it culminates at the top of the trend, to be quickly followed by a confirming bearish signal, three identical crows. These two together make reversal very likely, based not only on proximity, but also on strong confirmation. Next, the downtrend bottoms out and begins moving sideways as a double bottom appears. Price then reverses again and begins trending upward. As it does so, a new resistance level is established, trending gradually higher through to the end of the period.

Figure 8.14 Proximity of signals, example 1, four months

The next phase is shown in the extended chart in Figure 8.15.

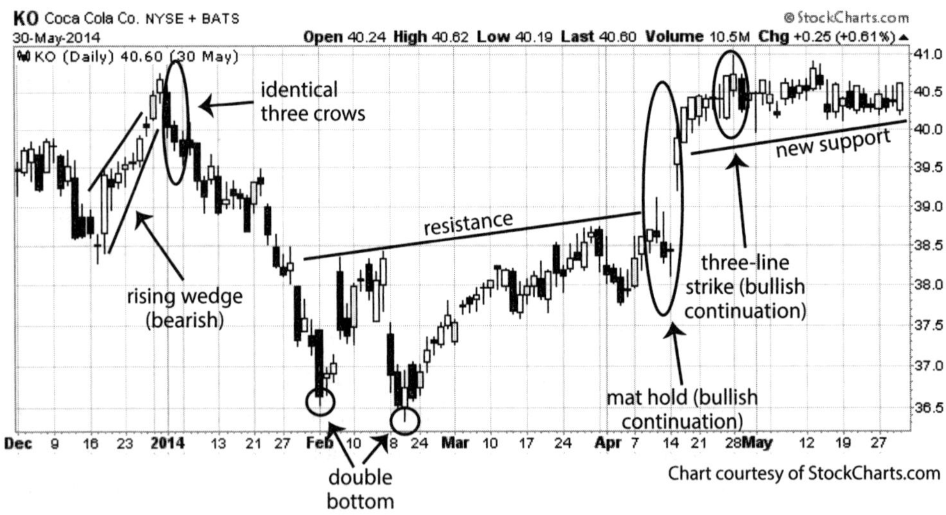

Figure 8.15 Proximity of signals, example 1, six months

The newly set resistance level continued into early April. At this point, an unusual pattern emerges. The mat hold is a bullish continuation; this one is exceptionally strong in two respects. First, it includes a very large upward gap; second, it moves above resistance.

By itself, this increases confidence of the uptrend moving higher. However, this is quickly confirmed by yet another bullish continuation signal, the three-line strike. As the price continues trending higher, a rising support level is set. This is a flip of the prior resistance. Normally, a flip is at about the same price, but this new support starts out higher. However, notice the slope of the rising support; it is identical to the slope of the prior rising resistance. This forecasts that the new support level is strong and is likely to hold as the uptrend continues. The trend did continue beyond the period shown into mid-July.

The KO chart was not especially volatile. Even with price movement, it covered only five points from top to bottom. Some cases of proximity-based signals are just as strong but with higher or lower volatility. One example of a chart with a similar price spread but more gradual trend movement is AT&T (T), shown in Figure 8.16.

Figure 8.16 Proximity of signals, example 2, four months

This is a busy chart. The falling resistance level was part of a downtrend first signaled by the three identical crows. Confirmation occurred rapidly in the form of a three-line strike, which is a continuation signal. The end of the downtrend was clearly forecasted with the bullish reversal morning star and immediately after this, the resistance level rose sharply.

The strength of the new uptrend was expressed both in the sharp angle of the uptrend and in the period it took, moving through the entire month of March. The next phase occurred in April and May, when the uptrend seemed to pause. This is shown in Figure 8.17.

Figure 8.17 Proximity of signals, example 2, six months

The continuation signal formed as an ascending triangle, predicting that price would continue on its upward path even as a new resistance level was set at $35.50. The price did continue to hold at this resistance level beyond the period shown, with sideways movement through June and then a renewed uptrend in early July. However, with such a rapid rise in price, other signals gave off a bearish warning. Specifically, the Relative Strength Index (RSI) moved into the overbought range in July, and immediately after this price declined back to the $35.00–$35.50 level.

This chart covers only a few points but within that range, volatility was a constant. So the longer-term future price for AT&T was not clear. However, the established resistance level did appear to be holding at least in the short term. All of the signals on this chart were strongest at proximity to the top of uptrends and the bottom of downtrends.

Flips

Beyond the proximity of signals is another aspect of support and resistance: the flip. When resistance converts over to become new support, it tends to set up a strong support level. This increases confidence in that level as a reliable floor for short-term price movement. The opposite is true as well. When old support converts to new resistance, confidence in that top price as a ceiling is increased. The flip adds an element of strength to the proximity at both the bottom and the top.

For example, the chart of Microsoft (MSFT), a long-term resistance just under $38.50 per share, lasted 3.5 months and held consistently with no price movement above that level. This is shown in Figure 8.18.

Figure 8.18 Flip (resistance to support), four months

Then, with a small upside gap on March 17, price moved through resistance in a rapid ascent. The big question at this point for traders was whether this move would quickly reverse or remain above the previous level. The appearance of the mat hold (a bullish continuation signal) increased confidence that a new support level had been established. This is a strong example of the value continuation signals provide. They do not mean only that price will continue to trend in the indicated direction. They also predict that the newly set level will remain; in this case, a resistance level flipped to support, and with the mat hold confirming the flip, it seems like the new level will hold.

The expanded chart confirms this forecast. Figure 8.19 held that support level, and the two failed breakouts below indicate that this is an exceptionally strong support price. The new sideways movement also set resistance at $341 per share.

The sideways trend continued beyond the period shown for another six weeks, until mid-July. Price then jumped up to $46 per share, a five-point move, in only four days. However, at the same time, the momentum oscillator RSI signaled an overbought condition.

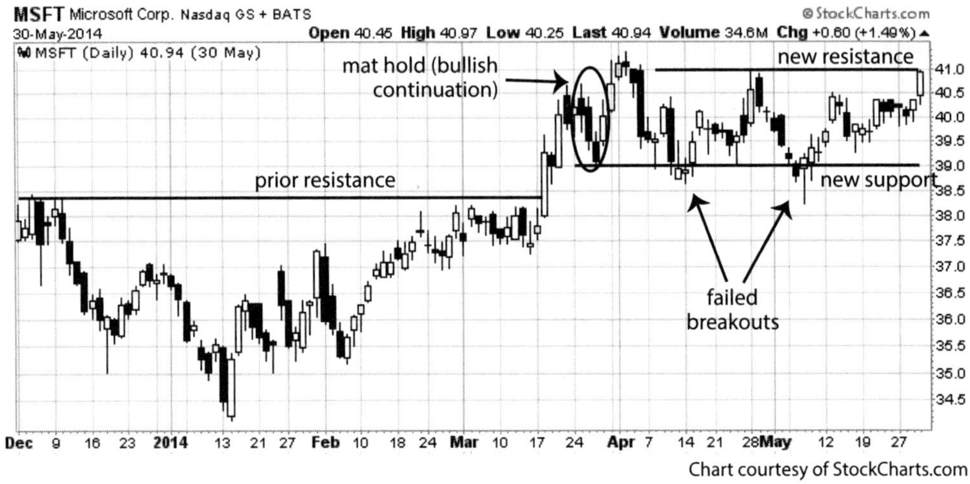

Figure 8.19 Flip (resistance to support), six months

The point to focus on with this trend is that the continuation signal confirmed the flip from resistance to support, and that new support level held. The fact that price appears to have moved too quickly by mid-July has to be understood in the context of that strongly set new support. If the price were to reverse, that support level of $39 per share is the point at which traders would expect the price to hold.

The opposite type of flip, from support to resistance, is located on the chart of Boeing (BA). This is an unusual flip in the sense that prior support was rising, but the flip to resistance was set at the starting point located at December 1. This is shown in Figure 8.20.

The beginning support price of just below $130 per share had been established a month before the period shown on November 1. As this level gradually rose to $135 in just under two months, the flip to the original price level and conversion to resistance seemed quite clear. It made the new resistance level exceptionally strong just by virtue of the flip.

The rising support level could be interpreted in a bullish manner, but a reversal was signaled by the bearish belt hold. This clearly forecast a price decline, which did occur ten sessions later, and in a convincing manner. The flip to the starting point of the rising support, flipping to resistance, set up the remainder of the chart with a strong, new price ceiling at close to $130 per share. The next phase in this chart is shown in Figure 8.21.

Figure 8.20 Flip (support to resistance), four months

Figure 8.21 Flip (support to resistance), six months

The resistance level did hold all the way until early May, while also establishing a support level of about $121.25 per share. Toward the end of May, the trend evolved into a new upward direction. Although support held into the next two months after the charted period, resistance did jump higher, only to retreat back into the range shown in Figure 8.21. In this example, the new resistance level set after the flip lasted for several months.

Are Support and Resistance Valid Price Predictors?

The examples of various behavior surrounding support and resistance raise a new question within the hypothesis of relative correlation. Can the support and resistance patterns be used effectively to predict price?

The answer depends on other factors. As long as indicators including price reversal and continuation signals, momentum, volume, and other sources for information are available, support and resistance are useful forms of information concerning the strength or weakness of the current range of trading and its breadth. Some specific patterns of breadth, notably when a shrinking breadth is taking place, are quite unreliable by themselves. However, this has to be further clarified to state that strength or weakness of the trend, the slope of price moves and the speed of change, proximity of signals to resistance or support, and the strength of candlestick and other signals all affect how strong or weak a support/resistance pattern is and how much traders may depend on the combined set of predictions.

Reversal itself is complicated by the shape, speed, and other attributes of dynamic support and resistance. With all reversal forecasts, you have to rely on placement, strength of the trend, and proximity. However, the strength of the signal itself and its confirmation ultimately determine whether a reversal creates high confidence or low. Does the likely reversal approach 100% or 50%? Or is it somewhere in the uncertain middle? Many reversals, perhaps a majority, will be found and confirmed in the middle zone of certainty; this is where confirmation based on the support and resistance trends can help to further confirm the likelihood of the reversal occurring.

In the case of continuation signals, the same caveats apply. However, based on support and resistance shape and duration, confirmation takes on a new meaning. This usually is thought of as confirmation of a trend. A confirmation signal forecasts that the trend will continue. But there also are times when confirmation leads to sideways movement and confirms not the trend but the newly established resistance or support level. Once price breaks through above resistance or below support, a confirmation signal might not predict a continued price movement, but rather the likelihood that the new resistance or support level will hold.

So the hypothesis of relative correlation can be further modified with an additional theory concerning continuation signals, and this may add new strength to continuation itself, recognizing that it may relate more to a newly established trading range after breakout, and less to the direction of the trend. The revised observation is as follows:

A continuation signal may predict further movement in the existing trend. It may also add high confidence that a newly established support or resistance level will hold based on the proximity of that continuation signal. This may apply even when the price pattern enters into a sideways movement rather than continuing the prior trend.

This concept may be applicable to many instances of breakout, notably when the range flips from resistance to support (bullish) or support to resistance (bearish). This gives greater significance to the continuation signal beyond the predicted trend direction. For traders managing a longer-term holding period, continuation takes on a new definition. It may be trend-related or, with a breakout, it may be trading range-related.

Coming chapters move beyond the focused attributes of patterns (traditional analysis, candlesticks, reversals, continuation, combined Western and Eastern, confirmation, and support/resistance). The remainder of the book focuses on how combinations of signals add strength to the candlestick reversal or continuation. No one signal or set of signals is adequate for making informed and timely trades. However, when you combine exceptionally strong candlestick and Western price indicators with other forms of information, confidence can be significantly increased and may add more ways to approach the elusive 100% level. The next chapter begins this more detailed analysis of signal and confirmation with the study of moving averages.

9

Moving Averages—Finding Statistical Correlation

A moving average (MA) is a set of tracking lines that represent the average of past prices, normally based on the closing price of each session. These lagging indicators provide value in some configurations, specifically at crossover points. When the averages cross each other or evolve above or below the current price, you can use an MA as a confirming signal.

You need two MA lines to gain value from crossover; the most popular among the combined two-MA systems are 50-session and 200-session MAs. These MA(50) and MA(200) lines interact not only with price, but also with each other. An MA may also track support or resistance as a secondary means for identifying trading range and the level of strength it provides as trends develop.

Some traders discount MAs as worthwhile indicators because they are nothing more than a summary of past prices. Although this is true, it is not just the use of averages that provides value, but also how the two MA lines act together and opposite of one another. MA is one of many forms of confirmation; it should not be used exclusively as confirmation, but as a secondary indicator.

Types of Chart-Based Moving Averages

MAs consist of two types. The simple moving average (SMA) consists of adding up the values in a set number of sessions, and dividing by the total. So a 50(MA) is the sum of the last 50 sessions' closing prices, added together and then divided by 50. This involves a lot of math, but fortunately modern online charts calculate MAs for you.

The SMA is used in all of the examples in this chapter, which is the most accepted method for the default of 50 and 200 sessions. As a comparative method between different charts, this consistently aids in developing opinions about the relative strength or weakness of an MA, and the reversal or continuation conclusions you reach as a result.

This is especially important for the types of indicators based on an MA—crossover of one MA with another, price interaction with an MA, tracking support or resistance, and the use of a specific indicator (this chapter includes a section on Bollinger Bands, which uses MA analysis to identify price attributes that may signal reversal).

Beyond the SMA is a more complex form of MA called exponential moving average (EMA). This is a popular method used in many statistical applications because it adds greater weight to the most recent entries to the field of sessions studied. However, even a slight distortion created by weighting may distort signals popularly used by chartists. The SMA is preferred for two-signal analysis, in recognition of a basic problem with EMA. Because longer-term averages tend to be less responsive to current changes, the lag factor can become a problem in comparative analysis. A shorter-term average—50 periods, for example—will be more responsive to current change, and this is why two-average analysis provides reversal signals worth noting. But that same lag factor distorts the comparative analysis in crossover study. Because the longer-term average is less responsive, EMA could exaggerate the impact of a 50-period weighted average.

Using the simple moving average overcomes the lag effect created by weighting. The lag still occurs, but with SMA the relative values are more accurate when observing double crossover and price interaction. In addition, the SMA is more accurate for tracking support and resistance.

Two-Line Averages and Double Crossover

The first MA reversal signal, and perhaps the most popular among chartists using MA analysis, is the double crossover. This is the situation in which the shorter-term MA moves above the longer-term (bullish crossover) or moves below (bearish). In the bullish crossover, both MA lines will be found below the price, and in the bearish version, both are above the price range. So the current trading range is a comparative point of analysis, with the significant event being the crossover itself.

The double crossover can be especially effective as a confirming signal when prices whipsaw, creating higher-than-average short-term volatility. The MA provides a smoothing effect and crossover shows where price begins trending too far in one direction. An example of a bullish double crossover working as a confirmation signal is found in the chart of General Mills (GIS), shown in Figure 9.1.

This set of signals began with three white soldiers after a downtrend, and this strong bullish reversal marked the point where the trend turned. It also occurred immediately after price moved below declining support, a move that failed and reversed very quickly.

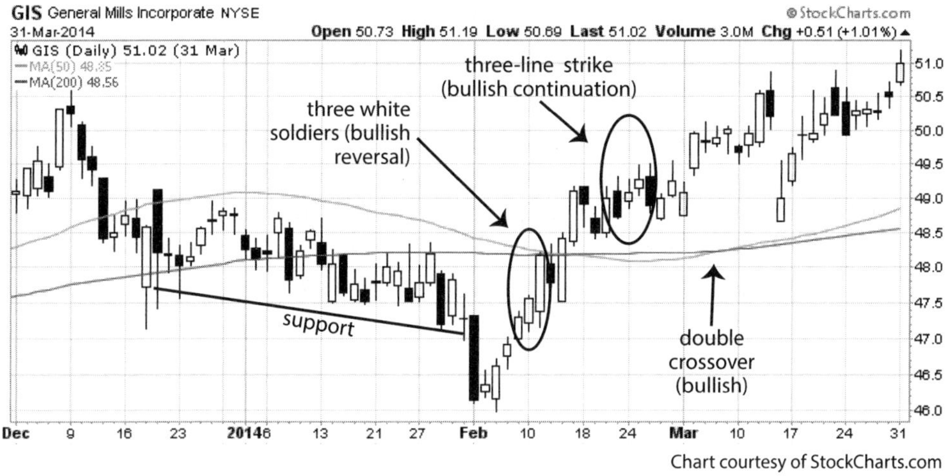

Figure 9.1 Double crossover (bullish), four months

The three white soldiers is a strong signal, without doubt. But it needs to be confirmed. The first confirmation signal was the bullish three-line strike that followed the initial reversal. This bullish continuation signal is a strong and convincing one that raised confidence of more bullish movement to come. The bullish double crossover was a second form of confirmation. Although this was a lagging indicator, it implied stronger bullish movement to continue.

The next phase in this trend is seen in the expanded chart, shown in Figure 9.2.

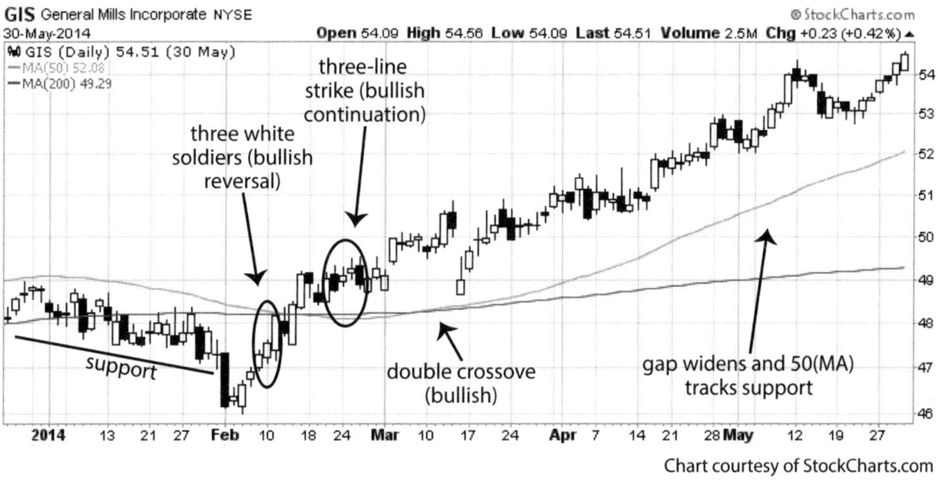

Figure 9.2 Double crossover (bullish), six months

Price did continue upward and as it did so, the gap between the two MA lines widened. The 50(MA) line tracked support, adding strength to that level as the dynamic trading range expanded its bullish trend.

A bearish version of the double crossover is located on the chart of Herbalite (HLF), shown in Figure 9.3. The initial signal for reversal was relatively weak due to proximity. A double occurrence of a bearish engulfing pattern normally is considered exceptionally strong. However, both of these were moderate in size and shape. They also both occurred after a period of sideways movement, with the actual downtrend located a full month earlier.

Figure 9.3 Double crossover (bearish), four months

The doubt this weak proximity and signal created was alleviated by the double crossover that confirmed a bearish move. This took place at the conclusion of the charted period and after a bearish price response to the engulfing signals. The next phase in this price action is seen in the expanded chart, shown in Figure 9.4.

The double crossover confirmed the candlestick double signal, but the resulting price movement was not convincing at all. This is a case proving a point observed earlier: When an initial signal is weak, confirmation is not likely to make resulting price movement stronger. Weak signals lead to weak confirmation. So although a double crossover in the right position may confirm price direction, if the prior trend was weak and reversal signals and confirmation were also weak, the entire forecast is unpredictable.

Chart courtesy of StockCharts.com

Figure 9.4 Double crossover (bearish), six months

Price Interaction with Averages

The double crossover, like so many signals, is either strong or weak depending on proximity, strength of the preceding trend, and the type of reversal signal that occurs. By the same logic, price interaction relies on strength of the preceding trend and proximity of the initial reversal signal. This occurs when price is higher than the 200(MA) and then moves above the 50(MA) (bullish)—or when price is lower than the 200(MA) and then moves below the 50(MA) (bearish).

An example of the bullish price interaction is seen in the chart of ConocoPhillips (COP), shown in Figure 9.5.

The chart began with price movement developing into an uptrend. The preceding downtrend was strong enough to add weight to the reversal, and the signal, a morning star, appeared at the right proximity. However, this signal was not perfect. The expected pattern is a middle session in the form of a doji, and this was a near-doji. In the morning star, the wider the gaps, the stronger the signal. These gaps were minor. However, even with the weak reversal, proximity was reassuring that a reversal was under way.

This was confirmed initially by the mat hold, a bullish continuation signal, and then by the bullish price interaction. Note that this occurred after price rose above the 200(MA) on February 24, and then also rose above the 50(MA) starting on March 10. The reversal and double confirmation sets up a likely bullish trend expected to continue beyond this period. The expanded chart (shown in Figure 9.6) shows that the forecast was accurate.

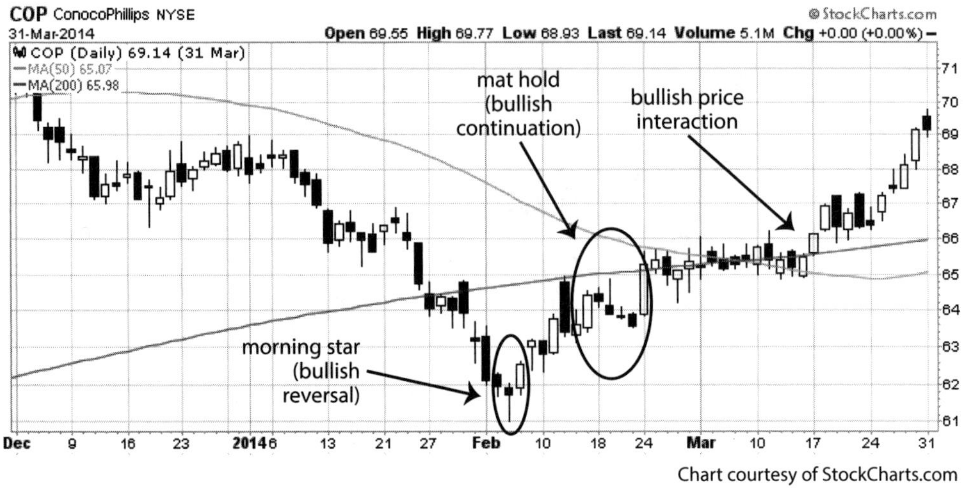

Figure 9.5 Price interaction (bullish), four months

Figure 9.6 Price interaction (bullish), six months

The longer-term chart puts the overall trend in perspective. As the bullish price movement continued, the gap between the MA lines widened. Because the shorter-term MA is more responsive to price changes than the longer-term MA, the widening gap further confirms the bullish trend.

A bearish price interaction pattern works in the same manner, but with price trending in the opposite direction. Figure 9.7 shows the chart of BlackBerry (BBRY), which contains very specific and clear signals with perfect proximity. This began with a belt hold occurring close to resistance. The belt hold, characterized by a brief uptrend culminating in a black session with no upper shadow, is a bearish reversal signal. This is easily missed because it consists of primarily white sessions and often looks like a three white soldiers, as it does in this case. However, there is no downtrend to reverse, so there is no actual bullish signal taking place.

Figure 9.7 Price interaction (bearish), four months

The identical three crows that quickly followed set up a second bearish reversal, confirming the forecast that the preceding uptrend had ended. As price did begin to decline at the beginning of March, the bearish price interaction added additional bearish confirmation. As with most MA-based signals, this was a lagging indicator. It consisted of price below the 200(MA) and then trending below the 50(MA) as well. After the initial interaction, price moved sideways, distorting the interaction, and then it fell well below, establishing the bearish confirmation strongly.

The next phase in the trend is seen in Figure 9.8.

Price continued to decline with falling resistance to the end of the chart, and with support forming at about $7.25 per share. The establishment of support and sideways movement beginning at mid-April indicates that the bearish trend was coming to a conclusion.

Figure 9.8 Price interaction (bearish), six months

Combining Moving Averages with Support and Resistance

The 50(MA) often tracks support and resistance very closely and consistently. When this occurs, it strengthens the line setting up a trading range border. However, because the MA is a summary of the price action itself, it is an oddity, an average of the prices it tracks. So with this in mind, a tracking MA(50) should be acknowledged as a secondary form of confirmation. It verifies that the level of volatility is stable and that the support or resistance trend is reasonable, notably when it is evolving as a dynamic price level.

For example, the 50(MA) tracked resistance on the chart of Buffalo Wild Wings (BWLD) as that resistance level fell. In this period, the 200(MA) was far below the trading range shown, which is typical for companies whose stock is as volatile as BWLD. The chart is shown in Figure 9.9.

The pattern is a revealing one. Resistance was on the decline at mid-chart and the 50(MA) rose above price and then followed resistance in its decline, and then the MA trended below price. Support established at about $131 per share. The bearish engulfing signal had good proximity, with price moving through resistance. The signal itself is also quite strong with a small first session and a considerably larger second session.

The next step is shown in Figure 9.10 in the expanded chart.

Chart courtesy of StockCharts.com

Figure 9.9 MA tracking resistance, four months

Chart courtesy of StockCharts.com

Figure 9.10 MA tracking resistance, six months

Several important developments are noteworthy here. A second bearish engulfing confirmed the first, and this was also a strong signal with good contrast between the breadth of the two sessions. The price level declined as expected. The previously established support level was tested briefly and held. And a second example of the 50(MA) tracking resistance was found as well. With resistance trending upward in this example, and with support well established, the signal here indicates a potential uptrend to follow. In fact, during the month that followed the period shown, price levels rose 20 points to the mid-$160s.

MAs also may track support and provide added confirmation of the trends under way. The chart of Wells Fargo (WFC) includes good examples of this, as shown in Figure 9.11.

Chart courtesy of StockCharts.com

Figure 9.11 MA tracking support, four months

The overall trend during this period was bullish, with prices on the rise throughout the period. Two distinct bullish continuation signals were highlighted. Adding confirmation was the tracking of support by the 50(MA). With the exception of a brief retracement at the beginning of February, price remained above the MA line, indicating that support levels were reliable.

The next phase is shown in Figure 9.12.

The strength of this uptrend held throughout the additional period reported, showing that support was trending upward with confirmation from the 50(MA). The value of this confirmation signal is twofold. First, as long as price remains above the 50(MA), the forecast is for a continued growth in the trend. Second, if price does fall below the 50(MA), it could signal a coming change. If this change is supported by other reversal signals, the forecast could be for a reversal or setting of a plateau in price levels.

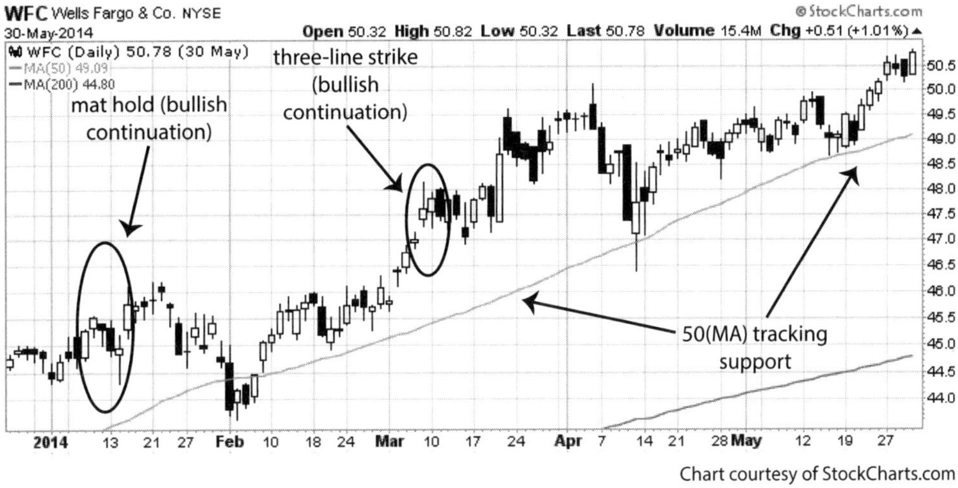

Figure 9.12 MA tracking support, six months

Moving Average Signals: Bollinger Bands

Tracking of the support and resistance levels with the 50(MA) is effective and a worthy form of secondary confirmation. Another indicator combines three different moving averages into a range analysis called Bollinger Bands.

This indicator was developed in the 1980s by John Bollinger. It includes three parts. The middle line is a 20-day average of price. The upper band is two standard deviations above the price average; the lower band is two standard deviations below the price average. So the indicator has three bands forming a range at and away from price levels.

Standard deviation adds a twist to the study of MA and its trends. This is calculated in six steps:

1. Calculate the 20-day simple average.
2. Find the deviation, equal to closing price minus the average price.
3. Square each session's deviation.
4. Add the 20 squared deviation totals.
5. Divide the result by 20 (number of periods).
6. Find the square root of the result to arrive at standard deviation.

This is a complex set of steps, especially because 20 periods are involved. Fortunately, free online charting services include Bollinger Bands and instantly compute the indicator's three lines, usually expressed as an overlay of price.

Bollinger Bands can be employed in several ways. When the bands are close together and then begin to trend farther apart, it implies growing price volatility. However, as with all MA indicators, Bollinger Bands is a lagging indicator and confirms other signals of coming reversal. It can, however, occur at approximately the same moment as another reversal signal.

Another use of the bands is to mark a likely reversal point, again as a lagging indicator in most instances. Some traders see price touching an upper or lower band as the signal point; others wait for price to move above the upper band or below the lower band as a sign of coming reversal. This alternative is stronger than a mere touch of price to upper or lower bands.

An example of Bollinger Bands is shown on the chart of Philip Morris (PM), shown in Figure 9.13. The first signal of interest is the three white soldiers, which showed up right at the bottom of the downtrend, making proximity excellent. Immediately before the downtrend ended and the three white soldiers appeared, the price moved below the lower Bollinger Band level. The final move of the downtrend contained two important and distinct features. First, it was a long black candle day. Second, Bollinger Bands were strongly violated by price, marking the end of the trend.

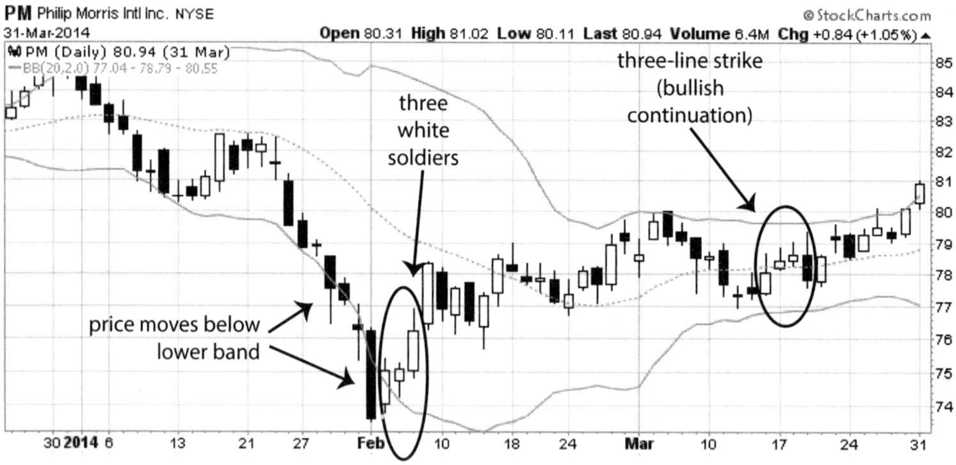

Figure 9.13 Bollinger Bands, four months

The next move was a very modest and slow uptrend, leading to the three-line strike, a bullish continuation signal. For the most part, price was contained within the range from upper to lower bands, with a few single-session violations but nothing strong enough to offset the continuation signal or a reversal.

After this initial period, price moved upward rapidly and another continuation signal appeared, this time a mat hold. Price continued rising, as forecast, through the end of the charted period. By mid-June, price rose above $90 per share before it signaled overbought conditions and reversed back to the $84.50 price level. This is shown in Figure 9.14.

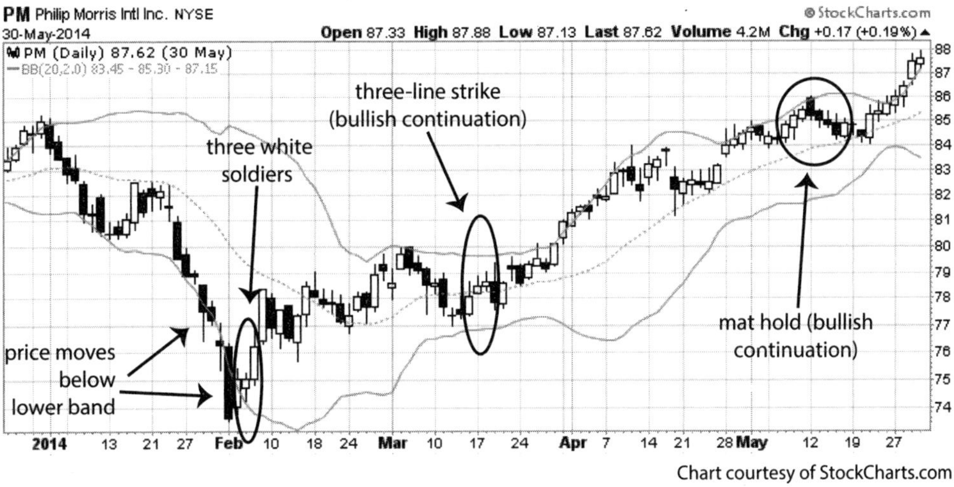

Figure 9.14 Bollinger Bands, six months

The use of Bollinger Bands and other MA tools as lagging indicators provides confirmation for existing trends, but the longer-term value is not clear. No indicator reveals the likely duration of a confirmed trend, although it does provide confirmation for the moment. MA signals strengthen what other signals and confirmation forecast, but MAs should never be confused with stronger leading indicators and confirmation.

The next chapter examines the role of volume indicators as confirmation (or leading indicators) for candlestick signals. Volume indicators come in several different types, and can add great value to the observed price trend and pattern seen on charts.

10

Volume Indicators—Confirmation of Price

Some traders believe that volume leads price, whereas others observe the nature of volume indicators to be more likely to lag than to lead. The fact is that volume is a key confirmation indicator, but its timing is inconsistent. At times, volume spikes or indicators coincide with strong reversals; at other times, volume diverges from price trends. At these times, acknowledging the value of the volume indicator over price makes sense—if and when the indicated turn in direction is confirmed. The role of proximity plays a role in these divergence cases as well.

Because volume is an uncertain indicator, it has to be evaluated in context. In finding an inconsistent correlation between volume and price, traders have to rely on proximity and confirmation before accepting a price forecast (reversal or continuation) based on volume alone or on volume in divergence with the price indicator.

Volume Spikes

The first type of volume worth studying is the singular spike. By definition, a volume spike should contain several attributes if it is to add value to the process of finding and confirming reversal. The spike will invariably identify a strong reversal point when these attributes are in place:

1. The spike must be a singular exception in size compared with sessions before and after.
2. To qualify as a true spike, volume levels must return to previously "typical" levels.
3. The spike should appear at proximity to support or resistance in order to signal a likely reversal. Lacking an existing trend, there will be nothing to reverse. As a consequence, spikes appearing during or after a period of sideways movement cannot serve as reversal indicators because no dynamic trend exists.

4. Spikes are not associated with continuation patterns, but they invariably accompany other reversal signals.
5. Reversal signals must also appear in nonvolume forms, relying on volume spikes (and possibly other confirming signals) to generate a trade with high confidence.

The volume spike is easy to spot because it is a visually exceptional event. For example, the chart of Yum Brands (YUM) shown in Figure 10.1 presents an example of a volume spike. It appeared at the point that price broke through below support and bottomed out. The volume spike was prominent and was followed immediately by a large upside gap and a return of price above support.

Chart courtesy of StockCharts.com

Figure 10.1 Volume spike, four months

In this example, the move below support was framed by the spike, which marked the point where the price decline was nearly certain to end. A volume spike is not especially unusual, but when it appears in this proximity (price breaking out below support), the likelihood of a reversal is quite high.

The gap that followed moved confidence to nearly 100%. A combination of the volume spike below support and an upside gap implied that the breakout was nearly sure to fail.

After this charted period, this belief was further confirmed. An expanded chart is shown in Figure 10.2.

Figure 10.2 Volume spike, six months

Support was reestablished two points above previous support and was confirmed immediately by the bullish continuation signal, the mat hold. This overall price pattern demonstrates that the strength of the volume spike in the ideal proximity for reversal is strongly confirmed in several ways. The large upside gap returned price into range, and the bullish continuation affirmed that the newly established, higher support level was likely to hold for the near future.

The spike is a single-session, visual type of signal favored by many day traders and swing traders. It is recognized as one of the three primary reversal signals (the other two including a narrow-range day, or NRD, and a directional turn day). When any two of the three appear, a day or swing trader is most likely to enter a trade based on the information. These three signals are rudimentary and do not take into account the role of many other signals, including candlesticks and traditional price patterns, momentum oscillators, or moving averages, for example. Although all of these play a role in confirming likely reversal in a swing trading program, the volume spike is most easily spotted and contains the greatest likelihood of an immediate reversal.

Why is the spike such a convincing signal? It all has to do with proximity and trader behavior. The spike is caused by increased activity among sellers and buyers, which is most likely to occur when the price point has reached its maximum level for the prevailing trend (lowest price acceptable to sellers in a downtrend or highest price acceptable to buyers in an uptrend). So the dramatic event is the price point at its proximity, which leads to much heavier trading than average. The volume spike is the visual expression of this event.

On Balance Volume (OBV)

Compared with the simplicity and visual clarity of the volume spike, more complex signals pertaining to volume are not as easy to spot or to interpret. On balance volume (OBV) is one of the more popular volume indicators because it adds value to trends, notably when divergence between OBV and price appears.

This indicator was introduced by Joseph Granville, the well-known bear on the market who predicted a market collapse over many years. Although Granville and his theories were criticized widely, and his track record was quite poor, OBV has survived as a valued volume indicator.[1]

OBV calculates levels of accumulation and distribution to compare volume and changes in price. When the closing price for a session is higher than the previous (white candlestick), that day's volume is added to the ongoing and accumulated volume number. If the day's price is lower (black candlestick), volume is subtracted. An immediate flaw in this indicator arises in the absolute decision to add or subtract *all* volume regardless of the extent of a price's rise or fall. For example, if price rises only a fraction of a point, it is considered a plus day; if volume rises a substantial number of points, the result is the same. So the degree of change is not taken into account, only the price direction.

When the market is ranging in one direction or another, OBV takes on a clear signal. If OBV rises, it forecasts an upside breakout above resistance. If OBV declines, it alerts traders to a potential downside breakout below support. Whether or not these events come to pass relies on finding more signals than OBV, which is most likely to add value in the role of confirmation rather than as a leading reversal signal. The "rule" of interpreting OBV should be tempered further by observing the importance not only of confirmation, but of confirmation and proximity to the levels of support or resistance.

Traders are likely to observe that OBV is a directional indicator of dubious value. Given its absolute treatment of daily volume regardless of the extent of a price move, OBV may not be the best volume indicator for either reversal or primary confirmation. However, where OBV does gain strength is in divergence. When OBV moves opposite the direction of price, it may foreshadow a weakness in the price direction. This could mean an apparent price move is only a retracement. However, in those instances where OBV will be relied upon over price direction, confirmation is essential. If confirmation agrees with what OBV shows and contradicts price, then the divergence should favor the OBV direction. A bullish divergence may identify a bottom of a downtrend, and a bearish divergence may mark the top of an uptrend. Although divergence is potentially stronger than agreement between volume and price, confirmation and proximity should rule the way that OBV is included in the price analysis.

The formula for OBV is simple. In rising price days, the total volume is added to the previous accumulated OBV, and in falling price days, volume is subtracted. Focusing on divergence, some interesting observations may emerge in a chart, although the interpretation will not always result in the same outcome. For example, on the chart of UPS shown in Figure 10.3, there are two examples of OBV divergence, one that anticipates a price move and another that lags behind.

Chart courtesy of StockCharts.com

Figure 10.3 On Balance Volume, four months

So OBV may act as a leading indicator in some cases and as a lagging indicator in others. But traders cannot know whether the indicator is reliable until it finds confirmation of a change in price direction, and unless this occurs in proximity to support or resistance.

On this chart, falling OBV anticipated the move from uptrend to downtrend by a single session; for traders paying attention to trends and using proximity analysis, this makes the OBV turn a valuable indicator. In that single session prior to the turn, a bearish divergence forms. It does not last long, but for the timing of trades, it is long enough—assuming the reliance on OBV is strong enough prior to locating the confirmation it needs. That appears in the form of the identical three crows bearish reversal. Proximity was excellent here, as reversal occurred at the top of the uptrend as price moved slightly above resistance and then quickly reversed.

The second OBV signal was not as useful for timing of a trade. The downtrend ended clearly as price moved below the newly established support. This support is not especially strong because it lasted less than two weeks; however, the appearance and proximity of the bullish reversal morning star marked the trading range's level. In this case, proximity was not apparent as long as the trading range was falling dramatically; it became clear only with the appearance of the bullish reversal. These developments are shown in Figure 10.4.

Figure 10.4 On Balance Volume, six months

The OBV in this case was unclear in its significance, making it a poor addition to the sharp turn in price direction. The rising OBV marked on the chart lagged behind the newly established bullish trend. Because OBV was lagging in this example, it demonstrates the limitation in this indicator as anything more than a confirmation signal. The likely divergence found in some instances often is too fast and limited in duration to add a convincing signal to the trend.

For example, the last divergence marked on the chart demonstrates a case in which OBV diverges from the downward retracement by a single session, and points to a likely resumption of the uptrend. This confirms the two ascending triangles, which are bullish continuation signals. However, given the very brief nature of the OBV divergence, it is speculative whether OBV added enough value to this trend. The second ascending triangle could be interpreted as confirmation of the first, adding strength to the possibility that prices may rise above resistance successfully. This occurred beginning on May 12 when the price level rose above $99 per share and remained there for the rest of the period shown. During this period, OBV did not add to the confirmation of the trend.

Accumulation/Distribution (A/D)

Expanding on the OBV indicator and correcting its major flaw is Accumulation/Distribution (A/D). Although OBV is blind to the degree of increase or decrease in price, A/D solves that problem by considering the range of prices in a session between high and low, and between the opening and closing price.

A/D acts as a leading indicator, the formulated expression of the widespread belief that volume leads price. The value of A/D is found in locating divergence with price direction. Once divergence appears, price is forecast to follow the direction A/D points to and to reverse its direction. The divergence itself uses volume to point to a declining momentum in the current trend, and anticipation of the reversal likely to follow.

A bullish divergence (when A/D rises and price falls) is a strong leading reversal signal, which, if confirmed by candlesticks and other indicators, is expected to lead to a bullish change of direction. A bearish divergence (when A/D falls and price rises) has the opposite indication: that prices are likely to follow A/D and turn to the downside.

The formula for A/D is more complex than OBV. It creates and adjusts an index based on the following calculation:

$$(\text{Close} - \text{Open}) \div (\text{High} - \text{Low}) \times \text{Volume}$$

This daily calculation is added to or subtracted from the previous A/D index level. This creates a volume trend that normally tracks price direction, but at times diverges from it. At those times, divergence provides the strongest reversal signals from the A/D index.

For example, the chart of Las Vegas Sands (LVS) shown in Figure 10.5 demonstrates how bullish divergence acts on the chart.

Figure 10.5 Accumulation/Distribution—bullish divergence, four months

At the point that price declined to a new low, the A/D index rose. This divergence anticipates a bullish move in price. This is partially confirmed by the long lower shadow at the bottom of the trend, indicating lost momentum among sellers. Support appeared to be set at approximately $72 per share based on the days preceding this bottom; at the same time, A/D gave a clear bullish divergence signal. The resulting uptrend culminated at over $86 per share when price momentarily moved through resistance. This proximity was perfect for a bearish reversal, which was signaled immediately by the identical three crows that quickly followed.

This chart combined a strong A/D bullish divergence signal with a resulting bullish move and proximity just above resistance leading to a bearish signal. The next phase is shown on the expanded chart in Figure 10.6.

Chart courtesy of StockCharts.com

Figure 10.6 Accumulation/Distribution—bullish divergence, six months

A second bullish divergence appeared in mid-May as price declined and formed a three-line strike, which is a bearish continuation signal. However, at this same moment, A/D rose, presenting a dilemma for traders. Do you follow the strong candlestick bearish continuation or react to the bullish divergence in A/D? Based on the chart-wide support level at approximately $72 per share, the evidence favors the A/D bullish divergence over the bearish continuation. Although strong continuation implies that a breakout is likely to hold, it is noteworthy that price did not continue to decline contrary to the bearish continuation signal. The price action beyond the period shown reveals another attempt to move price below $72, which failed. It also appeared to establish resistance at about $78 per share. So the contradiction between the three-line strike and the bullish divergence in A/D led to a period of uncertainty. Conflicting signals—especially two very strong signals located at proximity to support—create this uncertainty. Just as strong preceding trends and signals tend to lead to strong response (and weak preceding trends lead to weak response), it often occurs that contradictory strong signals lead to uncertainty in subsequent trends. The original hypothesis may be further adjusted to observe:

Contradictory strong signals occurring at proximity tend to create uncertainty in subsequent price trends and may offset one another to create temporary sideways price movement. The stronger each contradictory signal is and the closer their proximity to support or resistance, the longer the period of sideways price movement is likely to last.

A/D also provides instances of bearish divergence, in which the volume index moves downward in spite of price trending or continuing upward. For example, the chart of Tesla Motors (TSLA) in Figure 10.7 shows a strong example of bearish divergence and confirmation at proximity to resistance.

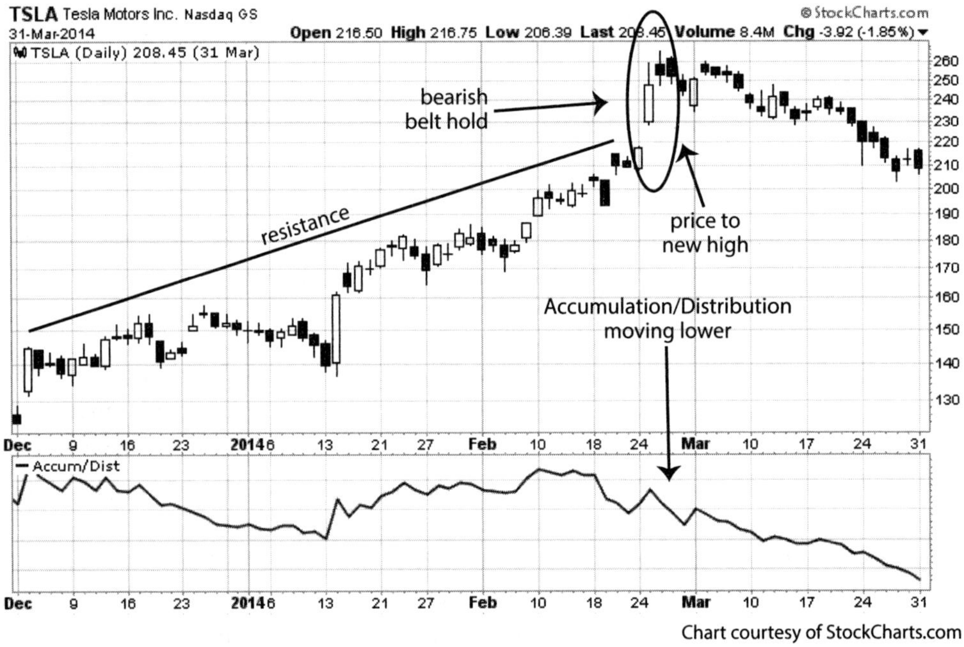

Figure 10.7 Accumulation/Distribution—bearish divergence, four months

Resistance rose to the high point where a bearish reversal signal appeared in the form of a bearish belt hold. This signal occurred as price gapped and rose above resistance—exactly the proximity and placement you expect to see for reversal with high confidence.

Confirming the reversal was a bearish divergence in the A/D index. As the price gapped upward and advanced for three days, A/D declined for those same three days. The expanded chart in Figure 10.8 reveals what happened next.

Figure 10.8 Accumulation/Distribution—bearish divergence, six months

The anticipated downtrend developed throughout the chart until mid-May, when the decline stopped. It appeared that a reversal and new bull trend was developing; in fact, over the month after the period shown, price rose all the way above $240 per share before retreating back to the $230 per share level. So in this example, the strongly indicated reversal and downtrend developed as expected, and the combination of A/D bearish divergence and the bearish belt hold at strong proximity to (and through) resistance raised confidence close to 100%.

Money Flow Index (MFI)

The money flow index (MFI) takes the Relative Strength Index (RSI), a momentum indicator (see Chapter 11, "Momentum Indicators—The Exhaustion Point"), and weights it for the effect of daily volume. The result is a simple index that identifies overbought and oversold conditions just like RSI. Although the index levels can be adjusted, RSI is usually set up to identify an index value of 70 as marking overbought and 30 as marking oversold. MFI modifies this, using the 80 and 20 index values to mark overbought and oversold levels.

These levels may also be thought of as market tops for a stock (index above 80) or market bottoms (index below 20). A divergence signal may also occur and, based on the belief that volume leads price, divergence is a signal to enter a trade. A bullish divergence occurs when MFI trends upward but price declines; a bearish divergence is the opposite. However, in a majority of instances, MFI is more likely to track price trends—the value of MFI is in identifying overbought (market top) or oversold (market bottom) conditions.

To calculate, first derive the daily Raw Money Flow (RMF), which is calculated for each session as follows:

$$((\text{High price} + \text{Low price} + \text{Closing price}) \div 3) \times \text{Volume} = \text{RMF}$$

Next, calculate both positive and negative RMF for the past 14 periods, and divide the positive by the negative RMF to arrive at the Money Flow Ratio (MFR):

$$(\text{Positive RMF sessions} \div \text{Negative RMF}) \div \text{MFR}$$

(Note: The sum of positive and negative sessions equals 14.)

Finally, calculate the daily adjustment in MFI:

$$100 - (100 \div (1 + \text{MFR})) = \text{MFI}$$

Fortunately, you do not need to go through these calculations, as online charting services perform them automatically. However, it is instructive to understand how the indicator is developed. This formula demonstrates how the momentum of RSI is modified to add the impact of daily volume.

The most common value in MFI is that it marks areas where prices have topped as overbought or bottomed as oversold. This augments and emphasizes the key ingredient of reversal because MFI turning points are most likely to occur in proximity to support or resistance. Relying on an index like MFI solves the problem of identifying proximity in the moment. In hindsight, these turning points are easily spotted; however, as trends progress, it is not always a simple matter to spot these conditions. MFI helps in this. For example, a case of MFI helping to identify proximity and likely reversal is seen in the chart of Intel (INTC), shown in Figure 10.9.

Throughout December, price was trending strongly upward. By January 1, it might be difficult to know that price was topping out. The first strong signal that the price was topping is seen in MFI, which moved into the overbought area above the index value of 80. Although resistance began declining immediately, no confirmation was found until price jumped upward with gapping price action. The three sessions above resistance formed a candlestick indicator called the evening star. This is a bearish reversal that is accurate

72% of the time; this was not included in the list of ten key candlesticks used in this book. Even so, it is a very strong reversal forecast. Combined with the MFI signal and declining resistance, confidence should be high that bearish reversal is under way at this point.

Figure 10.9 Money Flow Index (MFI), four months

The next signal occurred as the support trend line bottomed out and MFI declined into the oversold index value below 20. Price rose and MFI returned to mid-index. The new uptrend was confirmed with the continuation three-line strike. From that point onward, a new dynamic trading range was marked with rising resistance. The next phase in this chart is shown in Figure 10.10.

Although trading range leveled out in most of April and May in a narrow one-point range, a second bullish continuation signal appeared in another three-line strike. Even so, price did not immediately continue upward. In the period following that shown, price did trend strongly upward, climbing from the $26–$27 range up to $35 and higher by mid-July. However, this pattern included two large upside gaps accompanied by volume spikes and a clear overbought condition. The second bullish continuation signal shown on the expanded chart in Figure 10.10 was accurate even though the result was delayed; however, the bearish warning signs that followed were equally strong.

Figure 10.10 Money Flow Index (MFI), six months

In this case, the role of MFI clearly indicated the price direction in two instances, one following an overbought condition and another after an oversold condition.

Chaikin Money Flow (CMF)

The Chaikin Money Flow (CMF) indicator, developed by stock analyst Marc Chaikin, is based on the previously discussed Accumulation/Distribution (A/D) indicator (also introduced by Chaikin). In this expanded indicator, coming breakouts may be anticipated and forecast. The CMF indicator is based on a belief that a bullish move is first forecast by higher-than-average volume and closing prices in the top half of daily breadth of trading, and that with increased volume and closing price in the bottom half of the daily breadth, a bearish forecast is likely to develop.

Although this indicator adds value to the analysis of stock prices and the effect of volume, it also contains specific flaws. First, when gaps appear, CMF does not make adjustments; so an especially large gap is likely to distort the calculated result. Second, when volume or price moves substantially, this tends to become exaggerated in what CMF forecasts. So this signal has to be used cautiously and only as a confirming indicator. Although the volume-based signal may precede price, it also tends to display as a lagging indicator.

The general rule for using CMF is that when it turns positive as price breaks out above resistance, it is a bullish signal; when CMF turns negative when price breaks out below support, it is a bearish signal. Divergences also may apply. A bullish divergence indicates time to go long, and vice versa.

The calculation of CMF is as follows:

$$[((\text{Close} - \text{Low}) - (\text{High} - \text{Close})) \div (\text{High} - \text{Low})] \times \text{Volume}$$

The sums of these calculations are added together for 21 sessions and then divided by volume for the same 21 periods. This results in an index moving between +1 and −1. As with other indicators, this complex formula is calculated automatically when CMF is included on free online charts.

An example of CMF is found on the chart of Sears Holding (SHLD) shown in Figure 10.11.

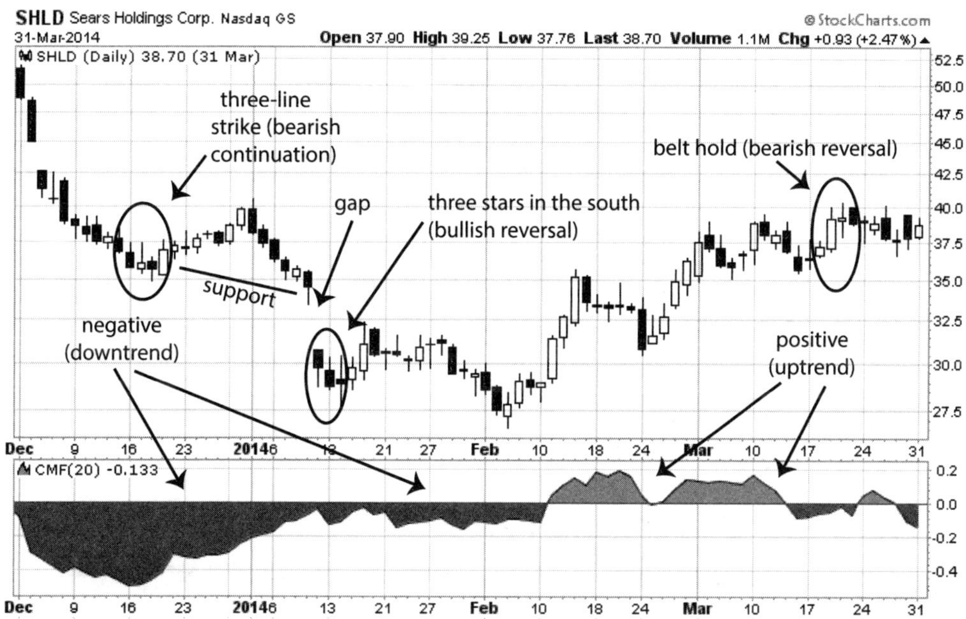

Figure 10.11 Chaikin Money Flow (CMF), four months

The first observation is that CMF tracks price direction very closely. In the first half of the chart, the bearish trend is matched by CMF, confirming a continued downward move. So overall, CMF provides added confirmation to this price move. However, there is more going on here as well. The bearish continuation three-line strike was accurate for only three weeks. It is always the case that a signal indicates likely direction but not duration. In fact, this downtrend ended with a strong set of bullish reversals. First was a considerable downward price gap taking price below support. This is the most likely proximity for reversal. This was immediately followed by the rare but strong bullish reversal in the form of three stars in the south. The combination of the gap below support and this reversal signal raised confidence to nearly 100%.

However, at the same time, CMF continued forecasting bearish moves for another month before it turned bullish. In this example, CMF was clearly a lagging indicator, with an exceptionally long lagging period. The bearish reversal belt hold appeared at a point where CMF fluctuated back and forth and added no confirmation or contradiction of any strength.

The next phase is shown on the extended chart shown in Figure 10.12. As price bottomed out by mid-April, CMF continued forecasting a downtrend, even as price rebounded to the upside.

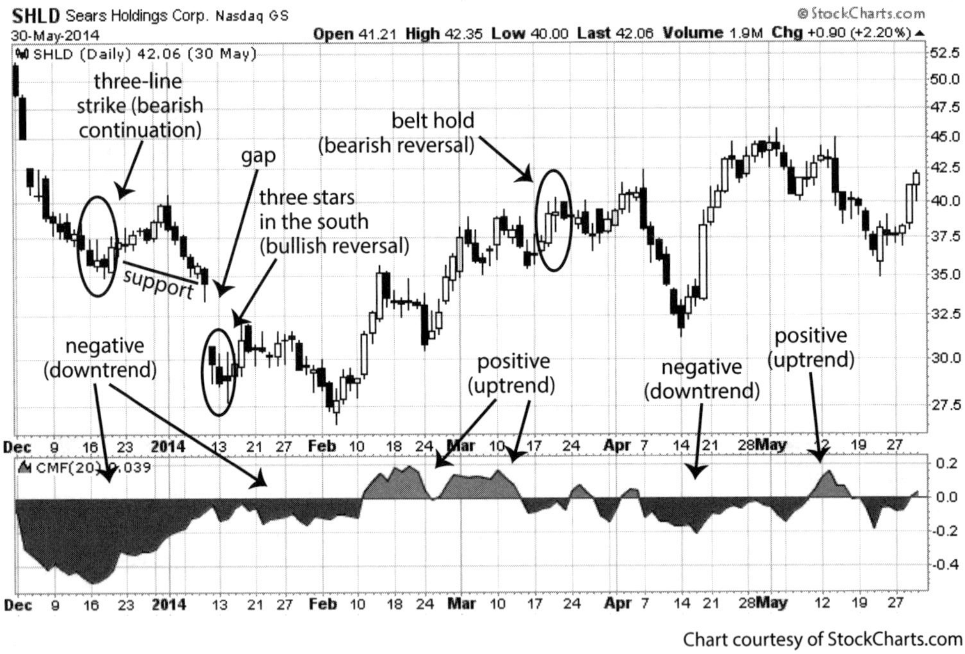

Figure 10.12 Chaikin Money Flow (CMF), six months

The remainder of the chart moved in an unclear direction and CMF also moved back and forth between positive and negative. CMF works as additional confirmation for reversals, but it is a cautionary indicator. It is often lagging and may not react for a considerable duration.

Chaikin Oscillator

Another indicator developed by Marc Chaikin is the Chaikin oscillator. This tracks money flow by comparing volume with price but through exponential moving average (EMA), which weighs later field entries more heavily than earlier ones. The calculation involves EMA for ten periods and for three periods. First, the Money Flow Multiplier (MFM) is calculated as follows:

$$[((\text{Close} - \text{Low}) - (\text{High} - \text{Close})) \div (\text{High} - \text{Low})] \times \text{Volume} = \text{MFM}$$

Next, MFM is added to or subtracted from the A/D index explained earlier in this chapter. And, finally, the adjusted A/D line is subjected to both three-day and ten-day EMA, and the longer EMA is subtracted from the shorter:

$$(\text{3-day EMA of A/D}) - (\text{10-day EMA of A/D}) = \text{Chaikin oscillator}$$

This adjusts Chaikin Money Flow (CMF) by using the EMA calculations. The most useful application of the oscillator is in locating and reacting to divergences. A bullish divergence occurs when the oscillator rises as prices fall; a bearish divergence is found when the oscillator falls as prices rise.

An example of bullish divergence in the Chaikin oscillator is found in the chart of Opko Health (OPK), shown in Figure 10.13.

The falling wedge is a bullish reversal signal. Price reaches a low at the spinning top (the doji session with long shadows). Even though the price trend remains unclear, moving sideways, the Chaikin oscillator began rising sharply. This is a bullish divergence pattern and should be seen as a strong confirmation of the bullish falling wedge.

During the uptrend, two sessions displayed long upper shadows, indicating that buying interest was weak. As these signals appeared, the Chaikin oscillator turned downward even as price continued its upward trend. This is a bearish divergence, a sign that the uptrend would not last. The final step was the belt hold, a bearish reversal. Given the long upper shadows, divergence in the oscillator, and then the reversal signal in the candlesticks, confidence that price would begin to fall was quite high. The next phase is seen in the expanded chart shown in Figure 10.14.

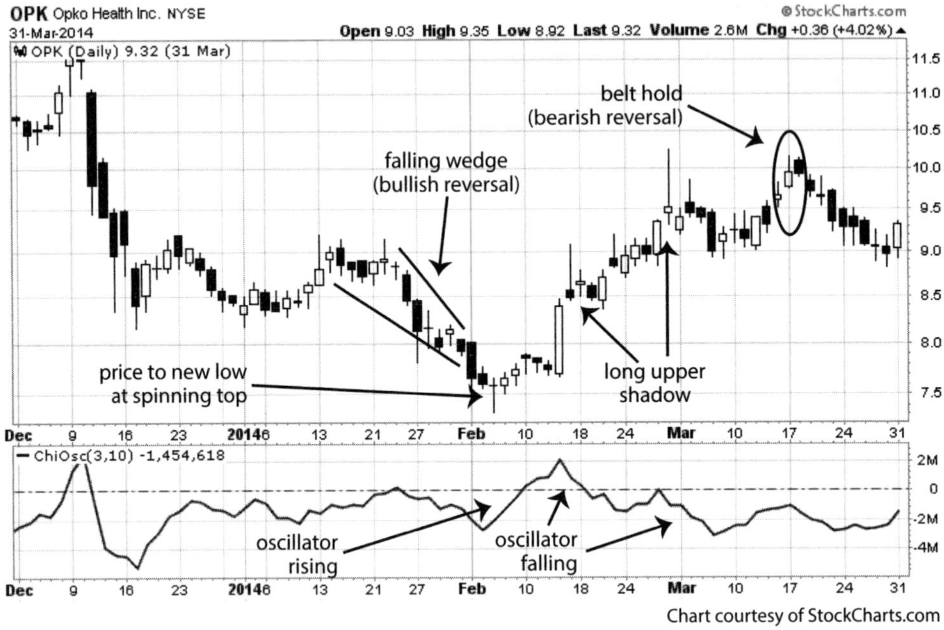

Figure 10.13 Chaikin oscillator—bullish divergence, four months

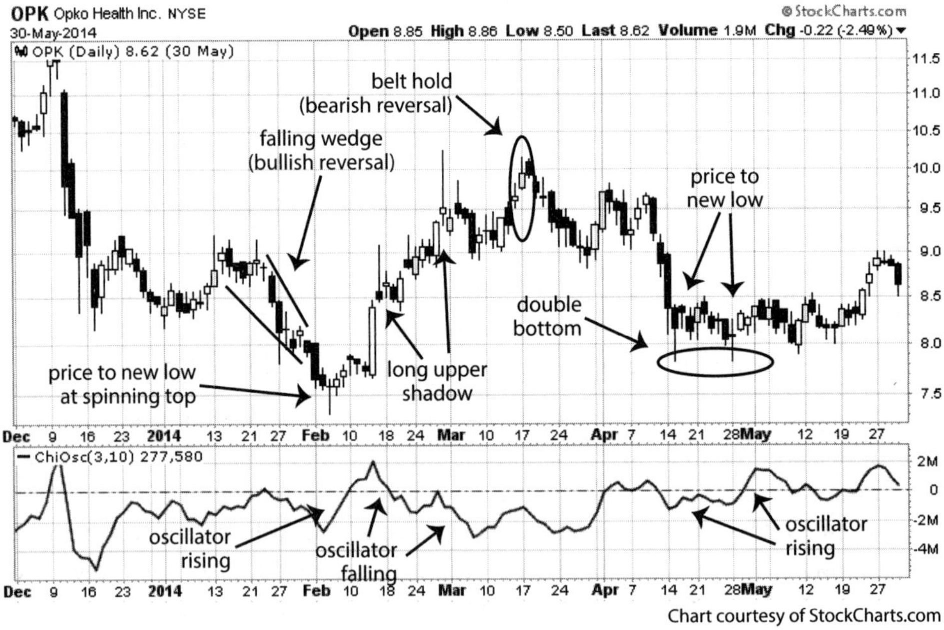

Figure 10.14 Chaikin oscillator—bullish divergence, six months

As forecast, price did fall, reaching a new low with a double bottom signal consisting of long lower shadow formations. However, even with prices declining and then flat, the Chaikin oscillator developed a new bullish divergence, heading upward.

A bearish divergence will follow a similar pattern. A good example is revealed in the chart of Amazon (AMZN), shown in Figure 10.15.

Figure 10.15 Chaikin oscillator—bearish divergence, four months

The oscillator turned sharply to the downside a full session before price gapped and declined. The bearish belt hold was the first signal of a coming bear turn. The large gap confirmed this; however, the strongest confirmation was seen in bearish divergence starting the day before the price decline.

The second bearish divergence pattern began several sessions before the downturn and was confirmed by a second bearish belt hold signal. At this point, the combined divergence and reversal signal raised confidence to near 100% that a bear trend was under way. The expanded chart confirmed this and is shown in Figure 10.16.

The price decline covered 90 points before bottoming out, a very strong bearish trend. It ended with the three white soldiers, a bullish reversal; however, the Chaikin oscillator began moving upward the day before, and was the first sign that the downtrend was over.

Even so, most traders would not make a move based solely on the oscillator's divergence, but certainly would have recognized the reversal once the three white soldiers made its appearance.

Figure 10.16 Chaikin oscillator—bearish divergence, six months

The many volume indicators are valuable in terms of trend tracking, but even more so when they also provide divergence to the price direction. The proximity of the volume signal is as crucial as any other reversal indicator. It will have great significance at or near support or resistance, and especially if and when it is strongly confirmed. The great confusion occurs when a volume signal contradicts a price signal that itself is exceptionally strong and at good proximity. In these instances, the divergence seen in a secondary signal may actually forecast a sideways price movement rather than either continuation or reversal. Such instances may also tend to lead to extended sideways movement when the contrary signals are stronger than average and when both occur at proximity to support or resistance.

The next chapter extends the discussion of relative correlation to momentum oscillators. Some of the volume signals in this chapter are closely associated with price momentum and even complement momentum oscillators. These oscillators are among the strongest forms of confirmation or even initial reverse signals.

11

Momentum Indicators—The Exhaustion Point

Trends never last indefinitely. They slow down at some point and eventually begin moving sideways or reverse and go in the opposite direction. This exhaustion factor applies to all applications of statistics, including trend analysis.

Momentum provides strong indicators about the nature of a current trend and potential reversal or continuation. Whereas a price signal identifies direction of the trend, a momentum oscillator is a signal designed to measure that trend's strength and speed. As a trend begins losing this momentum, a reversal is expected. This is especially true when the oscillator moves into an area of overbought or oversold condition.

These oscillators lead the price signals at times when the index of an oscillator moves out of midrange and forecasts reversal. This is worth noting because, if confirmed, price is likely to follow rapidly. However, at other times, the momentum oscillator will lag. It is not always leading or lagging, so the signal itself has to be studied as part of a broader analysis. When the oscillator acts as a leading indicator, it tends to lead to high confidence, assuming confirmation is found immediately. As a lagging indicator, it may act as an exceptionally strong form of confirmation for other signals.

Price Momentum Versus Trend Momentum

Price momentum refers mainly to direction of price movement. Some trends are quite gradual and slow. Others are volatile, with a large point breadth, and likely to go through big moves and retracements. These attributes define price in a particular manner, but trend momentum is not the same thing.

Trend momentum is not concerned with breadth of trading or volatility in price itself. It is more focused on two issues beyond price: strength and speed. A study of price charts reveals the differences in momentum among different stocks. Chartists also need to be aware of the breadth of trading in how momentum should be characterized. Some stocks move rapidly over dozens of points in a brief period of times. Others may appear equally volatile or more so, but maintain a narrow breadth of trading, often in single-digit breadth.

Momentum oscillators result from an index assigned to price averages, or from analysis of moving averages in relation to one another. Although these are usually based on closing prices, during an active session the momentum oscillator is updated for every change in price. The formulas are calculated instantly and automatically in online free charts, simplifying your role in tracking and understanding momentum.

When the oscillator moves into "overbought," it means that the trend has evolved above the midrange and a correction in price is expected, usually very quickly. The same is true when the momentum index moves into "oversold." This is interpreted as a signal of a coming return back into the expected midrange for the stock based on the current trend. When price breaks out above resistance or below support, momentum might reflect a likely reversal, or if price is strong enough to sustain the move, momentum might report midrange, indicating that the breakout is more likely to succeed. These attributes need to be confirmed by other signals, but the status of momentum should be kept in mind as an important consideration in judging the likelihood of success or failure in a breakout. The oscillator has the greatest importance in analysis when in proximity to support or resistance. These are the points where reversal is highly likely or—if confirmed—where continuation may also be forecast. This forecast at proximity relies on strong continuation signals and confirmation, and momentum oscillators are powerful indicators to include in this study.

A breakout below support or above resistance is most likely to reverse with large price gaps, exceptionally long candlesticks, or big upper or lower shadows. All of these attributes point to price volatility and likely reversal. When these price warnings appear at the point of breakout, they should rule the interpretation of price, even if momentum does not agree. Because oscillators are a reflection of price averages, a lack of overbought signal (at resistance breakout) or oversold signal (at support breakout) does not mean the breakout will succeed, especially if other reversal warnings are present.

At the point of breakout, price is at its most uncertain, and erratic behavior in price, volume, moving averages, and momentum is likely. This is why strong confirmation is essential at proximity to these all-important borders of the trading range. However, if momentum does not give off a reversal signal, this should not be seen as a sign of breakout success. The lack of a signal should not be taken as a form of confirmation.

Some specific momentum oscillators include Relative Strength Index (RSI), Stochastic oscillator, and Moving Average Convergence Divergence (MACD).

Relative Strength Index (RSI)

One of the most effective momentum oscillators is the Relative Strength Index (RSI). Its visual format is simple and straightforward, but it adds strong confirmation or leading reversal signals. The calculation creates an index valued between 0 and 100. When this index value moves above 70, the stock is flagged as overbought; when it moves below 30, it is oversold. The value of RSI is in the fact that a majority of the time, the index remains in the midrange of this index; so when it does moves above 70 or below 30, the signal tends to be strong.

RSI gains strength not only due to the index movement into overbought or oversold, but also in three other ways:

1. **The speed of movement toward the 70 or 30 index value.** When the index gradually inches higher or lower, it could predict a coming reversal. However, this tends to not be as strong a signal as a situation when the index line jumps strongly from midrange into overbought or oversold conditions. This is an exceptionally strong signal when it occurs in close proximity to support or resistance.
2. **Degree of movement above 70 or below 30.** If the index moves significantly higher than 70 or lower than 30, the reversal tends to be much stronger than the case in which the index is slightly over these lines. RSI is not a "yes or no" indicator; its strength varies based on how far the index value has moved.
3. **Amount of time RSI remains above 70 or below 30.** It is not unusual to see no moves above 70 or below 30 for many consecutive months. When the index value is higher than 70 or lower than 30, it is usually very temporary. However, when the index remains above 70 or below 30 for many sessions, it tends to add strength to the likelihood of reversal.

The calculation for RSI is normally based on 14 sessions and requires five steps:

1. Add together all upward-trending closing prices in the 14 sessions.
2. Add together all downward-trending closing prices in the 14 sessions.
3. Calculate the exponential moving average (EMA) for each of the results in steps 1 and 2.
4. Divide the upward close EMA total by the EMA for downward closing total to arrive at relative strength (RS):

   EMA (Up) ÷ EMA (Down) = RS
5. Arrive at the index value:

   100 – (100 ÷ (1 + RS)) = RSI

The result is the RSI index value between 0 and 100. Because this index compares advancing and declining prices, it makes sense that the index average will normally fall between 70 and 30. This is why any advances above or below these levels is exceptional and indicates a change in momentum favoring either a bearish reversal (overbought, above 70) or a bullish reversal (oversold, below 30).

An example of RSI's appearance and interpretation is found in the chart of Netflix (NFLX), shown in Figure 11.1. This involves two distinct instances of movement out of midrange, both occurring at proximity and both analyzed in the context of other signals occurring at the same time.

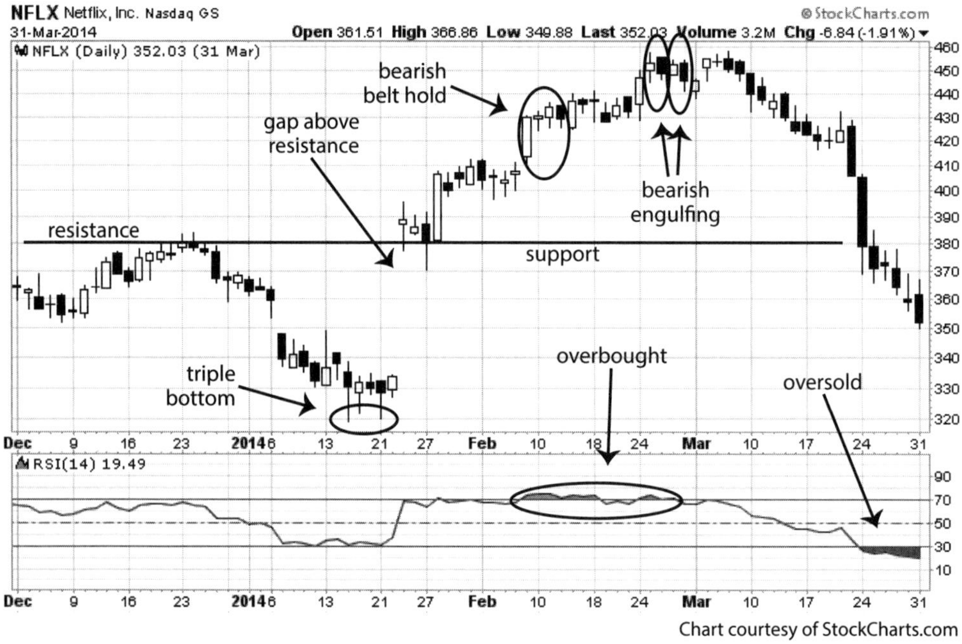

Figure 11.1 Relative Strength Index (RSI), four months

The first strong signal on this chart was the rare triple bottom, followed by a large upside gap. The triple bottom is far stronger than the double bottom, providing high confidence of a bullish reaction swing. That's precisely what occurred, but two events caused concern. First was the large upward-moving gap, and second was that the gap took price above resistance. Any gap through resistance (or support) is of great concern because a reversal is highly likely at that point.

Almost immediately after this breakout above resistance, a bearish belt hold and two consecutive bearish engulfing patterns appeared. Although the engulfing patterns were not especially strong, they confirmed the belt hold and appeared close together, a very unusual formation. The convincing bearish signal, however, was not the gap or the candlesticks, but the move of RSI into overbought status. This was unusual because the index remained above 70 for three weeks, an exceptionally long time for a momentum indicator to remain here. The more typical foray into overbought or oversold is a matter of only a few days.

This combined set of signals (three bearish candlesticks plus RSI) created high confidence that the price trend would decline, perhaps below the previously set resistance. And that is exactly what happened, as seen toward the end of the period charted. However, as the price declined below resistance, RSI quickly moved below 30 and into the oversold status. The next move is shown on the extended chart shown in Figure 11.2.

Figure 11.2 Relative Strength Index (RSI), six months

The RSI oversold condition continued through mid-April, and the bullish signal was confirmed by the double bottom in the last half of April. After this, price moved once again above resistance and RSI returned to the overbought status at the very end of the period. The entire month of June, following the period shown, was very bullish in spite of the overbought condition in RSI. In fact, price moved all the way to $470, 50 points above where it ended on the chart shown. However, throughout that month, RSI moved in and out of the overbought range.

The volatility of NFLX demonstrates that in some cases, momentum can remain in the overbought or oversold condition for an extended period of time. The need for strong confirmation and for focusing on proximity of these signals is especially crucial for highly volatile stocks. In this case, RSI provided good forecasts of reversal, but proximity and confirmation were the keys to accurate timing of trades.

Stochastic Oscillator

Momentum is measured by the Stochastic oscillator. This indicator calculates two separate moving averages based on high and low closing prices, one over 14 sessions and the other over three.

The word *stochastic* means randomly determined probability, statistically calculated based on data analysis. The result is an index with a value between 0 and 100. Overbought and oversold conditions appear in the same way as through RSI, but the usual identifying levels are 80 and 20 rather than the 70 and 30 used in RSI. As the index rises, indicating a time of accumulation, the likelihood of reversal and a new bearish direction increases, and the index value of 80 is seen as the point where this signal is strongest. On the opposite side, a decline is the Stochastic indicates a trend toward distribution, and the index value of 20 signals a likely reversal and new bullish trend. However, as with all indicators, the Stochastic-based momentum is one of many possible signals, and should confirm other indicators or, if it leads, it needs to be confirmed.

The indicator is designed to follow the speed and strength of the trend, and not to follow the price trend. Because the indicator is calculated based on moving averages of price at high and low levels, it normally serves as a leading indicator. If this is true, it should anticipate price changes and, if confirmed by other signals, may predict coming price reversals before they appear on the chart.

The indicator identifies two moving averages, a fast version called %K, based on 14 sessions, and a slow one, called %d, an average of the last three %K results. To calculate Stochastic, two steps are required. First, calculate %K:

100 [(cc – lc) ÷ (hh – ll)] = %K

cc = Current closing price

lc = Lowest close during 14 sessions

hh = Highest high during 14 sessions

ll = Lowest low during 14 sessions

The value of %d is based on the latest three %K index values:

%K (Three most recent sessions) ÷ 3 = %d

The results of these two calculations create the two-line Stochastic result. An example of this is shown in the chart of Mastercard (MA), shown in Figure 11.3.

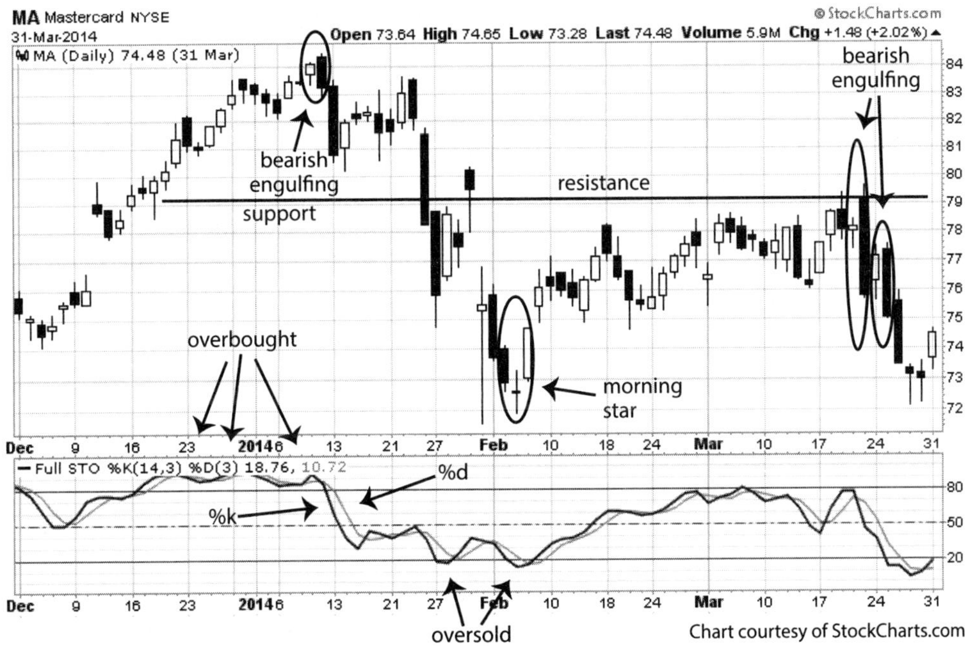

Figure 11.3 Stochastic oscillator, four months

The overbought or oversold condition is observed when the double lines move above 80 or below 20 on the index value. This makes Stochastic a visually simple indicator; however, unlike RSI, two specific differences should be noted. First, Stochastic tends to act as a leading indicator more often than RSI. Second, it is often more reliable due to the higher standards (80/20 versus 70/30) for action signals.

On this chart, Stochastic moves in to the overbought region and goes back and forth several times while price levels have reached a plateau. Looking at price alone, this is a condition of uncertainty. The trend could continue or reverse, and lacking evidence to reveal the next likely price direction, the sideways movement is unclear. However, the Stochastic move above overbought is a strong forecast of bearish reversal.

This is confirmed by the appearance of the bearish engulfing signal. Although this signal is not especially strong, it appears at the right proximity and confirms Stochastic. As expected, the price trend does reverse and head downward. Price moves strongly through support and gaps to new lows. The oversold Stochastic signal first appears just as price breaks through support. The second instance coincides with a strong candlestick bullish reversal, the morning star. Confidence is high at this point based on the strength and speed of the downward movement, Stochastic, and the candlestick reversal, all at the new low, making proximity perfect for a bullish reversal.

The Stochastic ends the period by approaching the overbought index value but without violating it. However, two exceptionally strong bearish engulfing signals then appear next to one another. These are strong due to their double appearance, and also because the breadth of the second session (especially in the first engulfing) is quite large. This point on the chart also clearly labels the flip from support to resistance. The flip makes this new resistance level very strong.

The next phase in this chart is shown in Figure 11.4. The bearish engulfing signals appearing at the end of the previous chart led to a downtrend of short duration and a return by Stochastic into the oversold region. Short-lived moves back into overbought hint at potential further price declines. In the period after that shown, price does seesaw back and forth during the following two months.

The Stochastic oscillator is effective because it includes two simple averages, and the second is an average of three sessions of the first. This means that the outcome is range-bound, so that any moves into overbought or oversold should be taken seriously. Traders seeking strong leading reversal indicators may rely on Stochastic. However, as with any average-based signals, strong confirmation and resistance, as well as support proximity, are key attributes required to prompt new trades. Use of candlesticks, volume, and Western indicators helps to confirm the strength and predictive value of Stochastic.

Figure 11.4 Stochastic oscillator, six months

Moving Average Convergence Divergence (MACD)

One of the more complex oscillators is the Moving Average Convergence Divergence (MACD). Developed by Gerald Appel in the 1970s, this combines three separate exponential moving averages, based on prices in 12 (fast), 26 (slow), and 9 sessions. The 9-day moving average (MA) is called the signal line. This appears as a bar graph, with the other two EMA lines appearing above or below that center. The relationships and crossovers among the three moving averages provide signals about the price momentum on the chart. This is a lagging indicator, so it is normally useful as a confirming signal, but rarely as an initial reversal signal.

MACD creates observed signals concerning the bullish or bearish forecasts provided by movements, divergence, and crossover of these averages:

1. **Crossover.** When both the 26- and 12-day averages are below the signal line and then cross over and above, it is a bullish signal. When both are above the signal line and then cross below, it is a bearish signal.

2. **Divergences.** Divergence in the form of gaps between the 26- and 12-day averages increases the forecast (bullish above the signal line or bearish below). Big swings in upward or downward direction increase the forecast (bullish for upward swings and bearish for downward swings).
3. **Signal line.** The signal line represents an average of the other two, so as the other two cross over the signal line, its average will be at or close to zero.
4. **Oscillator index value.** The range of MACD index moves from 1.0 to −1.0. The signal line is always set on zero (defining MACD as a centered oscillator), and the other two averages range above or below.

As a centered oscillator, MACD provides a starting point for understanding the degree of momentum. The distance from the 26- and 12-day averages from the zero point of the signal line articulates the speed and strength of the current trend, its momentum. Although a lagging indicator, MACD includes the signal line as the average of two other averages. For this reason, there are occasions in which MACD works as a leading indicator. However, proximity and confirmation are needed before acting on forecasts offered by MACD. However, if both 26- and 12-day lines cross the signal line ahead of any independent reversal signals, it could foreshadow reversal; if confirmed quickly by other price signals, the leading momentum indicator may lead to high confidence about the likelihood of reversal, as long as proximity and placement of these signals are correct. This crossover event, with both averages crossing the signal line, is a flag revealing a likely turn in momentum. By the same argument, when a price trend is under way but no centerline crossover is observed, it also is significant. When both lines remain well above the signal line (bullish trend) or below the signal line (bearish trend), MACD is providing a continuation signal. Only when those lines begin approaching the centerline does it indicate slowing of momentum.

The observation of a continuation signal in the form of MACD may be most valuable when the current price trend moves above resistance or below support. A lack of crossover by MACD strongly supports continuation, meaning price is likely to remain at its breakout level. This is an exceptionally strong signal if additional confirmation is also located at the same time or close to the MACD continuation. With RSI, this continuation feature is not as strong; the most likely outcome of RSI will be for the index to remain between 70 and 30 most of the time, and for movement into overbought and oversold to signal reversal as an exception. So the midrange RSI does not offer any specific continuation signals. MACD, on the other hand, is not based on midrange versus overbought or oversold, but on movement of the averages above and below the signal line. So, when a price trend is under way and the MACD trend confirms that trend, a continuation signal may result, assuming it can be confirmed independently.

So crossover of both 26- and 12-day averages signals reversal and lack of crossover indicates continuation. However, these observations oversimplify the interpretation of MACD. Proximity and confirmation are key attributes required before acting on what MACD reveals. However, the forecast, when viewed in context with other signals, may increase confidence in the likely next move for price, whether reversal and continuation. An example of MACD is highlighted on the chart of Lowes (LOW) shown in Figure 11.5.

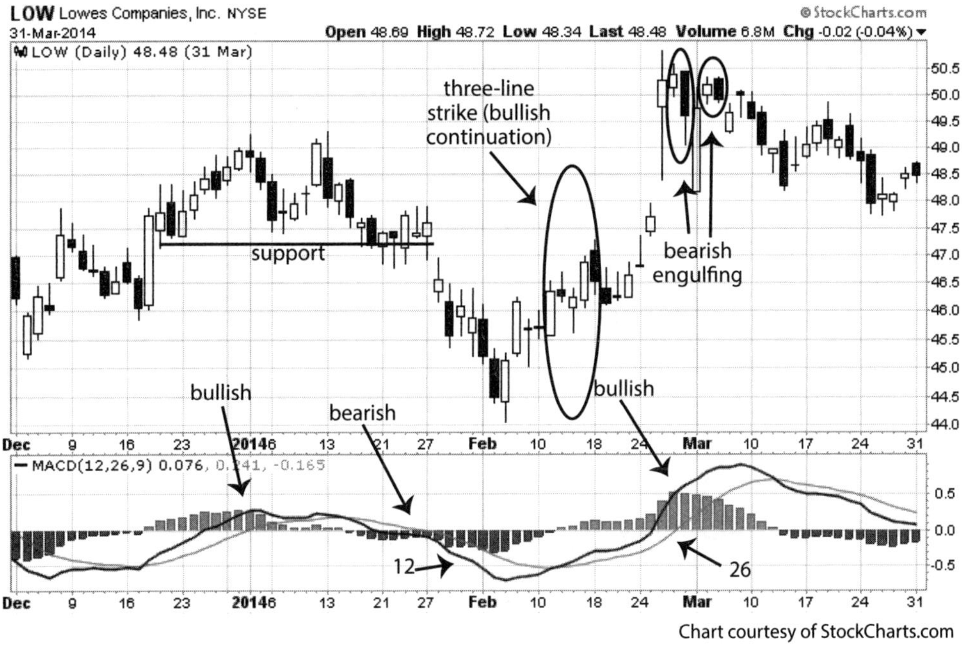

Figure 11.5 Moving Average Convergence Divergence (MACD), four months

The price trend established a line of support with MACD confirmation for a bullish trend. Setting support was a key attribute here because price began testing support and at the same time, MACD experienced a crossover and a resulting bearish reversal. As price bottomed out and then turned to the upside, a bullish continuation signal developed in the form of the three-line strike. This was confirmed by MACD as both moving averages once more crossed above the signal line. However, this lagged behind the price trend. Just as MACD acknowledged a bullish reversal, two bearish engulfing signals appeared. This led price to the downside, followed by MACD, with the two averages declining and moving toward the signal line throughout the month of March.

As shown in Figure 11.6, crossovers continued. In April, moves in the MACD averages crossed over the signal line, setting up a new bearish trend. This coincided with price moving below previously established support. The support level flipped and became the new resistance price. At the end of the chart, the double bottom signaled the end of the downtrend. Immediately after this, the MACD averages began moving upward toward the signal line, confirming the likelihood of another bullish reversal.

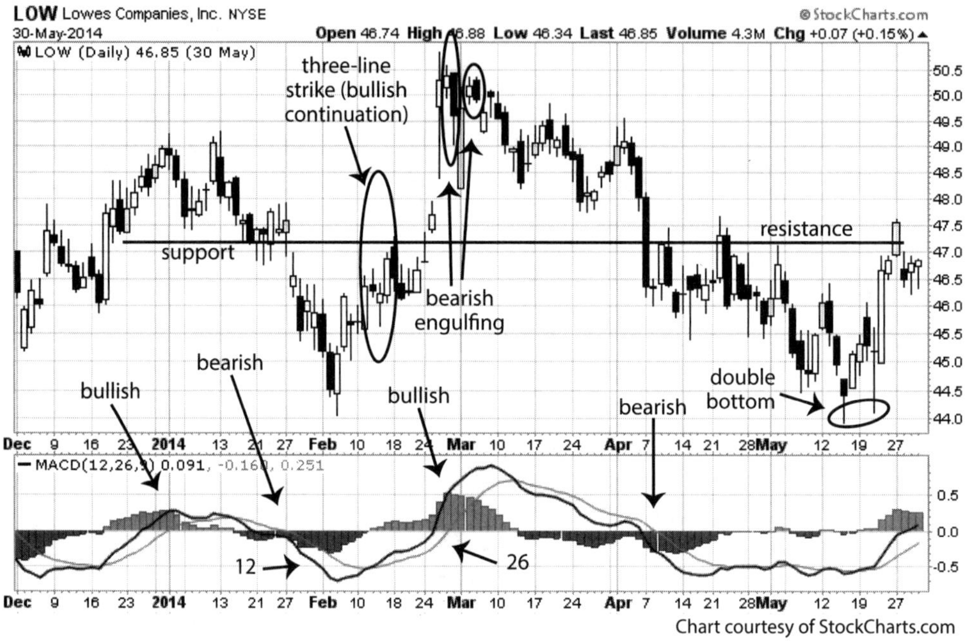

Figure 11.6 Moving Average Convergence Divergence (MACD), six months

This back-and-forth price movement appears volatile, but the entire six-month chart extends only six points from highest to lowest price. In this case, the exchange of bullish and bearish trends would be difficult to anticipate. However, tracking the MACD crossover of 26- and 12-day average works well in confirming the moves and distinguishing between reversals and retracements. It is noteworthy that most of the instances of MACD crossover occurred at proximity to support and resistance. In comparison, the retracements at several points on the chart were not in proximity to the borders of the range. For example, these retracements occurred at January 2–6, March 12–14, March 21–25, April 18–22, April 30–May 4, and May 8–12. All of these were at midrange on the price chart, and MACD did not respond to these momentary price moves. So the crossover of MACD averages as a confirming signal is quite effective.

One of the intriguing aspects of MACD, beyond the strength of crossover confirmation, is the clarity of continuation. This occurs when a trend is under way and the 26- and 12-day average lines remain above the signal line (bullish) or below the signal line (bearish). In this application of MACD, once these averages begin trending toward the signal line, it is an early warning that the trend may be ending. However, for as long as these both remain apart from the signal line, the continuation is strongly forecast.

For example, the chart of Kraft Foods (KRFT) shown in Figure 11.7 provides a good example of using MACD for continuation. This chart demonstrates how MACD appears in this context, but it must be confirmed by other continuation signals in order to be acknowledged.

Figure 11.7 MACD continuation, four months

Resistance trended upward and price moved through resistance. This could be seen as a reversal signal because the move initially failed. However, as price moved above this line, a bullish continuation pattern formed, in the three-line strike. Based on its proximity to resistance, this strongly forecasts continuation of the rising trend.

Price declined after this, so it looked like a reversal and new bearish trend. Even though the decline was quick, it lasted only three weeks and extended only four points. The bullish continuation was difficult to ignore. MACD dipped below the signal line, a divergence from the candlestick signal. However, it quickly reversed and turned bullish.

Price once again rose to resistance and then broke through. The pattern repeated with yet another three-line strike appearing at the point of proximity to resistance. This time, however, MACD moved strongly above the signal line, presenting a bullish signal and confirming the three-line strike. This continuation signal raised confidence in continuation, which not only did occur, but was further confirmed. Another three-line strike appeared in March, while the MACD averages remained well above the signal line in bullish territory.

Overall, the combination of candlestick continuation and MACD confirmation should tell traders that a reversal is not likely as long as these conditions continue. The next phase is seen in the extended chart shown in Figure 11.8.

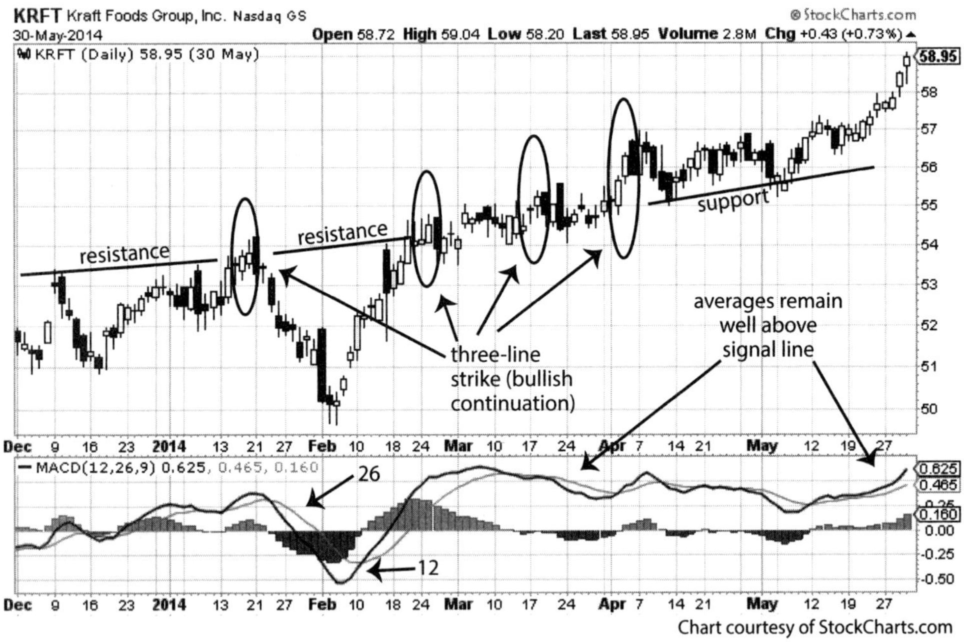

Figure 11.8 MACD continuation, six months

A fourth three-line strike appeared early in April. It is unusual to see four of the same continuation signals on a chart, but this occurrence adds great strength to the predicted continuation. This is confirmed for the remainder of the period by the status of MACD.

Both of the MA lines remained strongly in bullish territory until the end of the period. The rising resistance price also flipped and became a rising support level, adding more strength to the likely continuation of this trend.

This example of combining candlestick continuation with MACD confirmation solves a problem traders face in reading charts. As prices continue upward over the long term, the temptation to sell and take profits is constant. By combining price signals with momentum, it becomes clear that the trend did continue for an unusually long period of time. If the two MACD averages began declining and approaching the signal line, that would serve as a warning that the bullish trend might be coming to a conclusion.

* * *

Momentum oscillators reflect averages based on price, and as a result may be critically viewed as self-fulfilling prophecies. They are price averages meant to predict price reversal or continuation. However, when used in a greater context, momentum takes on a more powerful application. This context involves strong confirmation by candlestick and Western signals, occurring at proximity to support or resistance.

The reversal power of MACD confirmation adds order to an otherwise volatile and often unpredictable price trend. When the seesaw of short-term trends is under way, prediction without signals and confirmation is very difficult. The changes in momentum oscillators help to better understand how these price trends behave.

Using oscillators (especially MACD) to confirm a continuation price pattern adds tremendous value to initial continuation signals. It often occurs that a continuation pattern is confirmed only by proximity, meaning at the point of breakout above resistance or below support. This is troubling for every trader because continuation requires more than just an initial signal. It has to be confirmed. The proximity of a continuation signal increases confidence of a successful breakout, but proximity is not enough confirmation. This is where momentum oscillators can provide added forecasting. RSI and Stochastic, at the very least, should remain in midrange at such times, but this lack of change in the signal is not adequate. The MACD confirmation shown in the last section demonstrates an excellent method for confirming an ongoing trend and for tracking that trend and spotting the time when it begins to weaken and reverse.

The next chapter expands on these observations of reversal and continuation, proximity, and confirmation, by examining the nature of signal failures and false indicators. Many of these occur because signals are found in the wrong proximity, or because a reversal signal is assumed to work as continuation because it is found at midrange. The best way to minimize the effects of signal failures and false signals is to rely on strong placement and proximity as well as confirmation. However, even with the most thorough analysis, you will experience failures and false indicators in some cases. The goal of chart analysis based on candlesticks and other signals is not to eliminate these failure incidents, but to minimize them as much as possible.

12

Signal Failures and False Indicators—The Misguiding Signal

A common belief about signals—both reversal and continuation—is that they sometimes fail or are simply false. This belief that unreliable and inaccurate signals are random is misleading, however. Although signal failures and false indicators certainly are possible, it is more likely that a more in-depth examination of a chart will reveal that these occurrences can be explained.

A combination of flaws in patterns, proximity, or trends can be attributed to a majority of signal failures and false indicators. A typical pattern flaw is in a signal that meets the bare minimum to qualify for what it forecasts. Such signals are inherently less reliable than a stronger and clearer pattern to the signal. Proximity flaws include signals occurring midrange or long after a trend has peaked. These late reversals tend to fail, primarily because they are located in the wrong proximity to support or resistance. Flawed trends are those that are too short to truly count as a trend, or that are slow-moving, very gradual, and weak. In such cases of weak trends, signals are more likely to fail than in cases where trends are strong, fast, and long-lasting.

A related problem is contradiction of signals. Many signals may be contained within other signals, and give off opposite prediction (bearish reversal versus bullish continuation, for example). In these instances, which signal do you accept and which one do you reject? A great danger in chart analysis is a tendency for traders to see what they expect to see, and to not recognize instances of contradiction. The troubling close appearance of a rising wedge (bearish reversal) and an ascending triangle (bullish continuation) is an example of signals having patterns so close together that they can be interpreted in more than one way. The same problem is found with the falling wedge (bullish reversal) and the descending triangle (bearish continuation).

Among candlesticks, many patterns appear within the boundaries of other patterns, and provide contradictory signals. For example, a three-line strike (bullish continuation) concludes with a two-day bearish engulfing reversal signal. Likewise, a mat hold (bullish continuation) contains middle sessions that create the three black crows (bearish reversal). The fact that these contradictory signals are quite strong on their own creates a dilemma for traders. As a matter of interpretation, each trader has to decide between the contradictory signals.

This chapter presents an argument that failed signals, false indicators, and contradictory signals can be examined and demonstrated to not occur randomly. The hypothesis behind this argument is that in each case, the nature of trend patterns, confirmation, and the relative correlation of the broader picture all explain a majority of these enigmatic situations. The added hypothesis statement concerning signal failures and false indicators is:

> *Signal failures and false indicators can occur without explanation; however, inaccurate, contradictory, and failing signals and confirmation are most likely to be traced to a logical flaw in a pattern, proximity, or weakness in the trend. In a majority of cases, a failed signal or false indicator can be explained with analysis of the current trend, proximity, strength, or weakness of the signal and confirmation, or relative correlation between conflicting forecasts.*

Candlestick Indicator Conflicts

The first area of analysis is a situation in which conflicts are discovered between different candlestick signals. Some patterns, by definition, contain other patterns within their boundaries. For example, the chart of Alleghany (Y) includes a contradictory set of patterns. This is shown in Figure 12.1.

The three-line strike is a bullish continuation (shown within the oval). However, it concludes with a strong bearish engulfing reversal (highlighted with a rectangle). This appears twice. It could be interpreted as two continuation signals confirming continuation or two bearish reversal signals confirming reversal. So which is this, bullish continuation or bearish reversal?

The other attributes shown on the chart may clarify the issue, or only confuse it. The RSI signals first anticipated a bullish reversal, appearing at proximity to the bottom of the downtrend in the form of movement into the oversold area. RSI is normally very reliable in confirming turning points like this. However, RSI moved into the overbought at the same time that the conflicting signals appeared. So this indicates the stronger likelihood of a bearish reversal.

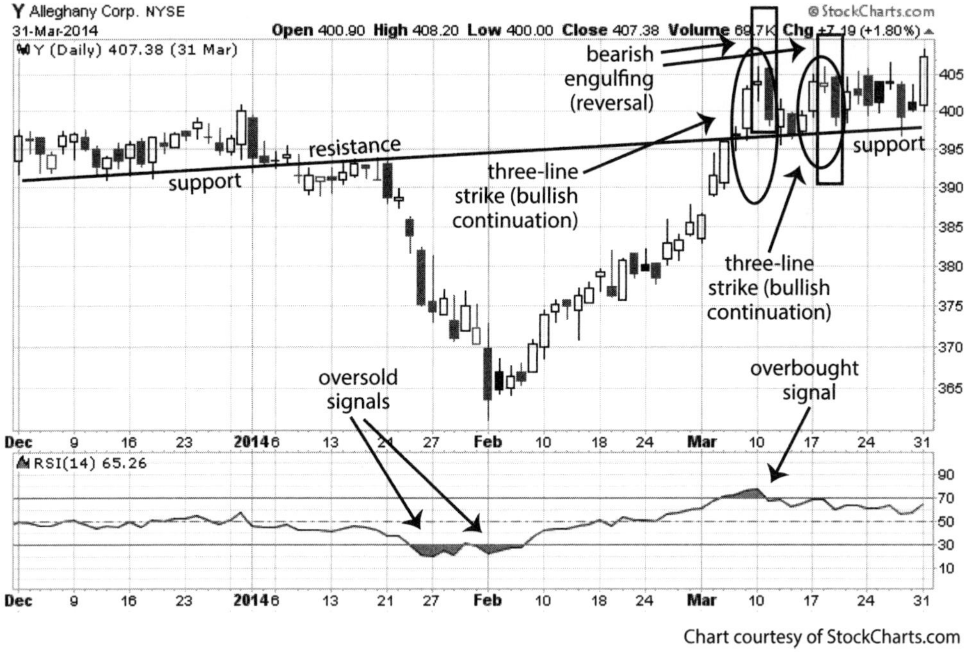

Figure 12.1 Three-line strike or bear engulfing, four months

However, at the same time, price was trending upward and broke through the previous resistance level. It appeared to establish a new line of support that continued the upward movement of previous resistance and support trends. The flip from resistance to support tends to make new support a strong border of the trading range. So the trend in resistance to support flip contradicts RSI's confirmation of the bearish engulfing reversal.

This situation is not easy to read. However, the combination of the resistance/support flip and the double occurrence of the bullish continuation signal appear stronger, at least provisionally. As long as the price remains above the line of support, interpreting the situation as bullish continuation is most likely. To see what happens in the expanded chart, see Figure 12.2.

The expanded chart shows that the line of support continued to rise and price remained above it for the remainder of the chart. No additional reversal threats appeared and RSI remained in its midrange through to the chart's end.

Figure 12.2 Three-line strike or bear engulfing, six months

This analysis reveals that there are ways to compare sets of signals that make sense. In this case, a strong resistance/support flip made a double continuation signal more compelling than the bearish engulfing (even though it also appeared twice). As long as the level of support held, the continuation turned out to be more likely. However, any signal of support testing, especially if confirmed by new bearish signals, would have quickly changed this interpretation.

Contradictory signals invariably present a great challenge. In this case, two very strong sets of signals presented a paradox for traders. No matter how this situation is interpreted, one of the possibilities has to fail. However, traders may take comfort in relying on the strength of the resistance/support flip as the deciding factor (as long as price remained above the newly established support level).

Continuation Versus False Reversal Indicators

Another version of contradictory candlestick signals involves the mat hold (bullish continuation) and three black crows (bearish reversal), which is found within the pattern of the mat hold. You could interpret this as a clear and strong continuation pattern, or you could focus on the strong bearish reversal and ignore the mat hold. The decision to move in one direction or the other is another dilemma, but as with the previous example, the right answer is most likely to be found in the other attributes of the chart.

For example, the chart of General Electric (GE) contains perplexing mixed signals for continuation and reversal. This is shown in Figure 12.3.

Figure 12.3 Mat hold or three black crows, four months

The end of the downtrend was marked briefly by the oversold condition in RSI. However, once price turned to the upside, the confusion began. The first signal is the mat hold, a bullish continuation (shown in the oval). However, within the mat hold, the pattern itself includes three black crows, a bearish reversal. Another three black crows appears in early March, indicating confirmation of a coming downtrend. However, support was rising and it held through to the end of the chart.

Accurate reading of signals is always subject to interpretation. One possible explanation of this chart acknowledges the strength of rising support. Both three black crows patterns do create very short-term moves downward. Most analysts would interpret these as retracements, and retracements normally are not associated with reversal signals.

However, a more important observation is the overall weakness of the pattern. After a strong downtrend preceding the second half of the chart, the trend moves upward, but not very convincingly.

Observing that weak trends are most likely to lead to weak signals, it is reasonable to discount all of the candlestick signals as also being weak. The continuation signal does lead to continuation, but it is weak continuation. The bearish three black crows patterns lead to very little price reaction. The only consistent attribute of this chart in the period after the strong downtrend is the price reversal confirmed by rising support. However, the outcome of this weak trend and questionable set of signals can be better observed only in the expanded chart, which is shown in Figure 12.4.

Figure 12.4 Mat hold or three black crows, six months

On this expanded chart, support continues to strongly support the price trend, even though that price trend itself is not especially strong. The appearance of another bear reversal signal, the engulfing pattern, led to the only attempt to move price below support. That breakout failed. The lack of movement in momentum (measured by RSI) into overbought indicates that this price trend is reasonable as a continuation pattern. However, this is not as much from any specific signals beyond support, but more from the lack of any successful bearish reversal signals to the contrary.

The entire chart displays weakness. The only strength is seen in two aspects, the initial strong downtrend during the month of January and the consistent rising support from February through May. The sole continuation signal was not compelling by itself, especially given the three contrary bullish reversal signals seen on the same chart. However, these were weak and led to weak and very short-lived downward movement and no success in breaking below support.

Confusion Between Triangles and Wedges

Another signal failure can be traced to the disturbing similarity between triangles and wedges, given their opposite meaning. A rising wedge is a bearish reversal, but if its rise is slight, a small adjustment could easily convert the wedge into an ascending triangle, which is a bullish continuation signal. The same problem is seen between the falling wedge (bullish reversal) and descending triangle (bearish continuation).

When the angles of the two sides of a wedge are sharp, the meaning is quite clear. So in order for a wedge signal to be considered reliable, it should be sharp and dramatic. A wedge that only slightly changes from a strictly sideways price movement can confuse and mislead. Because this situation involves opposite meanings, it requires extra caution in interpretation.

An example of the problem is seen in the chart of Kellogg (K), shown in Figure 12.5. The entire period was marked by consistently rising resistance, but the last week of January through mid-February presented contradictory and confusing information. Its meaning was open to interpretation.

Although the general trend appeared to be moving upward, the price dip at midchart created the contradictory signals. The pattern from late January through mid-February could be interpreted as an ascending triangle, which is a bullish continuation pattern, or as a rising wedge, which is a bearish reversal. Conditions favor the bullish continuation for two reasons. First, the rising wedge is poorly positioned. The prior price movement was moving downward gradually, so there was no uptrend to reverse, meaning proximity was very poor for bearish reversal. However, the price decline and turn back to bullish movement favors the longer-term concept of bullish continuation. The volume spike occurring at the very bottom of the price dip further confirms the bullish interpretation.

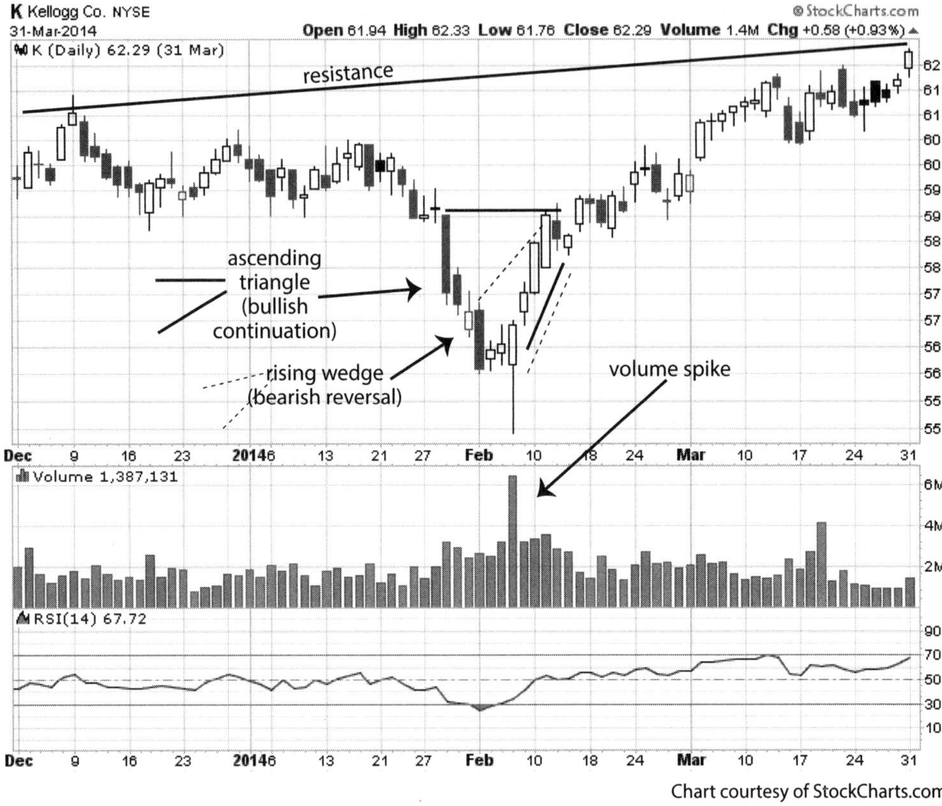

Figure 12.5 Ascending triangle or rising wedge, four months

Because price continued trending higher through the remaining period, the bullish take on this pattern was correct. However, to see what happened next, view the extended chart in Figure 12.6.

More confusion was caused by the volume spike occurring just as price moved above resistance. The volume spike is most often seen as proximity to resistance or support; in this case, the likely bearish reversal was also confirmed by RSI moving into the overbought region. At that moment, the signals all pointed to a bearish move to follow. However, price remained above the prior resistance line and flipped to form new support. So in spite of the strong signals, price did not reverse as anticipated. As with the previous example, it turned out that the trend in support and resistance may easily overcome what other signals forecast.

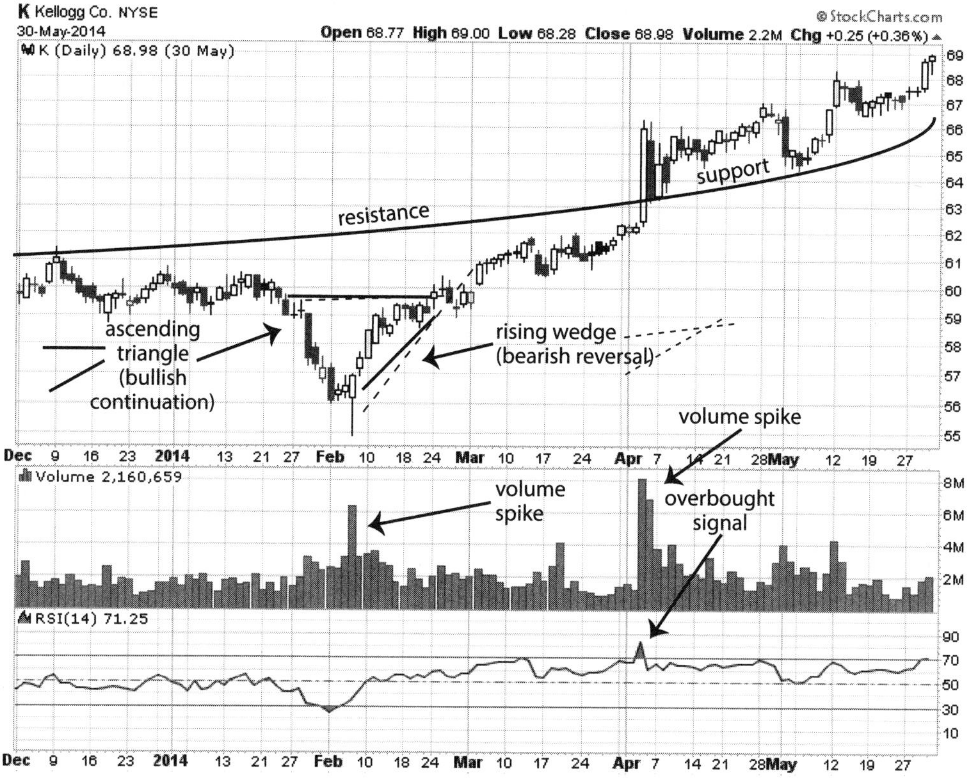

Figure 12.6 Ascending triangle or rising wedge, six months

This is troubling for those traders relying on candlesticks, volume, and momentum. It implies that these signals can and at times do simply fail without any visible cause. The one sign that a bullish continuation was more likely than a bearish reversal was the long white candlestick that appeared as price broke above resistance. In most cases of breakout without any other signals, you expect to see an immediate retreat; this did not occur. So even with the volume and momentum signals with excellent proximity (breaking above resistance), the price trend was strong enough to continue moving in the same direction. Resistance flipped to support and price remained above the newly established support through the rest of the chart.

A troubling aspect of this long-term bullish trend was also seen in RSI. Notice how the index approached the overbought level of 70 repeatedly. This forecasts potential weakness in the bullish trend. In fact, in the period after that shown through May 30, RSI did move above 70 and price tumbled over the next two months. So the confusing and contradictory signals did not prevent the uptrend from playing out, but eventually the trend was exhausted and a bearish reversal occurred.

This chart was difficult to read because of the contradictory indicators, the short-term weakness in price trends, and failure of the strong volume spike and confirming RSI to lead to reversal. This chart presents one case of price defying the signals. However, this occurs less frequently than more predictable cause and effect. In most instances of contradictory signals, analysis more often shows the way to the more likely forecast. This chart reminds traders that strong reversal signals and confirmation are not always enough.

The chart's initial focus was on the contradiction between the bearish reversal signal in a rising wedge, and bullish continuation in the ascending triangle. The opposite situation presents a similar dilemma. An example of a falling wedge (bullish reversal) and descending triangle (bearish continuation) is seen in the chart of BlackBerry (BBRY), shown in Figure 12.7.

Chart courtesy of StockCharts.com

Figure 12.7 Falling wedge or descending triangle, four months

The first important signal was found in MACD with a bullish crossover. But from mid-January through most of February, a confusing situation developed. The pattern was either a bullish reversal (falling wedge) or a bearish continuation (descending triangle). However, the key observation about this pattern is that it is poorly placed. You expect to see either of these after a strong uptrend. Although an uptrend preceded this pattern, the trend that began on January 21 was moving downward. Because this marked the beginning of either the wedge or the triangle, it could be interpreted as working in either interpretation.

In situations such as this, you look for confirmation. MACD remained above the signal line for most of this period, forecasting bullish continuation. Toward the end of the chart, MACD did decline into a bearish crossover, and price quickly followed by moving downward as well. So initially, this appeared to be the most likely interpretation of the signal. However, when the confusing wedge/triangle appears like this, it tends to obscure rather than strengthen the actual trend. What happens next makes this point, as shown in Figure 12.8.

Figure 12.8 Falling wedge or descending triangle, six months

The trend did go to the bearish side, price following MACD. After the crossover occurred, the two averages remained below the signal line for the remainder of the chart and price settled into a sideways range between $7 and $8 for the rest of the charted period.

This chart reveals that poor proximity tends to negate signals. The initial wedge or triangle was weakened by two factors. First, the proximity did not support either bullish reversal or bearish continuation because no actual downtrend had been established. Second, when these contradictory signals appear, they tend to offer little or no guidance of value. Just as the previous case of a rising wedge versus ascending triangle was confusing, this situation involving a falling wedge versus descending triangle did not add actionable information to the analysis. Traders can learn from these examples because there is one consistent message: Contradictory information points to the need for extra caution. On this chart, the only reliable forecasts came from MACD. However, price and pattern did not confirm what MACD anticipated. So when a contradictory set of signals appears, the prudent course to take is one of caution.

The signals in this case were lacking in confirmation, making the case even more doubtful. The previous example displayed a strong reversal and confirmation moment, but price did not respond as expected. In this current chart, MACD was accurate in its forecast, but that alone was not enough to forecast a reliable price direction.

A conclusion you may reach from the analysis of contradictory signals is that these occur in periods of uncertainty. They become visual expressions of confusion among traders and conflict about what direction is likely to occur next. Some traders like to look at the broader market in these situations, hoping to see marketwide trends that may lead price direction for an individual stock. This is a dangerous concept, however. Although marketwide trends do affect longer-term price trends, moments of reversal or continuation tend to be reliable only to the extent of what can be viewed and confirmed on the single chart. Traders may prefer caution over assumption in trying to understand the market for a stock in which neither buyers nor sellers control the trend.

Failed Signals Between Price and Volume

The failure of a signal most often occurs because it appears in the wrong proximity. This essential attribute for either reversal or continuation is overlooked too often. In spotting a strong signal, traders may react to the signal itself while ignoring the essential requisite of proximity. It does not matter how strong a signal is found; if there is no existing trend, then there is no trend to reverse or to continue. As obvious as this might seem, it is also easily overlooked.

A case in point is revealed on the chart of Macy's (M), shown in Figure 12.9, in which price and volume are compared.

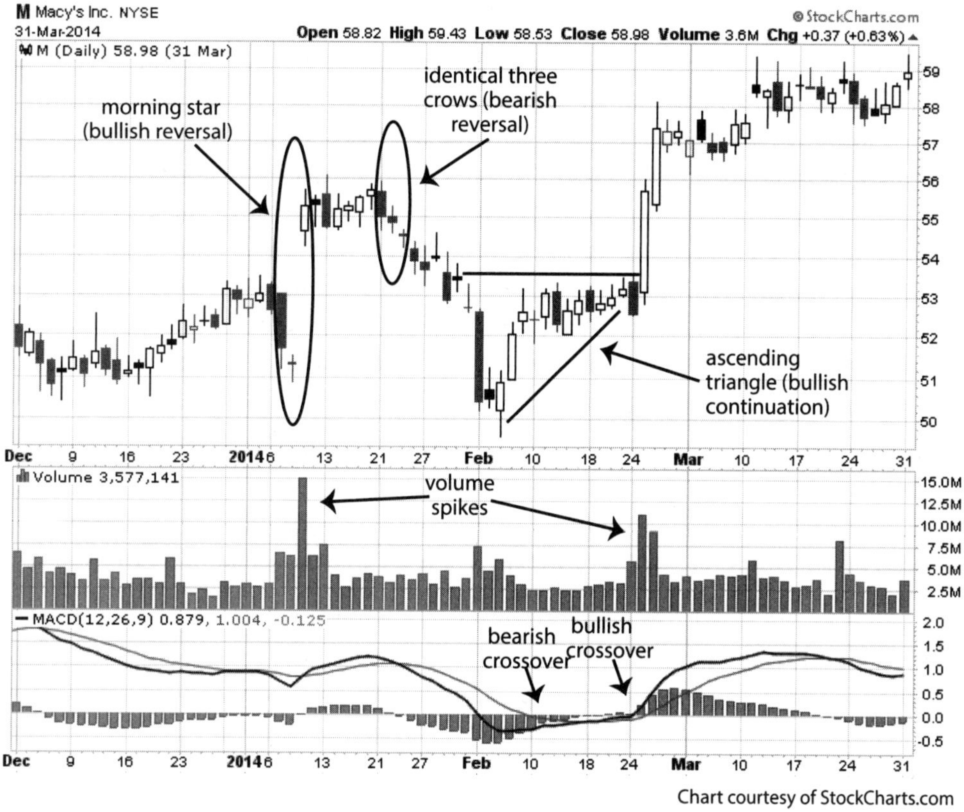

Figure 12.9 Failed signals—price reversals and volume, four months

The morning star showing up in the first half of January is exceptionally strong, based on the large price gap between the second and third session. In fact, this formation is one of the strongest versions of this reversal signal you are likely to find. It is confirmed even further by the volume spike occurring at the same time.

The only problem concerns the trend. There was no downtrend to reverse. So this signal does not fail because no uptrend develops after it appears. It fails because there was no downtrend to reverse. Some analysts will assign this the attributes of a continuation signal, on the argument that when a bullish reversal appears without the proximity required, it must be a continuation signal. But without a downtrend, there is nothing to continue. The very slight uptrend preceding this signal did continue for the short term. But a bullish reversal cannot also act as a bullish continuation signal. So this morning star, as strong as it appears, is not a signal at all.

Immediately after this, a bearish reversal is found in the form of identical three crows. This reverses a rather weak and short-duration uptrend and the resulting downtrend extended for only two weeks. The next signal was an ascending triangle, a bullish continuation indicator. Once again, proximity does not work because there was no uptrend to be continued. This was also contradicted by a bearish crossover in MACD. So the combination of a bullish continuation with nothing to continue, and a bearish crossover with no bearish price response, makes these signals worth little in terms of new or continued trends. The confusion that prevails on this chart emphasizes what has been observed previously: Conflicting signals and signals appearing without proximity tend to serve no purpose and may mislead traders.

Shortly after the bearish crossover, MACD's two averages crossed once again in a bullish direction. At the same time, a volume spike also appeared, signaling possible reversal to the upside. In this case, agreement between the bullish signals did lead to a bullish trend. The chart expanded to reveal what happened next, as shown in Figure 12.10.

A falling wedge appeared. This is a bullish reversal. However, once again there was no bullish trend under way, so lacking proximity this is not a signal at all, but more likely a coincidence of price pattern. A confusing set of MACD crossovers, first bearish and then bullish, was accompanied by another volume spike as price did begin trending upward.

This chart contained numerous signals with lack of proximity. Considering how crucial proximity is, when it is missing, the signals are neutralized as a result. A reversal only works when an existing trend can be reversed, and continuation only works when the signal points to the same direction as the trend that is under way. If these conditions are not found, the signals will fail—not because of any other influences, but because the signals themselves lack proximity to be valid.

From this, you can conclude that many signal failures are not failures at all, but are in fact nonsignals. This is due solely to the lack of proximity. And in these conditions, a reversal signal cannot be explained away as a continuation signal, or vice versa. Proximity rules the strength of signals, and without proximity, the signal—no matter how strong its pattern—cannot be taken as a true signal. A "failed" signal is more often a nonsignal.

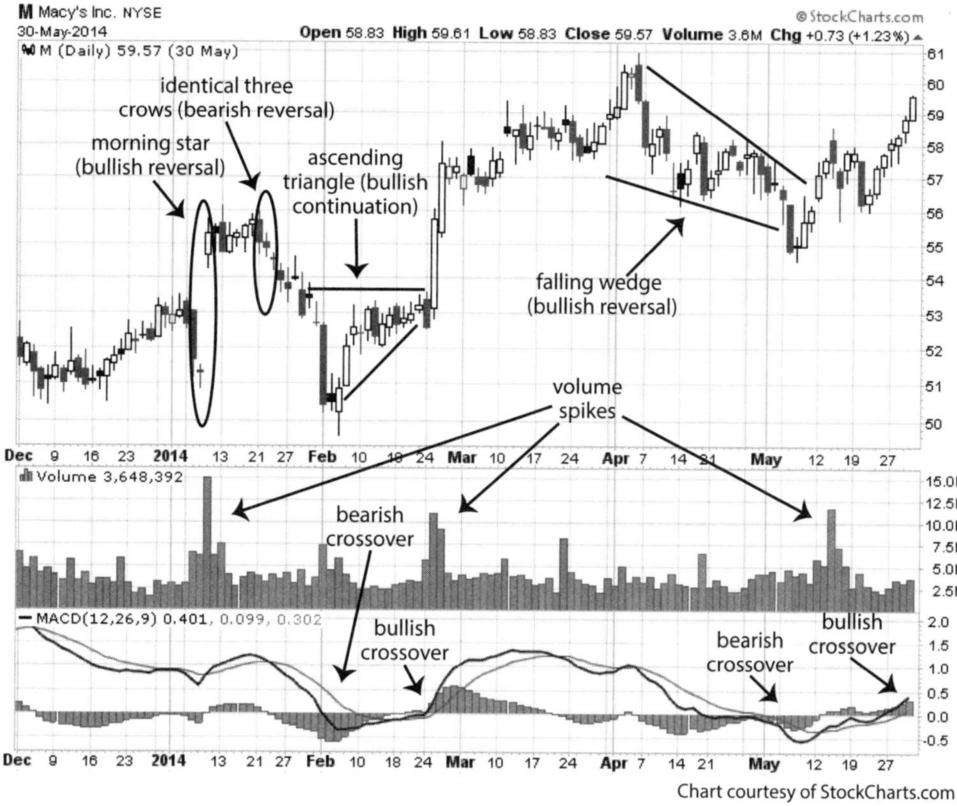

Figure 12.10 Failed signals—price reversals and volume, six months

Failed Signals Between Candlesticks and Momentum

The relationship between candlestick signals and momentum often is a strong one, with momentum providing reliable confirmation for both reversal and continuation signals. However, because momentum signals represent averages of prices over the recent past, strong price movement may create failed or false signals. As a consequence, momentum is not always a reliable form of confirmation; it may be necessary to seek additional sources of price forecasts before acting on what momentum predicts.

For example, in the chart of Lockheed Martin (LMT), a series of overbought forecasts provide false confirmation for what appears a series of bullish predictions. This is shown in Figure 12.11.

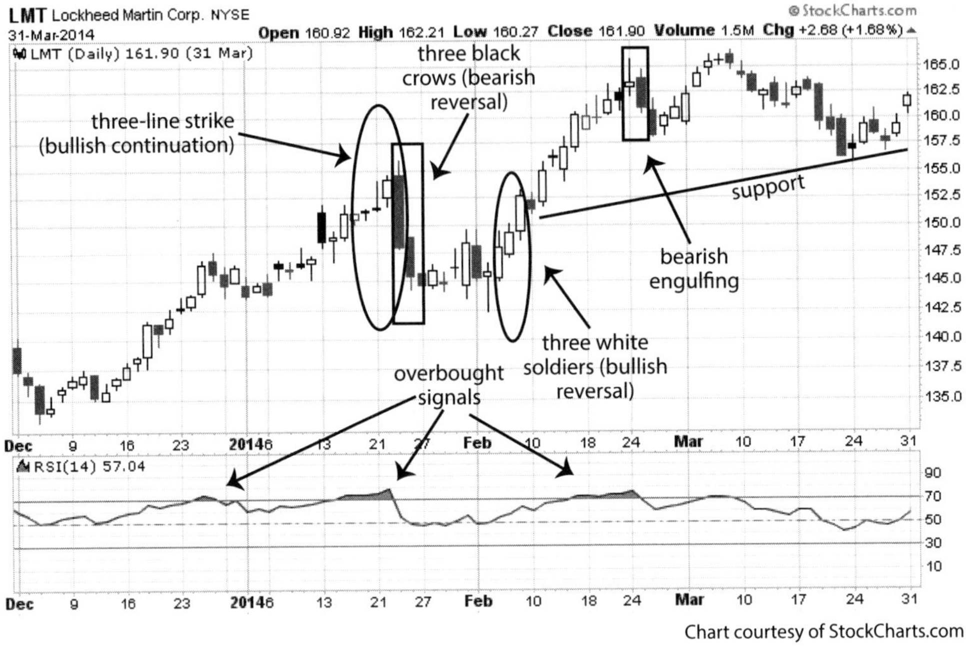

Figure 12.11 Conflicting signals—candlesticks and momentum, four months

The first problem is discovered in the contradictory appearance of the three-line strike (bullish continuation) and three black crows (bearish reversal). The bearish signal is contained within the bullish signal, so traders have to make a judgment call about which of these to believe. The tendency is to seek confirmation or contradiction in other signals, and momentum is the most likely source for this.

The RSI index moved into the overbought area above 70 on three separate occasions. None of these led to downtrends, so this draws into question the reliability of RSI, which normally is quite reliable for forecasting a coming turn in price. The three white soldiers may initially be considered as confirmation of a bullish trend; however, as a bullish reversal, this should appear at the bottom of a downtrend. Because it does not, this signal should be discounted as a confirming indicator. And like other examples of poor proximity, a reversal signal cannot be assumed to indicate continuation.

Toward the end of February, a bearish engulfing signal appears. This is at the top of the uptrend and shows up after RSI had moved into overbought, and then back into midrange. However, even though the signal had excellent proximity to resistance, price declined but remained above support. The RSI and engulfing signal and confirmation did not materialize.

The next phase in this chart is shown in Figure 12.12.

Figure 12.12 Conflicting signals—candlesticks and momentum, six months

The strong and rising support continued moving upward and had no instances of successful breakout. The sole move below support quickly returned into range. The bearish belt hold led to a few sessions of downward movement, but did not succeed in breaking through support. Likewise, a second bearish engulfing signal in mid-May was quite weak in terms of trading ranges and although it led to a few days of downward movement, support held.

This chart revealed many failures in signals. Most surprising among these was RSI, which tends to provide stronger signals than those seen during this period. The repetitive bearish reversal signals in the later part of the chart all failed to move below support, but more important, none were confirmed by other bearish signals. As a result, these reversals failed in spite of good proximity. The contradictory attribute of strong and rising support prevented a bearish move from taking hold during the period shown.

In instances of failed signals and false indicators, many factors are in play. The current news and competitive position of the company affects price movement, but you would expect to see this in the price, volume, and momentum patterns. Poor proximity is a recurring theme for these types of signals. Because proximity is not correct, the signals cannot be acknowledged as legitimate and often are merely coincidental. Lacking confirmation or associated with contradictory price movement, these failed signals are readily identified either as nonsignals or as signals that are just poorly placed.

Although failed signals are troubling to traders wanting to believe in the reliability of signals and confirmation, a few sound guidelines will help prevent problems in timing trades. These include:

1. **Be cautious when signals are contradictory.** Signals that contradict one another are symptomatic of uncertainty and confusion. They create an environment in which confidence is not high, and in which relative correlation of signals is absent or weak. This also applies to signals that can be interpreted in different ways, such as rising wedges (bearish reversal) versus ascending triangles (bullish continuation), or falling wedges (bullish reversal) versus descending triangles (bearish continuation). Even with strong proximity, a particular pattern may easily be interpreted as either of these opposite forecasts. As a consequence, additional confirmation is a requirement in such cases.
2. **Rely on proximity as a first requirement to define signals as legitimate.** The location of signals close to resistance (bearish reversal or bullish continuation) or close to support (bullish reversal or bearish continuation) defines the reliability of signals. This is especially true when the initial signal gaps through resistance or support. A strong trend with strong signals and confirmation increases confidence to nearly 100%, demonstrating that proximity is the key attribute for the relative correlation of all of the relevant signals.
3. **Reversal signals are not interchangeable with continuation signals.** A mistake made by many traders is to assume that reversal signals may act as continuation signals when proximity is not correct, or that continuation signals may serve as reversals for the same reason. This is a mistake. In spite of commonly held beliefs to the contrary, a test of the theory demonstrates that relative correlation of a reversal signal does not translate to continuation in an opposite trend, and that relative correlation of a continuation signal does not translate to a reversal signal. The proximity of signals is inflexible. Reversal is expected to occur at the top of an uptrend or the bottom of a downtrend; when a reversal signal is located elsewhere, it should be ignored as a false signal or a pattern coincidence.

4. **Weak trends tend to lead to weak signals, and weak signals are not reliable.** A clear and consistent relationship is observed in the inertia of trends, signals, and resulting price action. Weakness leads to weakness in a majority of cases. A weak trend is slow and gradual, or too short-term to provide high confidence in the direction. A weak signal barely meets the pattern criteria, or is located away from perfect proximity. Weak price action is nonresponsive to indicated reversal or continuation forecasts or does not react as expected. This cause-and-effect weakness is observed consistently in price patterns. This situation tends to lower confidence to nearly 50%.
5. **Strong trends tend to lead to strong signals, and strong signals tend to be highly reliable in predicting reversal or confirmation.** Inertia works in favor of strength, just as it works against weakness. A strong trend tends to lead to strong signals, both reversal and continuation. Strong signals tend to lead to strong price reaction. The relative correlation of trends, signals, and accurate forecasts raises confidence to nearly 100%.

The observations about strength or weakness in trends, signals, and results are generalizations. However, as this chapter demonstrated in its example, weak signals and poor proximity are likely to lead to unresponsive or contradictory price movement. So even generalizations provide degrees of confidence; when the signs are all strong, confidence is high due to the complementary relative correlation between trends, signals, and results. However, when the signs are marginal and weak, the relative correlation is weak as well, and the tendency is for unreliable and failed signals.

The next chapter moves a step further in the analysis of relative correlation, applying the principles of candlesticks and confirmation from other signals to swing trading. Swing trades are managed through the identification of strong trends and reversal signals; however, as with all types of trades, the key is timing. So swing traders seek strong relative correlation to raise confidence, so that their experience of successful trades will be improved over the random 50/50 outcomes of poorly timed trades. In this respect, relative correlation is demonstrated as an exceptional method for improving outcomes based on chart analysis.

13

Beyond the Signal—Candlestick Pattern Moves

Emphasis is invariably placed on candlestick signals, those one-, two-, and three-session indicators that traders rely on for reversal and continuation. Although these serve as the major force for recognition of trend direction, and for forecasting the next move, there is more.

Beyond the candlestick signal is the *pattern,* a set of signals or shape of high and low points in a trend that further provide forecasts of the next move. These rely on confirmation from other signals, but they often are overlooked due to the focus on individual signals. This chapter examines several of these important larger price patterns and shows how, when confirmed, they provide reliable forecasts of coming changes in price trends.

These patterns may extend over a few sessions or several weeks. Due to this variation in the duration of patterns, they are not always easy to spot. They might not be as reliable as more focused and short-term signals, but as this chapter demonstrates, these patterns can add strength to the timing of trade decisions. Just like the individual signals, longer-term patterns rely on both confirmation and proximity. They also support the previously offered hypothesis that strong trends tend to lead to strong signals, and that strong signals tend to lead to strong responses.

A *strong* trend consists of sharp angles, fast movement, and clear tops or bottoms. A *weak* trend is likely to be more gradual, with fewer points, or of very short duration; in other words, these trends may be arguably weak or not truly represent a trend at all. The strength or weakness of signals, especially candlestick signals, refers to the length of real bodies and shadows, especially in comparison between multiple sessions within one signal. The strength or weakness in response after the signal and confirmation refers to the speed of a reversal, strength of the new trend, resistance or support flips, and proximity. It also refers to what happens when price breaks above resistance or below support. In a strong reversal signal occurring at these points, confidence of reversal approaches

100%. When a continuation signal occurs and is strongly confirmed, confidence of price remaining above resistance or below support is also heightened and approaches 100%.

Another aspect of strength and weakness that affects reliability on signals is the problem of opposite signals having similar shapes, or contradictory signals occurring together. In this situation, the candlestick pattern may help to clarify which contradictory signal to accept as a more likely indication of the next move. These problematical situations include wedges with very slight angles and their similarity to ascending or descending triangles. The wedges are reversal patterns, and the triangles are continuation patterns with opposite meaning (rising wedge is a bearish reversal, whereas an ascending triangle is a bullish continuation, for example). These similarities create declining confidence because a slight move in a line or a slight change in actual price changes the entire meaning of the signal.

A problem further exists when indicators are contained within one another. For example, the mat hold is a bullish continuation signal, but within it is contained three black crows, a bearish reversal. And the bullish three-line strike is another continuation signal that concludes with a bearish engulfing pattern.

These contradictory signals present significant problems in interpretation because either of the contradictory signals could be adopted and acted upon. Traders have to rely on confirmation and strength or weakness of preceding signals; however, they may further determine the true meaning of signals by seeking larger candlestick patterns of the type described in this chapter.

Mood of the Market for Directional Change

The mood of the overall market (or, market *sentiment*) may affect individual stocks as well as index trends and overall price direction. This is not a reliable indicator at all times because individual stocks tend to set their own price trends and to reverse or continue on a basis not dependent on marketwide mood. However, this marketwide tendency is of value in deciding how much confidence to assign to specific signals, given proximity and confirmation.

This is a debatable aspect of technical analysis. Does the overall market affect individual stock trends and their strength or weakness? Or should marketwide trends be largely ignored in favor of trend and price patterns, proximity, and confirmation?

Short-term trends are widely acknowledged as emotional, chaotic, and unreliable. With this in mind, how much can a trader rely on changes in the moment? The many aspects of trade timing include emphasis on the crucial elements of strong trends, strong reversal or continuation signals, confirmation, and proximity to support or resistance. However, the market sentiment may further affect how reliable all of these attributes are in determining when to make a trade. A sentiment indicator will judge the overall market, but this may have little or nothing to do with the trends and direction of individual stocks. Sentiment indicators are among many tools traders may use, but unless trading is executed in index benchmarks, their applicability is limited.

On a marketwide basis, a contrarian view reveals a truth about the crowd mentality of the market itself. In the extreme regions of trends, the majority of traders tends to be wrong about its predictions of the market. Thus, more traders buy at the top of trends and sell at the bottom. The contrarian investor does not do the opposite just because of the belief that the larger market times decisions poorly. Rather, the contrarian makes trade decisions based on analysis and cold reason, rather than on emotion.

The best-known sentiment indicators are the well-known indexes such as the Dow Jones Industrial Average (DJIA), S&P 500, and NASDAQ. These all represent calculations of broader market trends based on sentiment, but a broad indicator does not reveal any specific trends in an individual stock. A measurement of the relationship between an individual stock and the market as a whole, or *beta,* is designed to assign the likelihood of how a stock's price moves with or against the market. So a beta of 1 reveals that a stock is likely to track marketwide movements closely. A beta below 1 implies a less responsive situation, and a beta above 1 implies a likely response stronger than marketwide movement.

A problem with beta is that it is calculated over long-term price trends. For the more immediate reversal or continuation that technical traders want to track, beta could be of little direct value. It is the clearest sentiment indicator available, but it does not reveal how a specific stock is going to track the larger market in the moment. A related problem is that stocks are not always trending, even when marketwide trends are strong. Stocks may be settled into a comfortable middle range for the moment, in which both buyers and sellers are content with the breadth of trading and price range. This sideways-moving tendency is a problem for chart analysis because there is no trend to reverse or to continue. This period of consolidation continues until a new direction becomes established. However, candlestick and other indicators are based invariably on an established trend and signals of reversal or continuation. Traders focus on proximity and breakouts to decide what is taking place and what is likely to take place next. So during consolidation, there is little anyone can do to anticipate the new direction price will set when it finally begins to move again.

In times of consolidation, some traders turn to sentiment indicators to try to determine the direction price will move in the near future. However, just as sentiment indicators do not affect short-term trends, they also are not reliable at predicting price direction to follow consolidation. This is a period in which reversal and continuation indicators cannot be applied because the horizontal trend is not a true trend at all, but merely a period of rest between trends.

Sentiment indicators are based on marketwide movement. These include opinions of advisors regarding bullish or bearish conditions, breadth indicators, the put/call ratio among options trading, volatility indexes (such as the VIX), and volume indicators for the entire market.

A problem with all of these sentiment indicators is that they do not reveal trends within individual stocks. They may provide contrarian signals or confirming signals of marketwide price trends, but a majority of traders relying on candlesticks and other price signals will not gain reliable intelligence from marketwide sentiment indicators.

As consolidation continues over time, specific price patterns may begin to emerge. When this occurs, traders using candlesticks will look for new trends with reversal or continuation signals. At these times, when newly established trends begin to emerge, it also aids in prediction to be aware of longer-term patterns. Even within a period of consolidation, some larger patterns may provide a strong forecast of price direction to come. Among these are the trends of 3s.

Candlestick—Trends of 3s

The first well-known trader in candlesticks was a rice merchant in Japan named Munehisa Homna (1724–1803). His name is variously also spelled Homma or Honma, and he was also known by the abbreviated named Sakata, after the city of his birth, Sakata, Japan.

He was so successful in developing and using candlesticks that he was given the title "god of the markets." He devised a series of patterns called Sakata's Five Methods, based on observation of 3s—three mountains, rivers, gaps, soldiers, and methods. These describe sets of candlesticks establishing directional patterns that either reverse or continue the established trend. These differ from candlestick signals because they are not limited to consecutive sessions in each case.

The first of these Five Methods is called three mountain top. It is similar to what Western technicians call the triple top and, when the middle "mountain" is higher than the first and third, it also closely resembles the head and shoulders pattern. However, as a pattern over a period of time, three mountain top can take a number of shapes and is more flexible than the relative rigid requirements of head and shoulders. As a test of resistance that does not succeed in breaking through, the three mountain top is a bearish reversal pattern.

The three mountain top is observed in the chart of Yahoo! (YHOO) in Figure 13.1. This begins with a support-to-resistance flip. Price immediately breaks through resistance on two occasions, but fails both times.

Figure 13.1 Three mountain top, four months

The pattern between the second week in February and mid-March peaks three times, forming a three mountain top. This is clearly a bearish pattern, which, as you would expect, leads to a strong price decline. This pattern is confirmed by the bearish engulfing reversal occurring at the peak of the third mountain.

The next phase in this trend is observed in the extended chart shown in Figure 13.2.

The extension of this chart reveals that the three mountain top pattern repeated in the subsequent price movements. The initial bearish forecast and confirmation led to a price decline; a second series of three mountain top, support/resistance flip, and bearish engulfing confirmation occurred to mirror the initial set of forecasts at a lower price range.

The three mountain top is a bearish pattern and its opposite, the three river bottom, is a bullish pattern. It is similar to the Western triple bottom or, given the shape of the middle decline, an inverse head and shoulders. However, the candlestick patterns such as these do not have to conform to rigid price shapes to provide strong signals.

Figure 13.2 Three mountain top, six months

An example of the three river bottom is found on the chart of Verizon (VZ), which is shown in Figure 13.3.

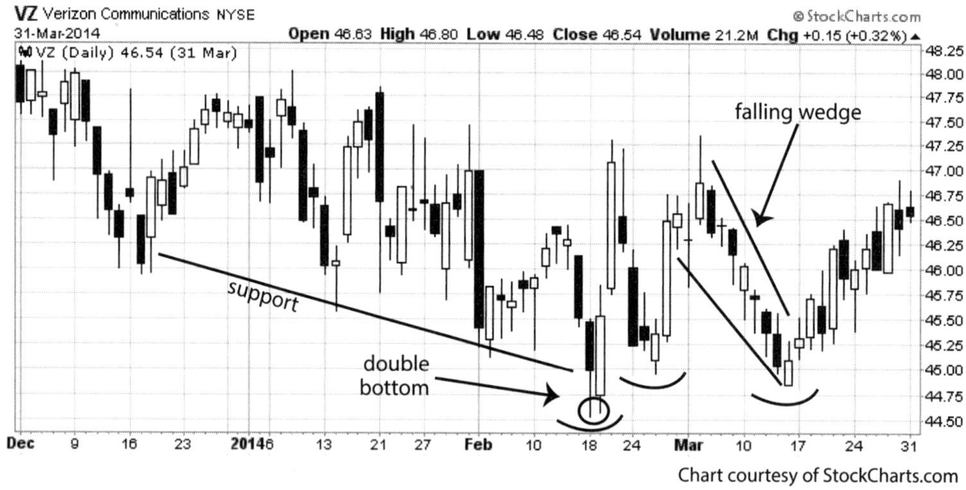

Figure 13.3 Three river bottom, four months

A declining line of support concludes with a double bottom. This also forms the first of the three river pattern, which confirms a bullish reversal. After a rise in price, a falling wedge ends with the third entry of the three river bottom. This pattern is similar to the

Western triple bottom; however, in the triple bottom, it is more common to see single spike sessions, and the three river bottom tends to consist of a rounded set of several sessions.

After conclusion of the falling wedge (a bullish reversal) and the conclusion of the three river bottom, a strong bullish trend begins. The next phase is shown in Figure 13.4.

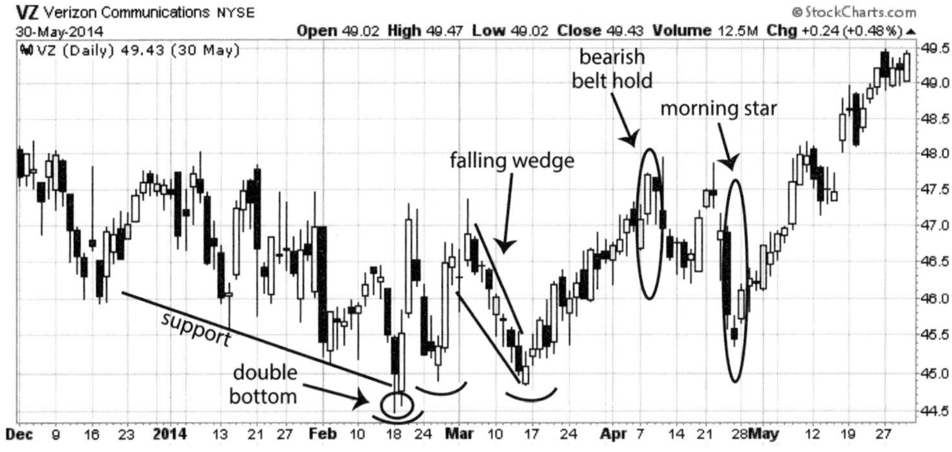

Figure 13.4 Three river bottom, six months

Prices rose for three weeks, topping out with a bearish belt hold, a reversal signal. The downtrend was brief, lasting under three weeks. The morning star signaled the end of this trend and reversal into a new bullish move. The price changes during March and April could be viewed as a series of short-term trends (up, then down, then up), or as retracement periods in a longer-duration uptrend. That uptrend began at the end of the three river bottom and continued through to the end of the period shown.

This chart provides an example of how price trends are interpreted. In the short term, traders look for signals. Proximity and speed of reversals has to be acknowledged, but in these instances the duration of the trends also points out that the big picture often has more significance. Although it is not visible as prices evolve, a look back over the chart allows the interpretation of a single and strong bullish trend with a set of interim retracements.

The next set of 3s is the three gaps pattern. Although gaps are found frequently, a set of three gaps moving in the same direction is not as common. It indicates reversal because price is moving in one direction too strongly (indicated by the repetitive gaps) and is setting up for a change in direction. This is especially true when proximity to resistance (in the bearish three gaps) or support (in the bullish three gaps) adds strength to the reversal. If confirmed by independent signals, confidence in a fast reversal should be quite high.

An example of the bearish three gaps is seen on the chart of BlackBerry (BBRY), shown in Figure 13.5. After a strong uptrend, breadth of trading settled into a narrow range. However, the end of the uptrend was clearly marked by the first three gaps pattern. The sideways movement in a narrow breadth was further marked by a second three gaps. Finally, two sets of identical three crows confirmed a coming bearish move.

Figure 13.5 Three gaps, bearish, four months

This is an interesting pattern. It includes two initial reversal signals in the form of three gaps and two sets of confirming bearish reversal signals in the form of identical three crows. Given the strength of the initial uptrend, this delay in reversal reaction is unusual. However, the next phase, shown in Figure 13.6, clarifies the trend.

The price does decline after a long pause, falling and remaining below previously established support. Price remained below that level for the remainder of the period shown on the chart.

The bullish version of the three gaps pattern should be equally strong in the indicated reversal as a downtrend concludes. An example is seen in the chart of Pfizer (PFE), shown in Figure 13.7.

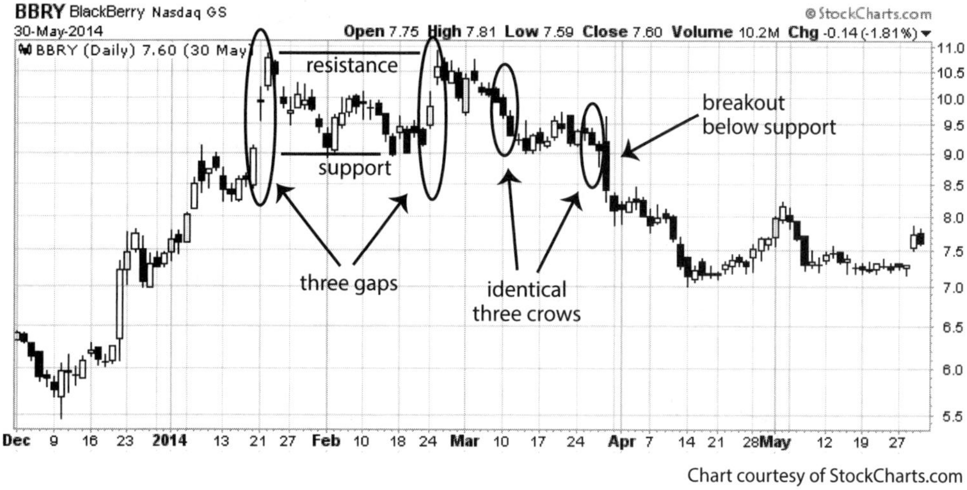

Figure 13.6 Three gaps, bearish, six months

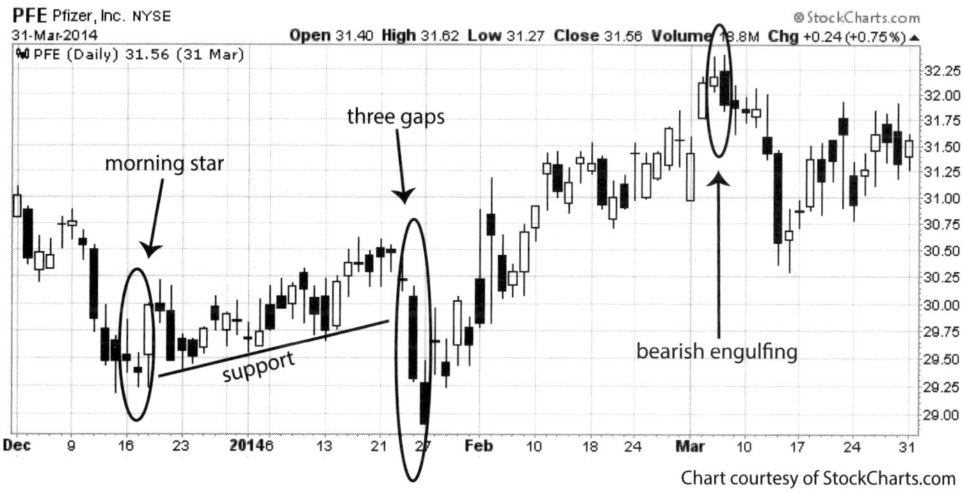

Figure 13.7 Three gaps, bullish, four months

The first signal of bullish reversal was seen in the morning star. However, after this appeared, support and prvice levels rose gradually. The appearance of the three gaps with a downward move confirmed the morning star and, although the response was delayed, this did lead to a strong reversal and uptrend. This ended at the beginning of March when prices topped out and a bearish engulfing pattern appeared, marking a bearish reversal. Proximity for this signal was excellent, at the peak of the bullish trend.

The bearish reversal occurred, and the next step in this trend is seen in the extended chart, shown in Figure 13.8.

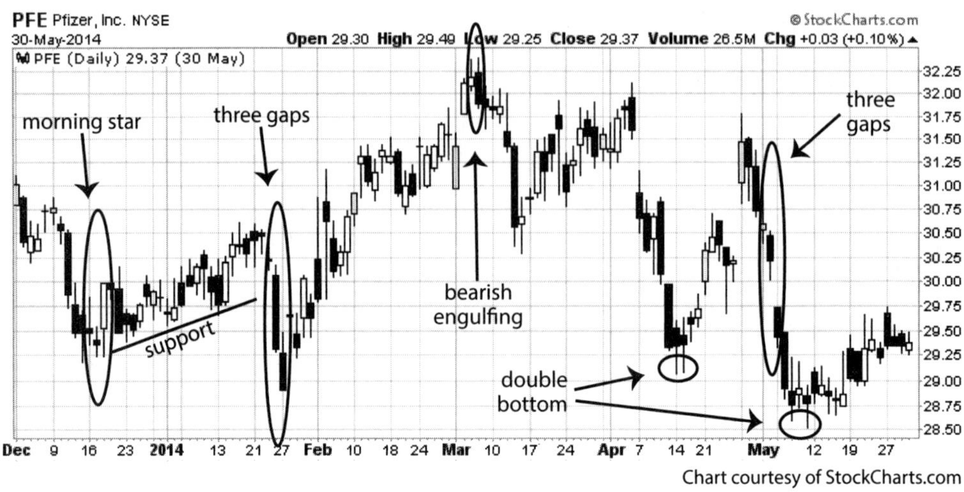

Figure 13.8 Three gaps, bullish, six months

Price dropped rapidly over two weeks but then rose just as strongly. Interpreting this chart could be difficult, but a few clear signals made sense of the volatility. First, at both of the bottoms of the short-term decline, double bottom signals clearly marked a turning point. This was confirmed with the appearance of another three gaps, a bullish reversal signal. Prices did rise beyond this chart and through mid-July, before once again declining.

The final version of the 3s pattern is the three soldiers. Although these are found in both bullish and bearish versions, they are not the same as three white soldiers or three black crows. What matters in these patterns is the direction of movement, which may involve white or black sessions and strong gaps. For example, the chart of Macy's (M) shown in Figure 13.9 includes a rising line of resistance interrupted by a failed breakout.

Price declined to a new low in early February, and was immediately offset by a three soldiers bullish pattern. This moved price through resistance with a second and confirming three soldiers pattern, which as of the period covered, appeared to be holding. The next step is seen in the extended chart, shown in Figure 13.10.

Prices peaked in early March and were then shown to be declining gradually, until a second bullish three soldier pattern forecast another bullish move. Although the period ended with a bullish trend, over the next three months conditions were quite volatile, with price rising to progressively higher levels, offset by progressively lower declines. This indicates that candlestick patterns indicating price trends beyond consecutive-session signals might be likely to appear in volatile conditions. In this situation, reversals are likely to be strong, but the duration of trends will tend to be very short term.

Chart courtesy of StockCharts.com

Figure 13.9 Three soldiers (bullish), four months

Chart courtesy of StockCharts.com

Figure 13.10 Three soldiers (bullish), six months

A bearish three soldiers also suffers from the same tendency toward volatile price movement. An example is found on the chart of MasterCard (MA), shown in Figure 13.11.

Figure 13.11 Three soldiers (bearish), four months

The initial uptrend closes with the bearish engulfing signal. This is confirmed by the first of the bearish three soldiers, which moves price strongly down to new lows. A brief rally is ended with a bearish belt hold. This reversal is confirmed by a bearish engulfing signal and a second bearish three soldiers pattern. However, on this chart the signal and confirmation extended over six weeks, quite a long period for a reversal signal to materialize.

The next phase is revealed in the extended chart, shown in Figure 13.12.

Price declined below the rising support level, and that level flipped to form a new resistance line. The angle of resistance continued to rise until mid-July, but throughout the period the short-term trends and reversals were highly volatile.

A problem with the 3s is that they are not specific signals, but directional patterns. They appear frequently in times of high volatility and short-duration trends. This makes the overall forecasting more difficult, but without these patterns to augment what short-term signals predict, managing price trends would be more difficult.

Figure 13.12 Three soldiers (bearish), six months

Candlestick Top and Bottom Patterns

Another pattern class involves price behavior at the top and bottom of trends. All of these are reversal patterns and should mark the top of uptrends or the bottom of downtrends. When these signals appear as price levels break through resistance or support, the likelihood of reversal is strongly increased and confidence of reversal, if confirmed, is likely to approach 100%.

The first among these patterns is the tower top. This is a bearish signal appearing after an uptrend, characterized by a black candle session following a series of white, and representing a turning point in the trend. Swing traders call the appearance of such a session a *reversal day*; however, to qualify as a true reversal marking the end of the trend, it should appear in the proper proximity and should be confirmed as well. As with other patterns, the tower top does not form as a specific signal, but presents a black session in a configuration following an uptrend and a series of white sessions. An example is found on the chart of US Steel (X), shown in Figure 13.13.

Price moved above resistance at the beginning of this chart. This point in the trend is always troubling to traders, who do not know whether to expect reversal or continuation. The tower top is a strong signal of reversal and retreat back into the trading range. This may be interpreted as confirmation of the breakout not likely to succeed; however, this is not enough to serve as a convincing reversal confirmation. The single session showing up two days after the tower top is a more compelling form of reversal, a small white session with an unusually large upper shadow. This indicates that buy-side momentum is failing, and that a reversal back into range is likely.

Chart courtesy of StockCharts.com

Figure 13.13 Tower top, four months

As expected, price did retreat back into range, but by mid-February was poised to once again attempt a breakout. At that point, the bearish belt hold stopped the upward advance and forecast a further price decline. At the end of March, price once again broke through resistance, but chances for downside reversal were quite high, based on the immediate appearance of the bearish engulfing signal.

The next step in this chart is revealed in the extended period, shown in Figure 13.14.

Immediately after the breakout above resistance and appearance of the bearish engulfing, price levels hesitated momentarily. At that point, another tower top appeared, setting up a strong price decline. This decline formed into channel lines as the price levels fell in a narrow breadth of trading of only two points. This low breadth is a sign that volatility would not be high in coming weeks for this stock. In fact, volatility did remain low even as price direction reversed and a new uptrend began, lasting for seven weeks before gapping three points to the upside. So the predicted low volatility took effect but did not last very long.

The opposite pattern is the tower bottom. This also consists of an established trend with its end marked by a white candlestick session, another form of reversal day. An example of this pattern is seen in the chart of Apple (AAPL), shown in Figure 13.15.

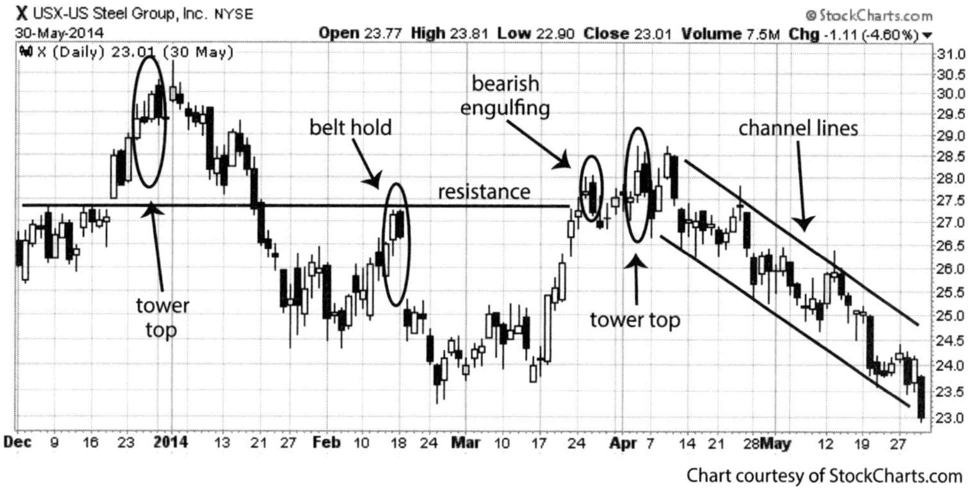

Figure 13.14 Tower top, six months

Figure 13.15 Tower bottom, four months

On this chart, even with numerous bullish signals, there is great reluctance of the price to move in a bullish direction. The bulls did win out, but only after repetitive reversal and continuation signals and the tower pattern. First was the large downside gap that took price well below support. When price gaps like this while breaking out of the trading range, reversal is very likely. The proximity for reversal is at its strongest.

Next, the tower bottom appeared. This set of down candle sessions concluding with one upward moving session (reversal day) clearly marks the bottom of the trend as well as the likely failure of the breakout. Price did advance back into the previously established range, but the uptrend soon turned and moved down for one week. Once again, a tower bottom marked a reversal point and the bottom of the short-lived trend. At this point, traders would expect to see a strong bullish trend become established. However, the trend moved very gradually, even with two strong continuation signals, the three-line strike signals.

The bullish trend did not take off strongly until late April, as shown in the extended chart in Figure 13.16.

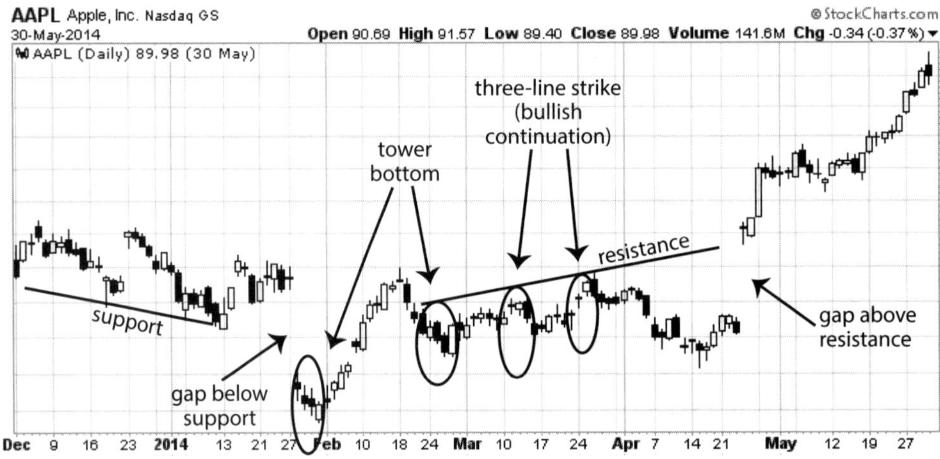

Chart courtesy of StockCharts.com

Figure 13.16 Tower bottom, six months

After the gradual rise in price levels, a strong upside gap appeared, taking price above resistance and looking much like the initial downside gap below support. Figure 13.17, the chart of Halliburton (HAL), reveals that during the month of May, the bullish trend finally took off strongly. In fact, by late August the price had climbed as high as $100 per share, ten points above the last price on the chart shown.

This chart demonstrates how the tower bottom (like the tower top) clearly identifies the end of the trend. This is a proximity pattern because with the reversal day moving contrary to the prior trend, the expected turn in the opposite direction is very likely. The tower patterns, when well confirmed as in this example, move confidence of reversal approaching 100%.

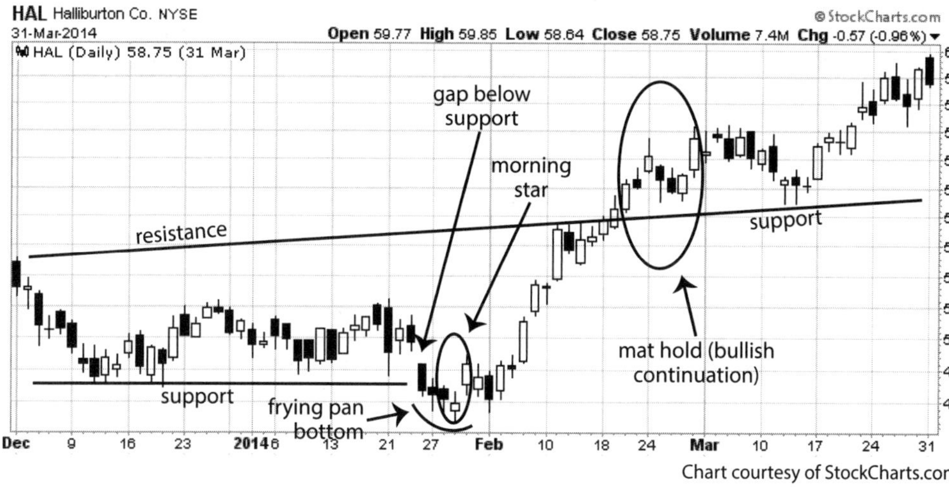

Figure 13.17 Frying pan bottom, four months

Another pattern identifying turning points in trends is the frying pan bottom. This is a pattern with a curving appearance that, like the tower bottom, includes a clear reversal day. The specific length and shape of each session varies, but the rounded bottom is a clear reversal day and—if confirmed—forecasts an uptrend with excellent proximity.

The downtrend in this chart was very slight and gradual, but support was clearly identified at approximately $49.75 per share. Price moved below this level with a gap and immediately formed a frying pan bottom. The last three sessions in this pattern also developed as a morning star, a bullish reversal. The number of signals, confirmation, and proximity all increased confidence to nearly 100% that a reversal was very likely.

As expected, price rose sharply and then moved above resistance. The bullish continuation signal (mat hold) occurred as price moved through resistance, forecasting a successful breakout. The next phase in this chart is shown in Figure 13.18.

The three-line strike further forecast a bullish continuation, and prices remained above the original rising resistance line through to the end of the chart. In this example, the strength of the frying pan bottom was revealed. The reversal day at the end of the pattern, as well as the bullish reversal taking place at the same time, gave the forecast of a bullish reversal a great deal of strength. Proximity of these signals, following a gap in price below support, made this a strong forecast that came to pass and lasted for the following four months.

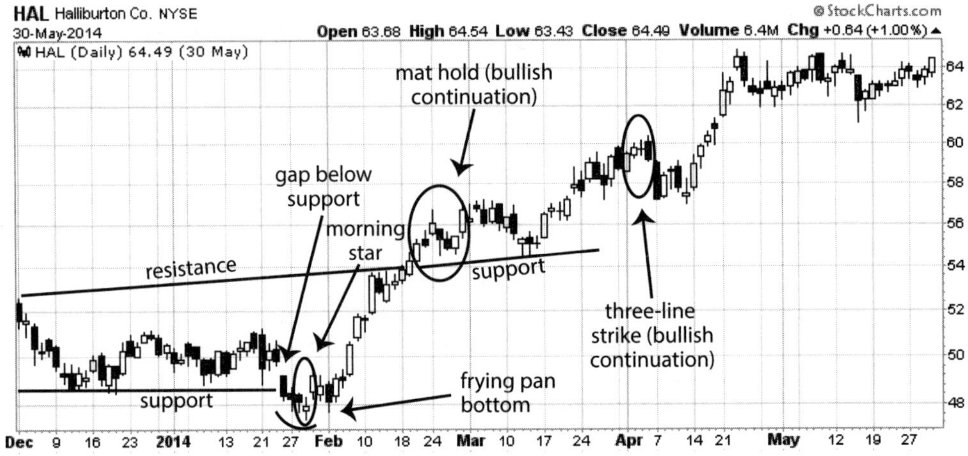

Chart courtesy of StockCharts.com

Figure 13.18 Frying pan bottom, six months

The opposite of the frying pan bottom is the bearish signal called the dumpling top. This is a rounded pattern found at the top of an uptrend that concludes with a reversal day. For example, the chart of Herbalite (HLF) in Figure 13.19 contains a clear dumpling top at the top of the uptrend in the first week of January.

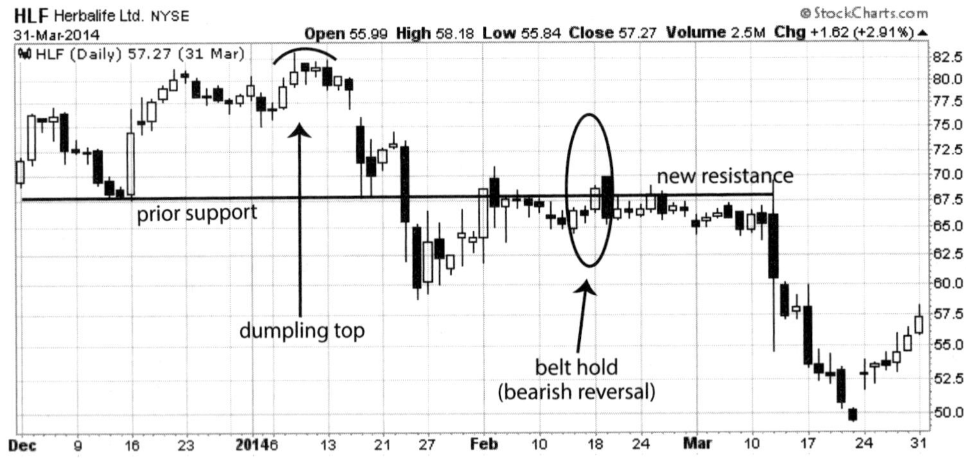

Chart courtesy of StockCharts.com

Figure 13.19 Dumpling top, four months

Over the next two months, price evolves so that prior support flips to new resistance. This adds strength to the forecast of a lower trading range, and the occurrence of the bullish belt hold after a three-week uptrend moves price through that newly established resistance level. This is excellent proximity for a bearish turn in price, which took place after three weeks of sideways movement in a very narrow breadth.

The next phase in this chart is shown in Figure 13.20, where prices remained below the newly established resistance through mid-April. At that point, an upward-trending channel appeared, setting a five-point range as price moved higher.

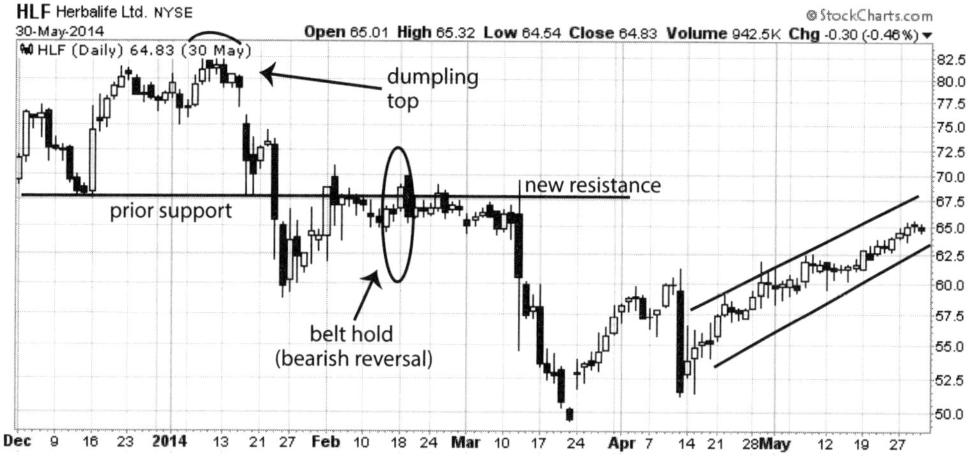

Chart courtesy of StockCharts.com

Figure 13.20 Dumpling top, six months

However, the important note concerning this chart is that the original dumpling top appeared in perfect proximity to the top of the uptrend and led to the forecast price reversal. Some confusion between the third week in January and mid-February was clarified by the confirming belt hold. This was followed by a clear move below newly established resistance.

Another pattern clearly marking top and bottom points in trends is called the gapping price pattern. The gapping price rising is a bearish signal showing up at the top of an uptrend and marking the likely point of reversal. It includes a breakout above resistance followed by an upward price gap. The gap indicates that the breakout is likely to fail. The chart of Tesla Motors (TSLA) in Figure 13.21 includes a strong gapping price rising pattern.

Figure 13.21 Gapping price rising, four months

This is confirmed by the overlapping belt hold, a bearish reversal, and a price decline with falling resistance soon after. This continues into the following period, as shown in Figure 13.22.

Figure 13.22 Gapping price rising, six months

The gapping price rising, when confirmed in this manner, has excellent proximity and increases confidence approaching 100%. The dumpling top, like the frying pan bottom, is not as obvious in appearance as many of the candlestick signals strongly forecasting reversal; however, both of these tend to appear at the right proximity for reversal. Proximity and confirmation are the two attributes that, when appearing together, clarify the trend.

The gapping price falling is the opposite, a bullish signal appearing at the end of a downtrend. An example is found in the chart of Lowes (LOW), shown in Figure 13.23.

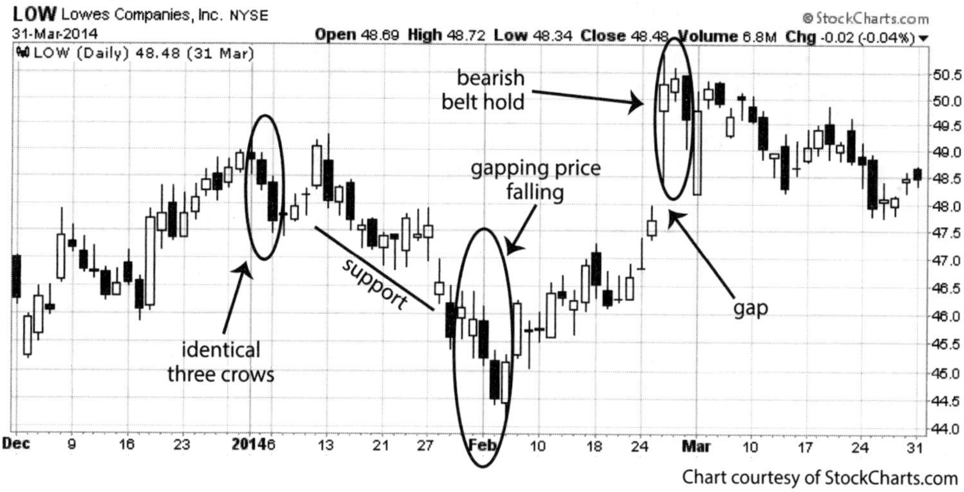

Figure 13.23 Gapping price falling, four months

The month of December saw an uptrend, whose end was marked by the bearish reversal, identical three crows. Support declined through most of December until price broke through below. At that point, a gapping price falling pattern developed. This is marked by a sharp price decline, a price gap, and a reversal day. This included several small gaps, identified by the changes between one session's close and the next session's open. Within the gapping price falling pattern, gaps appeared between each session, and although these were small, the number of gaps adds strength to the reversal forecast.

The resulting bullish price ended with clearly identified signals. These included a price gap and, at the very top of the trend, a bearish reversal in the form of a bearish belt hold. This forecast a turn to the downside, which did occur right away. The bearish trend continued until mid-May, as shown in Figure 13.24.

At the mid-May point, the bearish trend ended decisively. First, a new gapping price falling pattern appeared, this one with even more pronounced gaps than the first one. This pattern included a breakout below support with lower shadows forming a double bottom, providing bullish confirmation of the reversal. Overlapping this was another bullish reversal, the morning star. As with the first case of a gapping price falling, this reversal signal had excellent proximity to support, and the multiple confirmations of likely bullish reversal took confidence close to 100%.

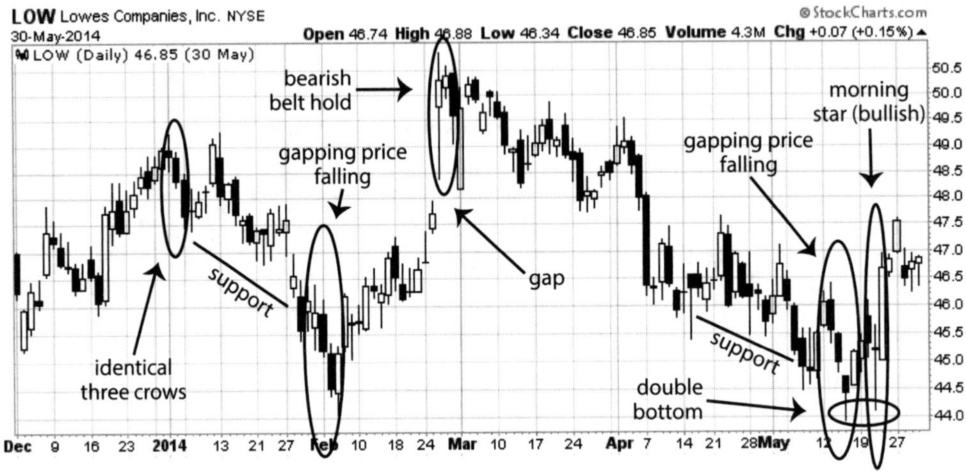

Figure 13.24 Gapping price falling, six months

A final top and bottom pattern is actually a one-session reversal signal. This is an oddity because the color of the real body does not matter—and also because although the appearance is the same whether it appears at the top or bottom, it predicts reversal from the current trend.

The pattern includes a real body of either color, little or no upper shadow, and a lower shadow that is longer than the breadth of the real body. When it appears at the top of an uptrend, it is called a hanging man. These are also called umbrella sessions. An example of this is seen on the chart of Las Vegas Sands (LVS), shown in Figure 13.25. These formations are not easily found, but in this chart three distinct hanging man sessions appeared in consecutive days. The multiple occurrences make the indicated bearish reversal exceptionally strong.

The resulting downtrend concludes with a gapping price falling pattern, a bullish reversal in good proximity to mark the end of the downtrend. The final long white session following the gap clearly marks this turning point. The uptrend that follows ends with equally clear proximity and turning point. The bearish engulfing forecasts a bearish reversal, which follows immediately.

Figure 13.25 Hanging man, four months

After this, the downtrend moves for less than three weeks and again turns to the upside, ending once three black crows marks yet another bearish reversal. This is shown in Figure 13.26.

Figure 13.26 Hanging man, six months

The chart continues to act in a volatile manner. After the three black crows, price declines for only one week before turning once more to the upside. Almost immediately, another bearish reversal is forecast by the belt hold. Although this chart is volatile and difficult to predict for any long-term trends, the turning points are clearly marked with reversal indicators. The initial three occurrences of the hanging man is the starting point for a volatile price movement to follow.

When the same umbrella pattern is found at the bottom of an uptrend, it is called a hammer. As with the hanging man, the color of the real body does not matter; it should be small and the lower shadow at least as long as the real body. Little or no upper shadow will appear. For example, the chart of Netflix (NFLX) shown in Figure 13.27 began by marking the end of a downtrend with two hammers.

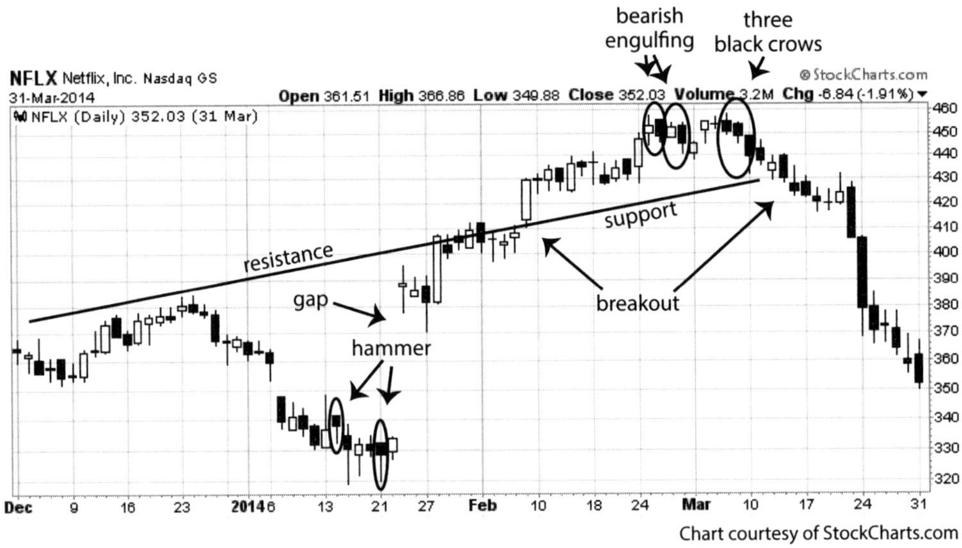

Figure 13.27 Hammer, four months

The first hammer is a weak signal, due to its appearance after a brief reversal. However, even though this signal was not clear, three sessions later another hammer appeared with much better proximity at the bottom of the longer-term downtrend. Additional confirmation was provided by the strong upside gap that followed right after the second hammer. Price next moved through resistance and, lacking any clear signals, the meaning at that point was not clear. However, price did continue moving upward, creating a flip from resistance to support.

The uptrend continued until two bearish engulfing patterns appeared at the very top of the trend, followed by a confirming three black crows. Confidence at this point was high that price was going to reverse and move downward. It is especially noteworthy that two breakouts framed this peak in the uptrend. First was the breakout above resistance leading to the flip; second was the breakout below newly established support, leading to a strong downtrend.

The next move involved considerable volatility. The downtrend lasted three weeks and concluded with a double bottom. However, in between price trended up 70 points and immediately retreated. This highly volatile swing made the trend unclear at the moment it appeared; in fact, while price was moving strongly upward, a bullish interpretation was possible. These expanded signals are shown in Figure 13.28.

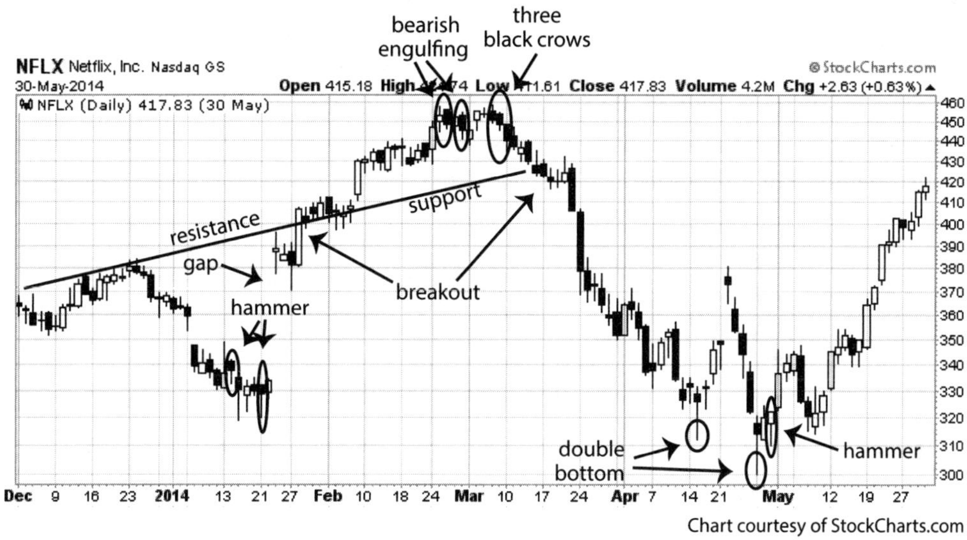

Chart courtesy of StockCharts.com

Figure 13.28 Hammer, six months

However, the repetitive gaps on the way up (and again on the way down) identified this as an aberration in the longer-term trend. The end of the prevailing downtrend was confirmed by the appearance of another hammer immediately after the second of the two double bottom shadows. The forecast uptrend reversal took place and moved price up 100 points in one month.

These top and bottom patterns add value to chart interpretation. They are distinct and separate from the more easily identified signals, which have specific formations in consecutive sessions. Patterns, in comparison, are more flexible, but add equally strong reversal forecasting and confirmation. As long as proximity is appropriate, these are shown to be highly reliable as part of a reversal analysis.

Candlestick Lines and Waves

Another type of price pattern consists of lines or waves marking reversal with more sessions involved than the more restricted candlestick reversal (normally involving two or three consecutive sessions). The first of these is the "eight lines" pattern. Because this pattern extends over many more sessions than a candlestick signal, its actual shape tends to be more varied, and includes at least eight sessions moving in the same direction. The ideal eight lines will occur without break, but some do include one or two sessions moving in the opposite direction.

The first of these is the eight higher price lines. This pattern consists of prices moving higher over eight or more sessions, often with repetitive gaps. The speed and duration of this pattern implies movement in an exaggerated manner, and sets up a bearish reversal. For example, the chart of 3D Systems (DDD) found in Figure 13.29 includes an 11-session example of the eight higher prices lines pattern. Sessions 5 and 10 move lower, leaving a net total of nine sessions trending higher.

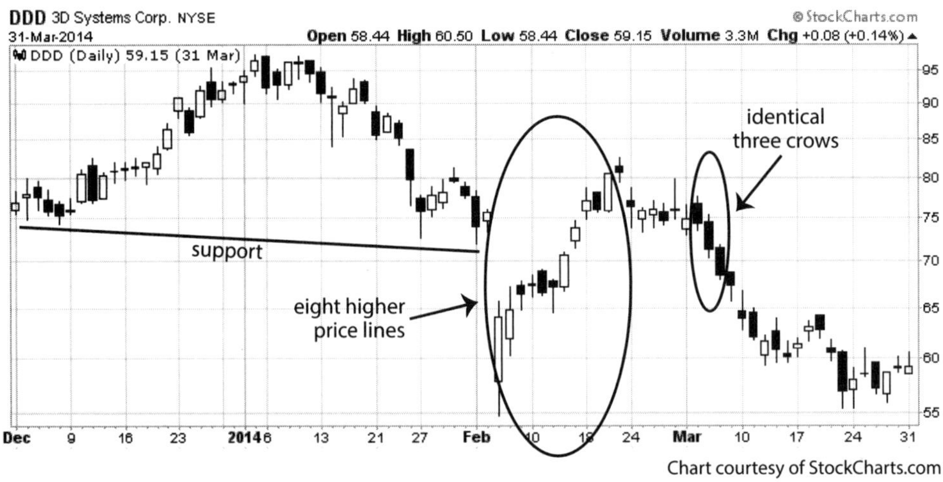

Figure 13.29 Eight higher price lines, four months

As this pattern appeared, price gapped below support before moving strongly back into range as part of the eight higher price lines pattern. This is a bearish pattern, characterized by rapid upward movement leading to a high likelihood of reversal. Price peaked immediately after the eight higher price lines pattern and then a bearish reversal appeared to confirm the next move. The identical three crows marked the beginning of the new downtrend. Proximity was excellent as this appeared immediately after the peak of the uptrend.

The next move was a decisive downtrend marked by falling resistance, until prices leveled out in May, as shown in Figure 13.30. This entire pattern was defined by the attributes of the eight higher price lines, a move that could be called an overly rapid upside move leading prices into an overbought condition.

Figure 13.30 Eight higher price lines, six months

The opposite pattern is called eight lower price lines. This creates a bullish condition due to the rapid decline in price, often taking price below support. This sets up excellent proximity for a bullish reversal, assuming confirmation also is found. For example, the chart of Kroger (KR), shown in Figure 13.31, includes an example of the eight lower price lines pattern.

Support declined for the first six weeks, until the eight lower price lines pattern moved price rapidly below support. This includes eight sessions, of which seven opened lower; however, the pattern's proximity set up a convincing turnaround signal. This was quickly confirmed with the bullish reversal signal, morning star. After this, prices continued moving upward, as shown on the extended chart in Figure 13.32.

Once the price level peaked, the breadth settled into a three-point range, quite narrow. In this example, all of the action occurred around the period of decline below support and the eight lower price lines pattern. The fall below support as this pattern developed, confirmed by the bullish candlestick reversal, provided good proximity and high confidence for the reversal that followed.

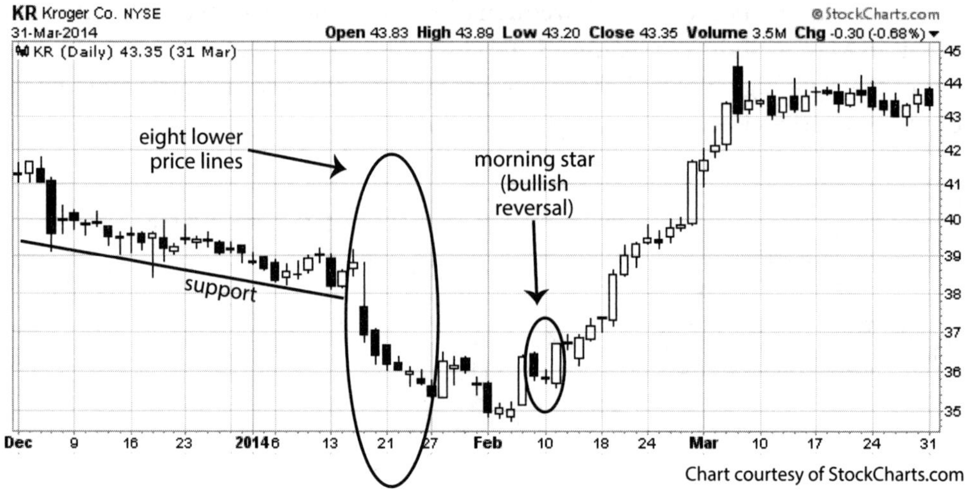

Figure 13.31 Eight lower price lines, four months

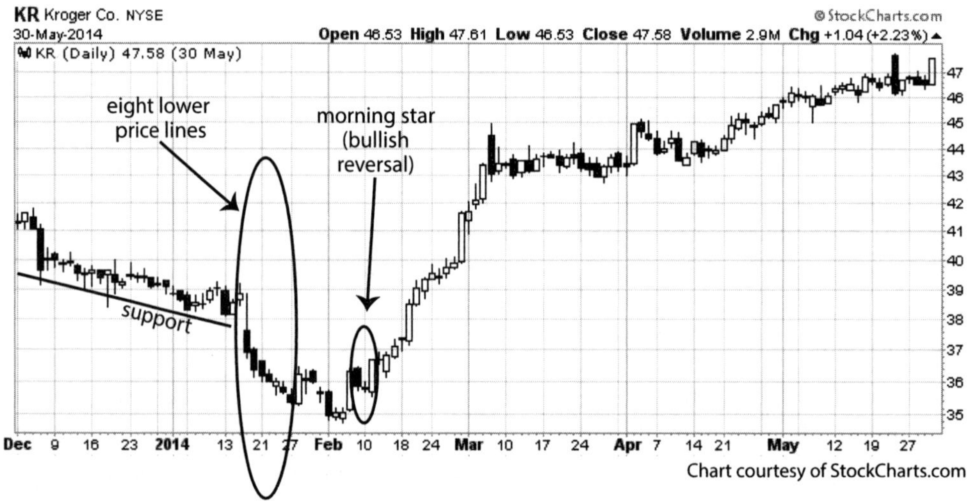

Figure 13.32 Eight lower price lines, six months

A final version of the lines and weave classification of patterns is the tweezer pattern. This is a two-session pattern with upper or lower shadows at the same level or very similar level, marking a clear reversal. This is similar to the double top or double bottom, but the tweezer tends to be restricted to consecutive sessions and with identical shadows.

For example, the chart of Buffalo Wild Wings (BWLD) displays a tweezer top in a highly volatile period, shown in Figure 13.33.

Figure 13.33 Tweezer top, four months

Support was clearly marked, and price moved below that level with a bearish signal, the belt hold. This was a weak signal, however, because there was only a slight uptrend to reverse, consisting of only three sessions beginning on January 8 and followed by three down sessions before the belt hold appeared. So proximity for this signal was not optimal. However, price did trend below support and continued until the exceptionally long black candle with its long lower shadow appeared.

Price next began a gradual move to the upside. The first signal of a reversal was the development of a tweezer top, marked at the end of February and first session of March. In a normal bearish reversal, traders hope to see an immediate decline. However, in this pattern of weak signals and uncertainty, price continued rising another 12 points before confirmation was found in the form of the three black crows signal. This series of signals and confirmation was weak, but the bearish reversal did confirm the bearish tweezer top. The next price move is shown in Figure 13.34.

Price declined after the reversal and confirmation, with the bottom of the downtrend marked by the black session with a long lower shadow. This led immediately to a bullish reversal identified by the ascending triangle. This chart was exceptionally volatile with big price swings, and characterized by weak signals and confirmation, poor proximity, and show price reaction to confirmed signals. This example verifies the previously observed tendency for weak trends to lead to weak signals—and for weak signals to lead to delayed response and weak subsequent price movement. The poor proximity of signals and delayed reaction time demonstrate that weak conditions may be found even in highly volatile price patterns.

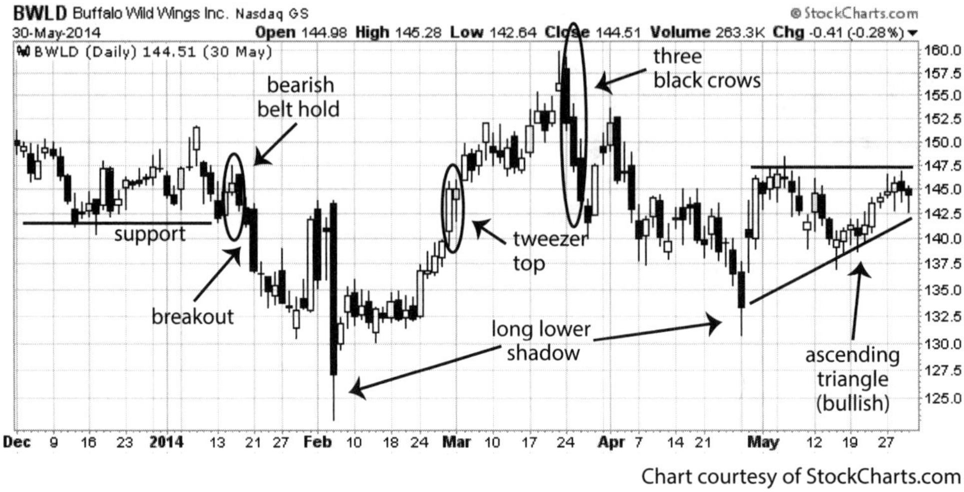

Figure 13.34 Tweezer top, six months

The opposite of the bearish tweezer top is the bullish tweezer bottom. An example of this pattern is found on the chart of Kraft Foods (KRFT), shown in Figure 13.35.

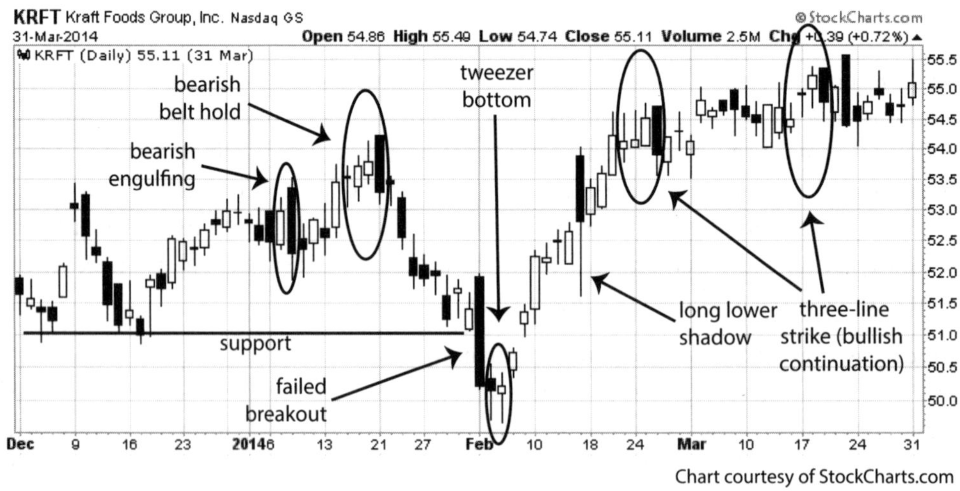

Figure 13.35 Tweezer bottom, four months

Compared with the tweezer top example, this chart displayed clear signals with excellent proximity and strong confirmation, as well as immediate responses in the price trend. The bearish engulfing appeared at a price peak, but reversal did not occur immediately; instead, it continued rising to a second price peak. At that point, the belt hold confirmed the coming reversal to the downside.

Price did decline as expected, and broke through support. This is where the tweezer bottom appeared (a double bottom). The proximity of this as a reversal signal created high confidence that price would rebound to the upside and return into range, which did occur very quickly. A few sessions later, the long lower shadow on the black candle session displayed a lack of momentum among sellers, unable to move price to the downside. The uptrend continued, further confirmed by the two three-line strikes, forecasting continuation of the bullish trend.

Although the tweezer bottom is a small and limited signal, it is a strong variation of the double bottom. The two lower shadows in consecutive sessions created this strong attribute, which is not seen in all double bottom formations. The strength of the resulting uptrend continued beyond the period shown, and the extended chart is revealed in Figure 13.36.

Chart courtesy of StockCharts.com

Figure 13.36 Tweezer bottom, six months

A third three-line strike confirmed the previous two continuation signals, taking price strongly upward through to the conclusion of the period shown. Starting with the tweezer bottom at the point of the failed breakout below support, the uptrend was strengthened by the repetitive continuation signals. This chart is an example of strong reversals, strong proximity, and creation of momentum to carry the trend forward for the next four months.

All candlestick patterns are contrasted with signals by their flexible, extended period covered and conformity to the hypothesis concerning strength and weakness. Weak trends lead to weak reversals (or continuations) and confirmation; weak reversals (or continuations) and confirmation lead to equally weak subsequent price patterns. This weakness is exhibited in both the degree and speed of price movement as well as by delayed response time. On the other extreme, strong trends tend to lead to strong reversals (or continuations) and confirmation; strong reversals (or continuations) lead to strong price movement and a likelihood of a quick response.

The difference between these patterns and more restricted candlestick signals is in two aspects of the pattern. Some patterns extend over a longer period than the consecutive-session signals. Other patterns involve placement of single-session indicators (like hanging man and hammer) or very small and confined patterns (like the tweezer) that, with strong proximity, may serve as exceptionally strong reversal indicators.

The next chapter concludes with a discussion of how charting techniques and observation of how reversals and continuation signals are confirmed are used to manage risk. A popular point of view is that charting and technical analysis as broad disciplines are high-risk trading strategies. However, if you observe the ways in which prices swing and in which trends begin and end, your trade timing can be greatly improved to reduce instances of poor timing and strongly improve the instances of profitable decision timing.

14

Risk Reduction Methods—Using Charting Techniques to Manage Risk

Risk is unavoidable. It cannot be eliminated entirely, but it can be managed and reduced. For many traders not using timing techniques based on chart patterns, trade timing is a high-risk venture that is very difficult, if not impossible to control. The methods examined in this book solve this problem.

Assumptions That Add to Risk

A series of assumptions are likely to increase trading risks and prevent application of sensible and effective techniques. This is true for charting and the use of signals or patterns to time trades.

Among these are the following:

1. **The "assumption of zero."** Traders may easily fall into the trap of opening trades with the mistaken belief that their price is the zero point, and that prices will move profitably from that point forward. Of course, this is not true. Prices are moving continuously, and may move in either direction. This is why in swing trading programs, it is important to reduce risk exposure by keeping dollar values of trades consistent, even with excellent signals and confirmation at the right proximity.
2. **Impatience.** It is easy to become impatient when strong signals do not appear frequently. Markets tend to move through cycles, and extended periods of low opportunity occur. In the desire to be in the market, traders may become impatient and make trades lacking proper signals and confirmation, and located at the wrong proximity. This is the root cause of many losses. As difficult as it is, developing patience is a worthwhile skill for every trader.
3. **Setting rules but not following them.** Another common error made by traders, whether experienced or not, is to fail to enforce their own rules. If your rules include seeking trades at the right proximity to support and resistance, with strong trends, signals, and confirmation, the theory states that your timing will

improve. However, for that to work, you also need to apply the self-discipline to follow your own rules.

4. **Failing to use the proximity rule.** Many traders are aware of the strength of signals at or moving through support and resistance. Both reversal and continuation are most likely at these key points in the trading range; in fact, these are the only points at which the hypothesis of relative correlation works. However, traders may decide to enter trades at midrange and even without adequate reversal or continuation signals and confirmation. This invites risk and often leads not only to poor timing of trades, but also to trades that fail in price direction.

5. **Not seeking strong confirmation.** An exceptionally strong signal at the right proximity is a compelling indicator; it is easy to make a trade quickly, aware that price can move rapidly. However, caution reminds all traders that confirmation is essential even with the other parts in place. Even if you find a strong signal and proximity is perfect, making a trade without that essential third ingredient of confirmation is a high-risk move. Relative correlation works only with all three parts: signal, confirmation, and proximity.

6. **Looking for reversal only and ignoring continuation signals.** Candlestick reversal signals are easily spotted and confirmed at the right proximity. Focusing on a short list of high-probability signals makes sense. The reversal signals used throughout this book are good examples of the type of reversals worth seeking. The bullish reversal signals in previous chapters are three stars in the south, three white soldiers, and morning star. The bearish reversal signals are three black crows, identical three crows, bearish engulfing, and bearish belt hold. However, it is easy to overlook continuation signals. In this book, continuation signals used include bullish and bearish three-line strike and the bullish mat hold. The danger in this risk is confusion among signals. If you seek reversal only, for example, you will spot the bearish engulfing in the last two sessions of the bullish continuation three-line strike; or you will see three black crows in the middle of the bullish mat hold continuation signals. Deciding whether a signal is bullish continuation or bearish reversal is one of the great challenges in chart analysis, and the solution is to focus on a combination of proximity and strong confirmation signals.

7. **Assuming retracement is reversal.** Interpreting a price pattern contains numerous pitfalls. Among these is mistaking retracement for reversal. In a retracement, it is more likely that volume will be small, whereas in a reversal, volume is more likely to grow and even to spike. In a retracement, you may also find continuation patterns contradicting the momentary price direction, and in reversals, strong reversal signals and confirmation will be found. Finally, retracement is an adjustment in the trend, and this can also be called confusion—you might notice erratic behavior and patterns in candlesticks during retracements. This could

include a mix of long and short candlesticks, price gaps in either direction, and long shadows.

8. **Tracking only a short number of favorite signals.** Another easy pitfall for traders is to focus on too few signals based on past success, but ignore others. For example, relying on momentum oscillators to identify movement into overbought or oversold index areas is a smart form of confirmation, but should never be used solely to time reversal trades. By the same argument, using only a short list of high-probability candlestick signals, but ignoring momentum, volume, or moving average signals also creates blind spots. Finally, use both Eastern and Western signals to spot reversal and continuation. Be especially cautious about signals with close design but opposite meanings (ascending triangle versus rising wedge or descending triangle versus falling wedge, for example). These are easily misinterpreted due to a difference of only a fraction of a price point in one or two sessions, so caution is always appropriate when using candlestick or traditional technical signals. Confirmation is the key because confusion between bullish continuation and bearish reversal (or bearish continuation and bullish reversal) is likely to occur at the proximity points. The indecision can be resolved only with strong confirmation, and preferably with multiple forms of confirmation. This applies when the angle of change between triangles and wedges is very slight, so more confidence is likely when the price angles are quite sharp and confusion is far less likely between continuation and reversal.

Technical Analysis Beyond Speculation

The reputation of technical analysis, broadly speaking, is that it is used primarily for speculative trading. Many fundamental analysts find security in the financial statements and reject technical analysis in the belief that either the efficient market hypothesis (EMH) or the random walk hypothesis (RWH) rule the markets. If either of these is true, then technical analysis has no value.

The truth, however, is that market behavior (meaning the behavior of traders active in the market) tends to follow predictable patterns, and this translates into price patterns that can be analyzed and tracked, so that forecasts of likely new movements become quite possible.

The efficient market hypothesis (EMH) is flawed. It assumes that all current prices have been adjusted for all known information about a company. Anyone who has studied price trends realizes that in the short term, price movement tends to represent overreaction to current news rather than as a reflection of that news. For example, when a company misses earnings projections by a few pennies, the stock price is likely to fall many points—only to correct and reverse within one to three sessions. This is hardly efficient.

Defenders of EMH argue that the fast return to more reasonable price levels proves the theory. However, in a truly efficient market, such price spikes would not occur.

The random walk hypothesis (RWH) would make any form of analysis hopeless if it were true. Under RWH, the theory states that there is no way to predict price trends, and that at any given moment, there is a 50% chance of prices rising or falling. It may apply under RWH that longer-term influences on price (such as earnings, for example) influence this randomness. But in the short term, no prediction is possible.

The hypothesis of relative correlation dispels the RWH hypothesis, as many previous studies have also done. It is quite clear that with critical testing, there is nothing random about price movement. Observed price behavior at proximity to support and resistance proves this point. When proximity is right (meaning price has approached or broken through support or resistance), reversal is at its highest likelihood as long as reversal signals are found and confirmed. By the same argument, if continuation signals are found and confirmed at the right proximity, then continuation is also very likely.

Another influence on these tendencies is the strength of the prevailing trend. Strength tends to lead to equally strong signals and confirmation, which tend to lead to a strong response in price. So given strength of movement (defined as speed and degree of change), proximity, signals, and confirmation, confidence about the predicted price movement approaches 100%. No one should ever expect absolute certainty. But as the examples in this book have demonstrated, confidence may approach 100% when all of the conditions are optimal.

This set of observations not only dispels both EMH and RWH as reliable theories, but it also raises the possibility that technical analysis may be applied to investment timing, even among the most conservative investors. As a general assumption, conservative investing is likely to depend on the fundamental strength of the company, and speculative trading is likely to depend primarily on technical patterns (candlesticks, Western technical price patterns, moving averages, volume, and momentum). However, the high reliability of properly applied relative correlation may also be applied by conservative investors to protect profits, time entry and exit into portfolio positions, and anticipate coming price trends in individual stocks.

For example, a conservative investor holding a permanent portfolio of value investments has to be aware of cyclical price changes. Such an investor is likely to want to take profits in the short term with the idea of either moving in and out of equity positions, or using other products (such as options) to take profits without selling stock. Options may also be used to protect paper profits rather than needing to close positions; so even conservative investors with a buy-and-hold approach to the market can use technical analysis to increase confidence in price projections and to take steps to avoid losses or take profits.

Relative correlation clearly provides advantages in trade timing. However, it is not limited to speculative and short-term trades. Some conservative theories suggest that shares should be bought and then held without worrying about short-term price cycles. However, this idea is going out of favor as investors and traders are able to make short-term trades for very little cost and make those trades online without relying on stockbrokers to execute trades for them. In 1960, the average holding period for stock was over eight years. Today, that average has fallen to under five days.[1]

For both traders and investors, this means that relative correlation of prices and forecasting of both reversal and continuation for prices and trends is a useful tool for timing of trades. These trades may involve movement in and out of stock positions, or the use of risk reduction tools like options to protect profits and reduce risks.

Applying Multiple Signals

Although many of the examples in this book involved a small number of signals, this does not mean traders should limit the indicators they use. The purpose of isolating signals to only two or three types has been to clarify examples. In practice, you might want to combine not only price signals, but also volume, moving average, and momentum signals to get the best forecasting signals and confirmation possible.

A danger in using multiple signals is the likelihood of finding contradictory indicators. This often is why traders tend to focus on a short list of highly reliable signals. For example, you might decide to limit your analysis to ten candlestick signals like those in this book, but in reality there are dozens of possible candlestick signals. However, because a large number of these are only about 50% reliable, relying on them is of questionable value.

This point brings up a related problem with candlesticks. Most literature identifies reversal and continuation signals very clearly, so it is easy to discover which type of signal appears and, if confirmed, how it should be used. However, the same literature also claims that a specific signal may act as reversal *or* continuation, depending on where it appears. So a strong signal like three black crows would act as reversal when appearing at the top of a current uptrend, or as continuation if it appears within a downtrend.

This assumption is rejected under this book's hypothesis of relative correlation. Under this hypothesis, candlestick indicators are either reversal signals or continuation signals; they cannot be either or both. Under the hypothesis of relative correlation, when a signal shows up in the wrong place, it is merely a coincidence of price pattern and should not be given any assumed value as a signal at all. A second belief associated with relative correlation is that candlesticks that are accurate only half of the time provide no actionable value whatsoever as reversal or continuation signals. These may be of value to the extent that they confirm other signals, but should not be used as a sole source of confirmation, given their 50% reliability.

While the belief in transferability of candlesticks between reversal and opposite confirmation is only a theory, it may be useful to focus on a small number of highly reliable signals and to not assume any transferability. This inflexibility adds to the strength of signals and confirmation that are observed; it also reduces the chances for timing errors based on potentially false indicators.

No system for projecting future price movement is going to provide absolute certainty in timing of trades, but it is possible to *approach* 100% confidence when all of the elements are present:

- Candlesticks with a high percentage of probability for expected outcomes
- Strong trends leading to strong signals and confirmation
- Proximity at (or through) support and resistance
- Signals beyond candlesticks that strongly support the forecast initially observed

Relative correlation is based on discovering and quantifying all of these elements. Testing the hypothesis has further demonstrated that when signals fail or when false signals appear, the underlying cause can be traced. Either proximity was flawed, or preceding trends were too weak to create reliable signals. False signals do not simply appear for no reason, but most often can be explained by weakness in one of the attributes of the price pattern. A weakness includes a slow trend or a trend whose duration is too short to represent a true trend, poor proximity of signals, minimal signal formation, or confusion between reversal and confirmation (bullish reversal versus bearish confirmation, or bearish reversal versus bullish confirmation). This confusion leads to many misinterpreted signals, notably in low-slope triangles versus wedges, and in contradictory candlestick signals (such as bullish three-line strikes containing bearish engulfing, or bullish mat hold continuation containing three black crows).

Because so many apparent signals, even those with high probability, can be interpreted in more than one way, relative correlation requires analysis beyond the immediate trend and signal. It depends on multiple confirmations and on seeking additional intelligence from candlestick patterns that extend over time rather than being restricted to consecutive signals.

All of the analytical skills required to increase confidence in likely forecasts are a culmination of study for all of the aspects of relative correlation. The greater the input of signals and patterns, both for price and trends, the higher the chances for improved timing of trades and reduction of trading risks.

A

Hypothesis Summary

Ten Key Western Signals (Chapter 2)

1. Double tops
2. Double bottoms
3. Price gaps
4. Ascending triangles
5. Descending triangles
6. Symmetrical triangles
7. Rising wedges
8. Falling wedges
9. Trendlines
10. Channel lines

Ten Candlesticks with High-Performance Rankings (Chapter 3)

	Performance Ranking Percentage	
	Bullish	Bearish
Three black crows		79%
Three stars in the south	100%	
Three-line strike (bullish)	83%	
Three-line strike (bearish)		84%
Three white soldiers	84%	
Identical three crows		72%
Bearish engulfing		82%
Morning star	78%	
Bearish belt hold		71%
Mat hold	78%	

Source: Thomas Bulkowski, *Encyclopedia of Candlestick Charts*

Relative Correlation Basic Hypothesis: Proximity and Strength (Chapter 1)

> *A candlestick indicator serves as an initial forecast of coming price reversal or continuation. However, it is not dependable, even with confirmation, unless and until it is analyzed in conjunction with proximity to the edges of the trading range and the strength of trend and price characteristics in play. At that point, the relative correlation of the candlestick indicator is a variable, and should be quantified before assuming that the indicated forecast direction is likely.*

Hypothesis Regarding the Strength of Reversal Signals (Chapter 7)

> *Strong reversal signals are likely to be accompanied by equally strong confirmation signals* ***if and when*** *the preceding trend was strong (meaning clear in direction and long in duration) and if and when proximity is maximized (reversal and confirmation appearing at or trending through resistance or support). When these conditions*

are present, reversal confidence is at its highest possible level, meaning a retreat from the previous trend and price movement in the opposite direction. A strong reversal is also most likely to lead to a strong reversal trend.

Hypothesis Regarding the Strength of Continuation Signals (Chapter 7)

Strong continuation signals are likely to be accompanied by equally strong confirmation signals. This is especially true when the preceding trend was strong and with maximum proximity (close to or at resistance or support). When these conditions are present, continuation confidence is at its highest possible level, meaning likely breakout above resistance or below support. A strong continuation is also most likely to lead to further movement with strength at least equal to the preceding trend.

Hypothesis Regarding the Nature of Weak Reversal and Continuation Signals (Chapter 7)

Weak reversal or continuation signals are likely to be accompanied by equally weak confirmation signals or even by contradictory signals. This applies in all levels of proximity and to all levels of trend strength (and most likely when the preceding trend was weak as well). The weakness of signals and confirmation are most likely to be located at midrange and not in close proximity to resistance or support.

Hypothesis Regarding the Nature of Continuation for Breakouts Versus Trends (Chapter 8)

A continuation signal may predict further movement in the existing trend. It may also add high confidence that a newly established support or resistance level will hold based on the proximity of that continuation signal. This may apply even when the price pattern enters into a sideways movement rather than continuing the prior trend.

Hypothesis Regarding Strong Signals That Contradict One Another (Chapter 10)

Contradictory strong signals occurring at proximity tend to create uncertainty in subsequent price trends and may offset one another to create temporary sideways price movement. The stronger each contradictory signal is and the closer their proximity to support or resistance, the longer the period of sideways price movement is likely to last.

Hypothesis Statement Concerning Signal Failures and False Indicators (Chapter 12)

Signal failures and false indicators can occur without explanation; however, inaccurate, contradictory, and failing signals and confirmation are most likely to be traced to a logical flaw in a pattern, proximity, or weakness in the trend. In a majority of cases, a failed signal or false indicator can be explained with analysis of the current trend; proximity, strength, or weakness of the signal and confirmation; or relative correlation between conflicting forecasts.

B

Hypothesis Testing

The author tested the hypotheses presented in this book, through trades made over a two-year period. The tests were performed on www.ThomsettOptions.com, and employed a combination of chart analysis and option trades. The following are all the trades during the period; these are also available for reviewing on the Web site and are open to the public. The overall net profits from this trading activity involved 582 trades and totaled $75,591 (unadjusted 38% per year) based on a hypothetical portfolio valued at $100,000.

The following are the results of the trades opened and closed in the virtual portfolio:

Opening Date	Stock Symbol	Yield	Days Held		Opening Date	Stock Symbol	Yield	Days Held
2012					15-Nov 2012	COP	19%	4
16-Sep 2012	IBM	91%	19		14-Nov 2012	SLV	30%	5
25-Sep 2012	MSFT	52%	3		20-Nov 2012	CAT	14%	1
14-Sep 2012	VZ	80%	3		20-Nov 2012	CAT	8%	1
12-Oct 2012	S	63%	16		20-Nov 2012	CAT	13%	1
29-Sep 2012	SPDR	5%	6		20-Nov 2012	CAT	19%	1
10-Oct 2012	JNJ	57%	7		9-Nov 2012	KO	0%	66
9-Oct 2012	MCD	281%	5		20-Nov 2012	CAT	21%	6
11-Oct 2012	X	43%	9		20-Nov 2012	CAT	18%	6
9-Oct 2012	K	45%	17		20-Nov 2012	CAT	9%	6
2-Oct 2012	GE	32%	17		15-Nov 2012	COP	33%	12
15-Oct 2012	VZ	51%	8		26-Nov 2012	IBM	38%	1
16-Oct 2012	MO	42%	7		28-Nov 2012	M	30%	1
16-Oct 2012	MO	46%	7		28-Nov 2012	M	13%	1
22-Oct 2012	X	36%	1		28-Nov 2012	M	22%	1

Opening Date	Stock Symbol	Yield	Days Held		Opening Date	Stock Symbol	Yield	Days Held
5-Nov 2012	VZ	57%	4		28-Nov 2012	M	14%	1
6-Nov 2012	K	42%	1		28-Nov 2012	M	10%	1
6-Nov 2012	VZ	45%	1		27-Nov 2012	COP	17%	2
6-Nov 2012	MO	40%	1		20-Nov 2012	CAT	59%	9
3-Oct 2012	MRK	35%	38		20-Nov 2012	CAT	37%	9
1-Nov 2012	MCD	60%	8		20-Nov 2012	CAT	27%	9
5-Nov 2012	IBM	33%	4		28-Nov 2012	M	31%	2
5-Nov 2012	COP	22%	1		28-Nov 2012	M	12%	2
4-Nov 2012	COP	12%	1		28-Nov 2012	M	19%	2
12-Nov 2012	CSCO	100%	4		15-Nov 2012	COP	78%	19
2-Nov 2012	YHOO	28%	14		28-Nov 2012	M	31%	6
15-Nov 2012	COP	41%	4		6-Dec 2012	M	21%	1
15-Nov 2012	COP	37%	4		8-Nov 2012	GLD	14%	70
15-Nov 2012	COP	21%	4		6-Dec 2012	M	22%	1
15-Nov 2012	COP	17%	4		6-Dec 2012	M	12%	1
15-Nov 2012	COP	13%	22		31-Dec 2012	IBM	28%	1
6-Dec 2012	COP	15%	1		31-Dec 2012	M	–52%	35
27-Nov 2012	COP	28%	10		4-Dec 2012	GLD	45%	3
27-Nov 2012	COP	55%	10					
19-Nov 2012	COP	24%	17		**2013**			
6-Dec 2012	COP	7%	1		7-Jan 2013	CMI	30%	39
15-Nov 2012	COP	5%	25		7-Jan 2013	BA	64%	28
16-Oct 2012	MO	46%	57		2-Jan 2013	IBM	61%	6
16-Oct 2012	MO	53%	57		8-Jan 2013	KO	32%	7
7-Nov 2012	ED	24%	35		20-Nov 2012	CAT	–107%	7
13-Dec 2012	WU	3%	39		11-Jan 2013	CMI	24%	7
14-Nov 2012	PDM	1%	28		12-Jan 2013	IBM	30%	7
6-Dec 2012	T	1%	6		10-Jan 2013	AMZN	38%	7
6-Dec 2012	CAT	24%	7		2-Jan 2013	MCD	–35%	7
6-Dec 2012	CAT	13%	7		23-Jan 2013	IBM	89%	2
6-Dec 2012	CAT	21%	7		24-Jan 2013	IBM	20%	8
6-Dec 2012	CAT	12%	7		26-Oct 2012	MCD	3%	8
6-Dec 2012	CAT	9%	7		10-Jan 2013	CAT	30%	8
6-Dec 2012	CAT	9%	7		18-Jan 2013	LVS	21%	8
12-Dec 2012	MCD	15%	2		24-Jan 2013	LMT	177%	66

Opening Date	Stock Symbol	Yield	Days Held		Opening Date	Stock Symbol	Yield	Days Held
6-Dec 2012	COP	10%	8		28-Jan 2013	KMP	53%	45
6-Dec 2012	M	29%	8		28-Jan 2013	AMZN	37%	40
6-Dec 2012	M	25%	8		1-Feb 2013	IBM	14%	3
6-Dec 2012	M	12%	8		6-Feb 2013	COP	103%	62
12-Oct 2012	S	-4%	66		6-Feb 2013	COP	72%	43
2-Nov 2012	YHOO	-100%	45		6-Feb 2013	AMZN	23%	43
7-Nov 2012	ED	-50%	40		6-Feb 2013	NFLX	27%	1
14-Dec 2012	MO	55%	3		8-Jan 2013	COP	25%	5
17-Oct 2012	IBM	40%	62		8-Feb 2013	AMZN	29%	4
5-Nov 2012	T	-89%	43		8-Feb 2013	NFLX	53%	10
5-Nov 2012	T	82%	43		28-Jan 2013	AMZN	16%	6
19-Dec 2012	MCD	24%	1		11-Feb 2013	WMT	35%	6
14-Dec 2012	VZ	93%	5		11-Feb 2013	WMT	22%	20
17-Dec 2012	K	50%	4		11-Feb 2013	WMT	21%	6
14-Dec 2012	IBM	32%	10		11-Feb 2013	WMT	69%	20
20-Dec 2012	M	44%	6		11-Feb 2013	WMT	45%	1
6-Dec 2012	M	21%	6		11-Feb 2013	WMT	64%	5
6-Dec 2012	M	59%	20		11-Feb 2013	WMT	45%	3
20-Dec 2012	M	23%	6		11-Feb 2013	WMT	42%	1
6-Dec 2012	M	49%	20		11-Feb 2013	WMT	37%	1
5-Nov 2012	IBM	4%	5		26-Feb 2013	XOM	-100%	18
22-Jan 2013	GE	-100%	51		26-Feb 2013	DE	6%	20
8-Jan 2013	COP	51%	5		26-Feb 2013	DE	-107%	20
25-Feb 2013	MO	59%	15		18-Mar 2013	MRK	20%	1
25-Feb 2013	AMZN	13%	94		27-Feb 2013	MO	36%	20
26-Feb 2013	CAT	54%	1		19-Mar 2013	IBM	15%	1
26-Feb 2013	CAT	45%	1		19-Mar 2013	IBM	5%	1
14-Sep 2012	VZ	3%	167		19-Mar 2013	IBM	12%	1
27-Feb 2013	LMT	19%	1		19-Mar 2013	IBM	3%	1
28-Feb 2013	AMZN	20%	1		19-Mar 2013	IBM	4%	1
11-Feb 2013	WMT	79%	22		19-Mar 2013	IBM	12%	2
11-Feb 2013	WMT	32%	22		19-Mar 2013	IBM	22%	2
11-Feb 2013	WMT	45%	22		6-Dec 2012	CAT	15%	105
28-Feb 2013	AMZN	29%	5		7-Mar 2013	BWLD	16%	14
4-Mar 2013	LEG	26%	1		7-Mar 2013	BWLD	9%	14

Opening Date	Stock Symbol	Yield	Days Held		Opening Date	Stock Symbol	Yield	Days Held
5-Mar 2013	CAT	17%	1		18-Mar 2013	MRK	32%	3
5-Mar 2013	CAT	20%	1		18-Mar 2013	MRK	20%	3
6-Dec 2012	CAT	9%	89		18-Mar 2013	MRK	16%	3
5-Mar 2013	CAT	19%	1		18-Mar 2013	LMT	26%	3
5-Mar 2013	CAT	16%	1		18-Mar 2013	LMT	-13%	3
5-Mar 2013	CAT	8%	1		19-Mar 2013	IBM	3%	2
5-Mar 2013	CAT	9%	1		19-Mar 2013	IBM	24%	2
6-Mar 2013	IBM	35%	1		19-Mar 2013	IBM	-17%	2
6-Mar 2013	IBM	26%	1		19-Mar 2013	IBM	15%	2
6-Mar 2013	IBM	20%	1		21-Mar 2013	AMZN	23%	1
6-Mar 2013	IBM	25%	2		22-Mar 2013	TIF	16%	3
6-Mar 2013	IBM	167%	2		18-Mar 2013	MRK	28%	7
7-Mar 2013	BWLD	12%	1		18-Mar 2013	MRK	11%	7
7-Mar 2013	BWLD	11%	1		21-Mar 2013	AMZN	13%	4
7-Mar 2013	BWLD	19%	1		25-Mar 2013	DOW	41%	1
7-Mar 2013	BWLD	10%	1		25-Mar 2013	DOW	28%	1
5-Mar 2013	CAT	25%	6		25-Mar 2013	AMZN	18%	1
5-Mar 2013	CAT	27%	6		26-Mar 2013	CAT	35%	1
5-Mar 2013	CAT	4%	6		26-Mar 2013	CAT	18%	1
5-Mar 2013	CAT	35%	6		18-Mar 2013	MRK	30%	15
5-Mar 2013	CAT	3%	6		22-Mar 2013	LMT	1%	16
4-Mar 2013	MRK	29%	9		4-Apr 2013	GLD	39%	1
4-Mar 2013	MRK	-198%	10		1-Apr 2013	EBAY	39%	4
14-Feb 2013	COP	4%	30		1-Apr 2013	EBAY	25%	4
4-Feb 2013	RAI	-100%	40		1-Apr 2013	EBAY	24%	4
1-Apr 2013	EBAY	23%	4		18-Apr 2013	XOM	41%	5
1-Apr 2013	EBAY	20%	4		23-Apr 2013	AMZN	66%	6
27-Mar 2013	AMZN	8%	9		26-Mar 2013	CAT	11%	34
1-Apr 2013	EBAY	18%	4		16-Apr 2013	DTV	20%	13
2-Apr 2013	CAT	-14%	7		10-Apr 2013	BWLD	19%	20
2-Apr 2013	CAT	20%	7		9-Apr 2013	MRK	11%	22
2-Apr 2013	CAT	-27%	7		9-Apr 2013	MRK	30%	22
2-Apr 2013	CAT	243%	7		29-Apr 2013	WMT	15%	2
2-Apr 2013	CAT	20%	7		29-Apr 2013	WMT	19%	2
9-Apr 2013	MRK	7%	1		26-Mar 2013	CAT	27%	38

Opening Date	Stock Symbol	Yield	Days Held		Opening Date	Stock Symbol	Yield	Days Held
9-Apr 2013	MRK	7%	1		29-Apr 2013	WMT	−1%	3
1-Apr 2013	EBAY	20%	9		3-May 2013	WMT	62%	2
1-Apr 2013	EBAY	11%	9		6-May 2013	BWLD	11%	3
1-Apr 2013	EBAY	0%	9		6-May 2013	BWLD	36%	3
1-Apr 2013	EBAY	1%	9		24-Apr 2013	AMZN	22%	15
1-Apr 2013	EBAY	10%	9		13-May 2013	GLD	6%	1
1-Apr 2013	EBAY	7%	9		6-May 2013	CAT	15%	9
9-Apr 2013	MRK	24%	1		6-May 2013	CAT	9%	10
10-Apr 2013	BWLD	21%	1		27-Mar 2013	CL	1%	58
10-Apr 2013	BWLD	34%	1		25-Mar 2013	DOW	1%	53
27-Mar 2013	AMZN	15%	15		2-Apr 2013	COP	100%	45
16-Apr 2013	DTV	47%	4		22-Apr 2013	WHR	−85%	25
16-Apr 2013	DTV	26%	4		23-Apr 2013	OHI	2%	24
16-Apr 2013	DTV	11%	4		28-Mar 2013	IBM	4%	53
16-Apr 2013	DTV	31%	4		10-May 2013	ED	1%	18
16-Apr 2013	DTV	26%	4		6-May 2013	MRK	−5%	22
16-Apr 2013	DTV	2%	4		6-May 2013	MRK	128%	22
16-Apr 2013	DTV	4%	4		4-Jun 2013	COP	15%	1
27-Feb 2013	MO	0%	51		4-Jun 2013	COP	17%	1
26-Mar 2013	GD	0%	24		31-May 2013	BWLD	13%	7
26-Mar 2013	GD	−100%	24		31-May 2013	BWLD	6%	10
26-Mar 2013	GD	72%	24		31-May 2013	BWLD	9%	10
11-Apr 2013	XOM	100%	8		5-Jun 2013	COP	33%	5
12-Apr 2013	GLD	−100%	7		5-Jun 2013	COP	22%	5
10-Apr 2013	AMZN	11%	12		5-Jun 2013	COP	16%	5
16-Apr 2013	DTV	9%	6		5-Jun 2013	COP	14%	5
16-Apr 2013	DTV	−1%	6		5-Jun 2013	COP	16%	5
16-Apr 2013	DTV	5%	6		5-Jun 2013	COP	77%	8
16-Apr 2013	DTV	5%	6		5-Jun 2013	COP	52%	8
17-Apr 2013	AMZN	10%	6		5-Jun 2013	COP	5%	9
17-Jun 2013	BWLD	33%	1		27-Jun 2013	GLD	28%	1
31-May 2013	BWLD	20%	48		1-Jul 2013	SLV	24%	10
17-Jun 2013	BWLD	6%	1		1-Jul 2013	SLV	10%	10
17-Jun 2013	BWLD	20%	1		18-Jun 2013	MRK	49%	23
17-Jun 2013	BWLD	11%	1		3-Jul 2013	MRK	49%	8

Opening Date	Stock Symbol	Yield	Days Held		Opening Date	Stock Symbol	Yield	Days Held
17-Jun 2013	CAT	14%	2		18-Jun 2013	MRK	–5%	23
17-Jun 2013	CAT	7%	2		3-Jul 2013	MRK	111%	8
17-Jun 2013	CAT	10%	2		1-Jul 2013	BWLD	18%	10
17-Jun 2013	CAT	7%	2		1-Jul 2013	BWLD	25%	10
17-Jun 2013	CAT	4%	2		1-Jul 2013	BWLD	21%	10
17-Jun 2013	CAT	3%	2		1-Jul 2013	BWLD	37%	11
17-Jun 2013	BWLD	13%	2		29-May 2013	LMT	1%	51
17-Jun 2013	BWLD	12%	2		21-Jun 2013	POXY	6%	28
17-Jun 2013	BWLD	13%	2		21-Jun 2013	SWK	8%	28
17-May 2013	COP	3%	79		21-Jun 2013	TUP	7%	28
17-Jun 2013	CAT	3%	3		21-Jun 2013	LVS	9%	28
17-Jun 2013	CAT	26%	3		21-Jun 2013	TIF	9%	28
17-Jun 2013	CAT	4%	3		21-May 2013	DB	2%	59
17-Jun 2013	CAT	14%	3		20-Jun 2013	PM	2%	29
18-Jun 2013	SLV	218%	2		21-Mar 2013	GIS	2%	120
18-Jun 2013	SLV	69%	2		1-Jul 2013	BWLD	35%	23
18-Jun 2013	SLV	114%	2		1-Jul 2013	BWLD	52%	23
18-Jun 2013	SLV	73%	2		17-Jun 2013	BWLD	8%	37
18-Jun 2013	SLV	106%	2		24-Jul 2013	GD	37%	1
18-Jun 2013	SLV	48%	2		29-Jul 2013	WYNN	22%	1
18-Jun 2013	MRK	62%	2		18-Jun 2013	SLV	79%	55
18-Jun 2013	MRK	38%	2		18-Jun 2013	SLV	14%	55
18-Jun 2013	MRK	23%	2		16-Jul 2013	KO	32%	27
18-Jun 2013	MRK	38%	2		6-May 2013	CAT	17%	100
18-Jun 2013	MRK	–118%	2		1-Jul 2013	SLV	–97%	46
18-Jun 2013	MRK	23%	2		18-Jun 2013	SLV	43%	28
18-Jun 2013	MRK	6%	2		18-Jun 2013	SLV	39%	28
22-May 2013	GS	0%	28		24-Apr 2013	AAPL	2%	50
30-May 2013	OXY	1%	22		15-Jul 2013	COP	–99%	32
31-May 2013	SWK	1%	21		16-Jul 2013	KO	–97%	31
11-Jun 2013	ADP	1%	10		24-Jul 2013	HAS	1%	23
13-Jun 2013	TUP	1%	8		30-Jun 2013	DUK	1%	16
17-Jun 2013	LVS	2%	7		12-Aug 2013	SYY	–88%	4
17-Jun 2013	TIF	2%	4		20-Aug 2013	URBN	13%	3
7-May 2013	AAPL	55%	45		13-May 2013	WHR	8%	106

Opening Date	Stock Symbol	Yield	Days Held		Opening Date	Stock Symbol	Yield	Days Held
16-Aug 2013	MRK	42%	12		26-Aug 2013	SLB	0%	53
26-Aug 2013	BWLD	31%	2		29-Aug 2013	LVS	1%	50
26-Aug 2013	BWLD	29%	2		11-Sep 2013	CMI	-100%	37
26-Aug 2013	BWLD	1%	8		12-Sep 2013	KR	-100%	36
26-Aug 2013	BWLD	13%	8		17-Sep 2013	BA	-100%	35
20-Aug 2013	DKS	22%	15		18-Sep 2013	FDX	-100%	34
16-Aug 2013	MRK	76%	25		16-Oct 2013	SWK	-100%	2
11-Sep 2013	OXM	45%	1		23-Sep 2013	VZ	1%	25
11-Sep 2013	AAPL	17%	1		10-Oct 2013	BWLD	0%	8
26-Aug 2013	BWLD	15%	17		10-Oct 2013	BWLD	38%	8
26-Aug 2013	BWLD	16%	21		19-Aug 2013	GS	100%	60
26-Aug 2013	BWLD	25%	21		21-Oct 2013	MCD	31%	1
2-Aug 2013	GHL	2%	45		18-Sep 2013	CAT	4%	34
15-Aug 2013	CSCO	-100%	36		3-Oct 2013	PG	53%	20
20-Aug 2013	BBY	-100%	31		23-Oct 2013	PG	6%	1
16-Sep 2013	OMC	1%	4		1-Oct 2013	CVX	20%	23
18-Sep 2013	CAT	27%	36		23-Oct 2013	CAT	13%	1
18-Sep 2013	CAT	-7%	36		23-Oct 2013	PG	29%	2
18-Sep 2013	MRK	21%	36		23-Oct 2013	PG	12%	2
18-Sep 2013	MRK	15%	36		23-Oct 2013	PG	14%	2
26-Aug 2013	BWLD	10%	35		23-Oct 2013	PG	8%	2
26-Aug 2013	BWLD	16%	35		23-Oct 2013	PG	7%	2
1-Oct 2013	CVX	1%	1		25-Oct 2013	AMZN	24%	1
1-Oct 2013	CVX	10%	1		19-Aug 2013	GS	0%	67
1-Oct 2013	CVX	3%	1		18-Oct 2013	GS	100%	7
1-Oct 2013	CVX	8%	1		23-Oct 2013	PG	26%	5
1-Oct 2013	CVX	14%	1		23-Oct 2013	PG	18%	5
1-Oct 2013	CVX	21%	1		18-Sep 2013	SLV	45%	42
1-Oct 2013	CVX	13%	1		30-Oct 2013	CMI	67%	5
1-Oct 2013	CVX	31%	1		7-Oct 2013	CTB	-100%	44
26-Aug 2013	BWLD	175%	37		11-Nov 2013	MSFT	21%	8
3-Oct 2013	PG	4%	5		11-Nov 2013	MSFT	21%	8
3-Oct 2013	PG	18%	5		11-Nov 2013	MSFT	12%	8
3-Oct 2013	PG	12%	5		11-Nov 2013	MSFT	13%	8
3-Oct 2013	PG	3%	5		10-Oct 2013	BWLD	50%	42

Opening Date	Stock Symbol	Yield	Days Held		Opening Date	Stock Symbol	Yield	Days Held
3-Oct 2013	PG	4%	5		11-Nov 2013	MSFT	30%	14
3-Oct 2013	PG	8%	5		11-Nov 2013	MSFT	32%	14
3-Oct 2013	PG	18%	5		11-Nov 2013	MSFT	20%	14
3-Oct 2013	PG	14%	5		11-Nov 2013	MSFT	24%	14
9-Oct 2013	YUM	48%	1		11-Nov 2013	MSFT	16%	14
11-Nov 2013	MSFT	27%	14		30-Jan 2014	XOM	123%	1
18-Nov 2013	SLV	49%	16		30-Jan 2014	XOM	55%	1
18-Nov 2013	SLV	1%	16		30-Jan 2014	XOM	23%	1
10-Dec 2013	MRK	18%	2		30-Jan 2014	XOM	6%	1
10-Dec 2013	MRK	12%	2		30-Jan 2014	XOM	60%	1
10-Dec 2013	MRK	19%	2		30-Jan 2014	XOM	35%	1
10-Dec 2013	MRK	7%	2		27-Jan 2014	BWLD	51%	9
10-Dec 2013	MRK	3%	2		4-Apr 2014	K	23%	3
9-Dec 2013	PG	14%	3		7-Apr 2014	MON	38%	1
9-Dec 2013	MSFT	65%	3		3-Feb 2014	CVX	26%	8
9-Dec 2013	MSFT	28%	3		13-Feb 2014	ATO	26%	1
9-Dec 2013	CVX	33%	4		18-Nov 2013	SLV	49%	88
9-Dec 2013	CVX	14%	10		30-Jan 2014	XOM	16%	15
10-Dec 2013	MRK	22%	13		11-Feb 2014	XOM	22%	3
10-Dec 2013	MRK	16%	13		11-Feb 2014	XOM	47%	3
10-Dec 2013	MRK	5%	13		30-Jan 2014	XOM	22%	15
19-Dec 2013	XOM	13%	4		14-Jan 2014	CBRL	-100%	38
20-Dec 2013	WAG	74%	3		23-Jan 2014	BBY	-100%	29
1-Oct 2013	CVX	12%	85		24-Jan 2014	INTC	-100%	28
9-Dec 2013	PG	40%	17		29-Jan 2014	BP	100%	23
27-Dec 2013	TWTR	8%	1		29-Jan 2014	BAC	-81%	23
1-Oct 2013	CVX	7%	87		30-Jan 2014	XOM	48%	22
30-Dec 2013	XOM	44%	1		30-Jan 2014	XOM	46%	22
31-Dec 2013	M	23%	2		14-Feb 2014	TRI	14%	7
10-Dec 2013	MRK	28%	27		27-Aug 2013	MCD	5%	184
10-Dec 2013	MRK	9%	27		27-Feb 2014	LMT	28%	1
					27-Feb 2014	LMT	19%	1
2014					27-Feb 2014	LMT	10%	1
1-Jan 2014	BAC	28%	14		27-Feb 2014	LMT	17%	1
9-Jan 2014	USO	15%	6		27-Feb 2014	LMT	8%	1

Opening Date	Stock Symbol	Yield	Days Held		Opening Date	Stock Symbol	Yield	Days Held
15-Jan 2014	PG	16%	1		27-Feb 2014	LMT	15%	1
13-Jan 2014	PM	9%	2		3-Mar 2014	PEP	22%	1
20-Jan 2014	SO	31%	1		13-Dec 2013	BWLD	37%	82
21-Jan 2014	BWLD	27%	2		12-Mar 2014	MCD	48%	1
9-Dec 2013	MSFT	8%	46		4-Mar 2014	RAI	7%	10
10-Jan 2014	M	9%	17		18-Mar 2014	VZ	27%	1
3-Oct 2013	PG	-100%	106		27-Feb 2014	LMT	19%	21
29-Jan 2014	OKE	34%	1		27-Feb 2014	LMT	9%	21
30-Jan 2014	ED	21%	1		27-Feb 2014	LMT	8%	21
18-Sep 2013	CAT	14%	134		27-Feb 2014	LMT	4%	21
27-Feb 2014	LMT	1%	21		9-Jul 2014	CMI	19%	1
18-Nov 2013	SLV	-100%	82		2-Jul 2014	TD	-49%	16
25-Feb 2014	WM	-100%	24		3-Jul 2014	DRI	-100%	15
28-Feb 2014	PPL	-100%	21					
27-Mar 2014	CBRL	10%	6					
1-Apr 2014	BMY	25%	1					
16-Sep 2013	MON	7%	198					
3-Apr 2014	COP	43%	4					
8-Apr 2014	PG	20%	1					
8-Apr 2014	PG	14%	1					
8-Apr 2014	PG	19%	2					
8-Apr 2014	PG	3%	2					
27-Feb 2014	LMT	21%	43					
10-Apr 2014	AA	12%	1					
11-Apr 2014	JPM	24%	1					
1-Apr 2014	CAG	-28%	15					
7-Apr 2014	UVV	-25%	9					
15-Apr 2014	CAST	16%	1					
26-Feb 2014	RAI	2%	51					
14-Apr 2014	CLX	48%	22					
29-Apr 2014	NSC	25%	9					
6-May 2014	WMT	15%	2					
8-Apr 2014	PG	39%	38					
2-May 2014	IBM	-100%	14					
8-Apr 2014	PG	30%	41					

Opening Date	Stock Symbol	Yield	Days Held		Opening Date	Stock Symbol	Yield	Days Held
20-May 2014	TWX	17%	1					
8-Apr 2014	PG	4%	56					
10-Jun 2014	LEG	11%	1					
9-Jun 2014	FDO	8%	4					
11-Jun 2014	ICE	19%	2					
3-Jun 2014	HD	142%	10					
5-May 2014	ED	30%	14					
6-Jun 2014	FLR	−100%	14					
23-Jun 2014	PM	37%	1					
24-Jun 2014	CP	28%	1					
9-Jul 2014	CMI	21%	1					
9-Jul 2014	CMI	26%	1					
9-Jul 2014	CMI	14%	1					
9-Jul 2014	CMI	24%	1					
9-Jul 2014	CMI	16%	1					

Endnotes

Chapter 1, "Charting Techniques—Predicting the Future"

1. Bachelier, L. (1900). *Théorie de la spéculation* (Doctoral dissertation in mathematics, University of Paris. English translation by Cootnerr, P.H. (ed.), 1964).
2. Fama, E. F. (1970). Efficient capital markets: A review of theory and empirical work. *Journal of Finance, 25*, 383–417.
3. Barberis, N., Scleifer, A., & Vishny, R. (1998). A model of investor sentiment. *Journal of Financial Economics, 49*, 307–343.
4. Kindleberger, C. P., & Aliber, Robert Z. (2005). *Manias, panics and crashes: A history of financial crisis* (5th ed.). (p. 47). Hoboken, NJ: John Wiley & Sons.

Chapter 3, "Candlestick Patterns—Recognizing Evolving Strength or Weakness"

1. Bulkowski, Thomas. (2008). *Encyclopedia of candlestick charts.* (p. 118, bearish belt hold; p. 308, bearish engulfing; p. 427, identical three crows; p. 552, mat hold; p. 598, morning star; p. 728, three black crows; p. 756, three-line strike bearish; p. 765, three-line strike bullish; p. 790, three stars in the south; and p. 794, three white soldiers) Hoboken, NJ: John Wiley & Sons.
2. Bulkowski, *Ibid.*, pp. 4–5, 909

Chapter 7, "Confirmation—An Essential Second Part of a Signal"

1. Morris, Gregory L. (2006). *Candlestick charting explained* (3rd ed.) (p. 211). New York: McGraw-Hill.

Chapter 10, "Volume Indicators—Confirmation of Price"

1. Granville, Joseph E. (1987). *Granville's new strategy of daily stock market timing for maximum profit.* Upper Saddle River, NJ: Prentice-Hall.

Chapter 14, "Risk Reduction Methods—Using Charting Techniques to Manage Risk"

1. Ro, Sam. (2012, August 7). Stock market investors have become absurdly impatient. *Business Insider.*

Index

D

O

P-Q

R

S